IMAGES
of America

ECHOES OF EDGECOMBE COUNTY
1860–1940

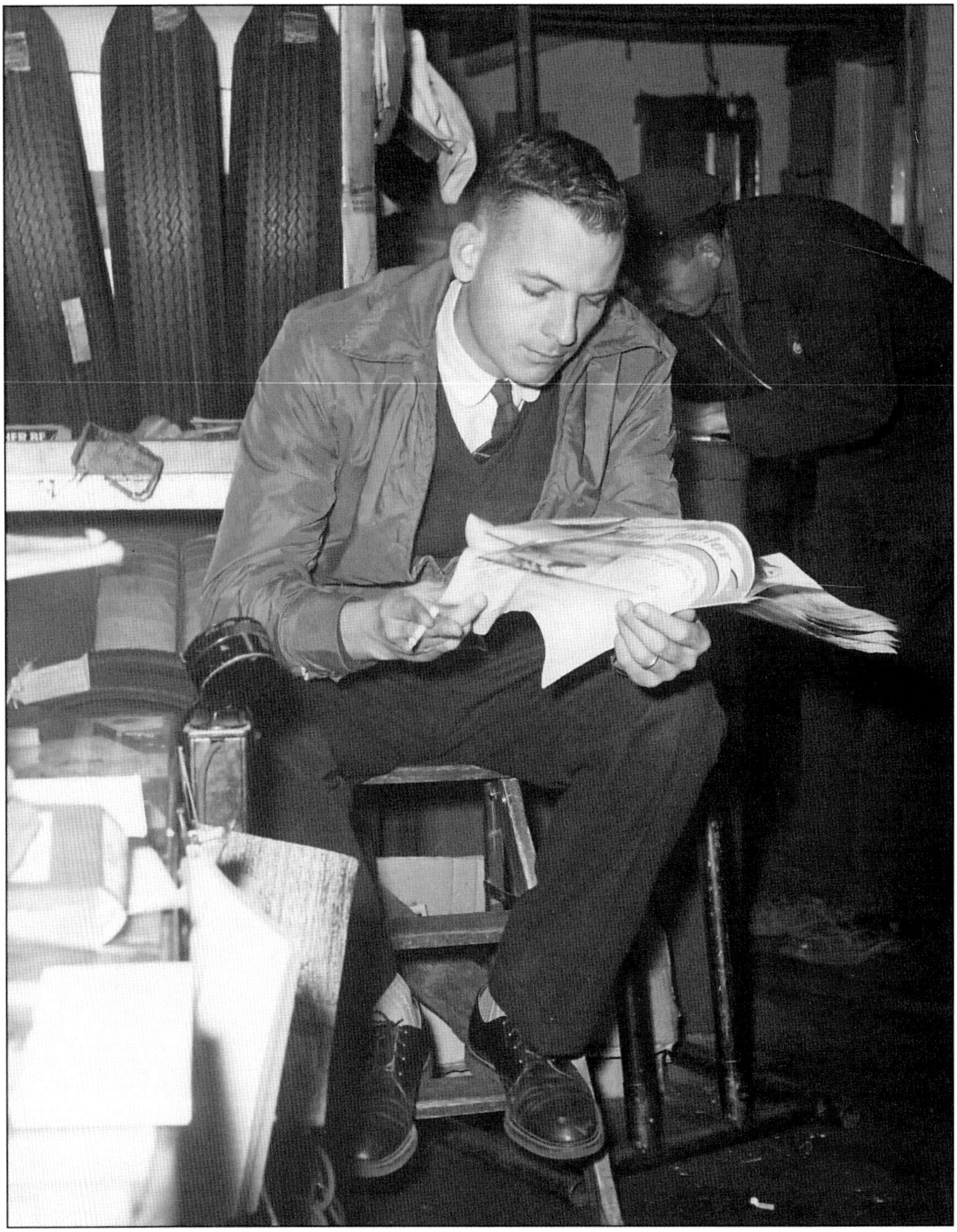

This book is dedicated to the memory of Baker Mabrey Bass Jr. (1925–1993), local historian and editor of the *Daily Southerner* for thirty-five years, whose collection of notes and photographs helped make this book possible. (BBH)

Cover photograph: The Town Hall was often the center of news and meetings. Here men are gathered to hear news of the Spanish-American War in 1898. (ECML)

IMAGES
of America

ECHOES OF EDGECOMBE COUNTY 1860–1940

Monika S. Fleming

ARCADIA
PUBLISHING

ISBN 978-07385-5337-5

Published by Arcadia Publishing,
Charleston, South Carolina

Printed in the United States of America

Library of Congress Catalog Card Number: 97134551

For all general information contact Arcadia Publishing at:
Telephone 843-853-2070
Fax 843-853-0044
E-Mail sales@arcadiapublishing.com
For customer service and orders:
Toll-Free 1-888-313-2665

Visit us on the Internet at www.arcadiapublishing.com

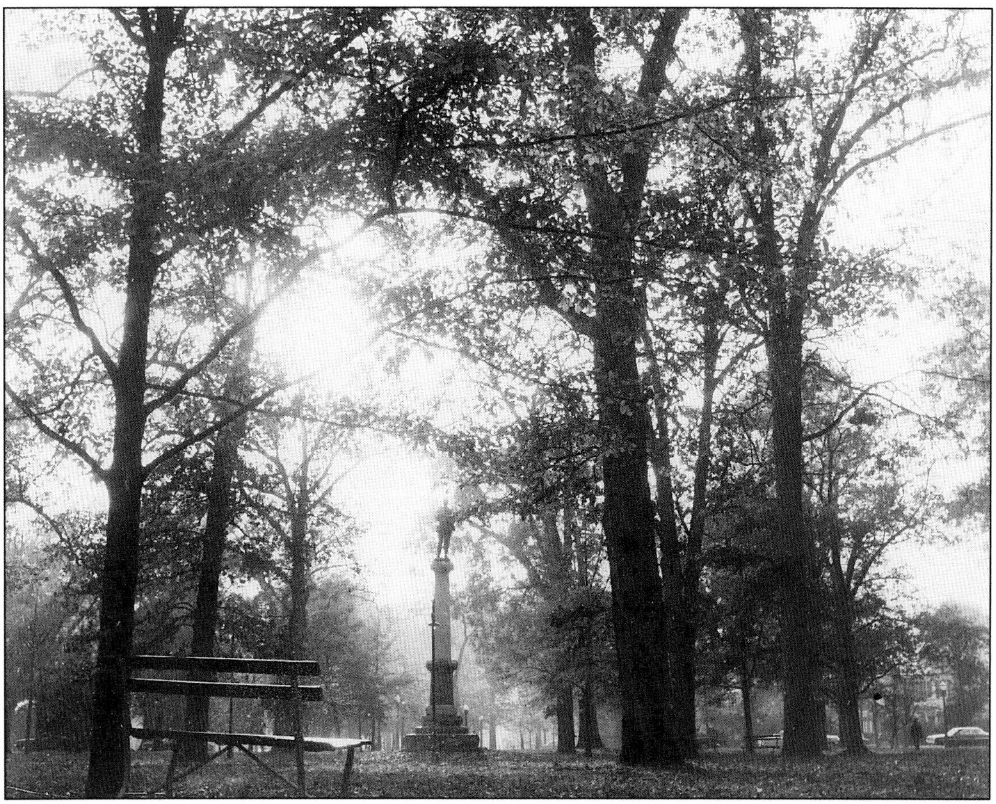

The Tarboro Town Common was created in 1760 by a legislative act that chartered the town. It is the second oldest town common in the United States. As in most Southern towns, a Confederate monument stands watch over the area. The monument was dedicated in 1904. (BBH)

Contents

ACKNOWLEDGMENTS

This book was created for the citizens of Edgecombe County; those of the present and those of the generations who have come before us. Many individuals generously gave their time and energy to help bring the project to completion. A special group of people willingly shared their knowledge of their families and communities and spent considerable time at the Blount-Bridgers House identifying old photographs: Arthur Edmondson, Nina Fountain, Bob Peters, Herb Taylor, and Joel Bourne. Others who gave invaluable assistance include Mary Howard, Jaquelin Nash, Betty Reason, and Bryant Jones.

Numerous county residents contributed family photographs. The donor of each image is indicated at the end of the text that accompanies each photograph with "PC" (for private collection) and the owner's surname. Thanks to the H.C. Bridgers family, Watson Brown, George Cherry III, Blanche and Henry T. Clark, Laddie and Elsie Crisp, the Jesse Bridgers Foster family, Whitfield Fountain, Lawrence Gulley, Mary Howard, Gladys Johnson, Donna Jones, Rudolph Knight, James Marrow, Bryan and Judy Mayo, Bill Murphy, Jaquelin Nash, Richard H. Parker, Oliver Curtis Powell, Helen Quigless, Betty Reason, Earl Roberson, Beverly Bridgers Short, Inez B. Simmons, Charles J. Spain Jr., Dick Stallings, Vera W. Stallings, Hack and Hassell Thigpen, Jo Webb, Wadie B. Winslow, and Jimmy and Josephine Worsley.

While many photographs in this book came from private collections, some are from Edgecombe County and North Carolina institutions. There follows a list of local and state agencies together with the abbreviations that have been used to identify each photograph throughout the book: Blount-Bridgers House (BBH)—the collections housed here include the files of the Edgecombe County Historical Society and part of Mabrey Bass' collection; Duke University Archives (DUKE); East Carolina University Special Collections (ECUSC)—thanks to Don Lennon and John McWatters for helping us meet our deadline; Edgecombe Community College Library (ECC)—thanks to librarian Lois Yoder and graphic artist Greg Dellinger; Edgecombe County Memorial Library (ECML)—thanks to director Dan Swartout and his staff, who were very cooperative with their files; Mordecai House (MOR); National Archives, Washington, D.C. (NA); North Carolina Department of Archives and History (NCDAH)—special thanks to Doug Owens and Steve Massengill, who located photographs of politicians and soldiers; Sprint/Carolina Telephone and Telegraph (CTT); Town of Macclesfield (MAC); University of North Carolina-Chapel Hill (UNC-CH).

Thanks to the entire staff of the Blount-Bridgers House—Carol Banks, Eric Greene, Susan Spain, and especially Meade Horne, who always knew who to call to get an essential photograph or piece of information. Edgecombe County is fortunate to have Meade as the director of the Blount-Bridgers House, and she as much as Mabrey inspired this work and kept me on track until its completion.

Finally, a special thank you to my partner in research and in life, my husband, Martin Fleming, who ran errands, tracked down information via the Internet, proofread the text, and made constructive suggestions.

INTRODUCTION

Over 275 years ago Tuscaroras roamed the woodlands of this area. In the mid-1730s, the first permanent European residents began settling along the Tar River in eastern North Carolina on land that would soon become Edgecombe County. The eastern and southern areas were settled first along Otters Creek (Autry Creek). After several years of dispute between the Royal Governor and the Colonial Assembly, Edgecombe County was finally recognized in 1741.

Settlement of the area took place so quickly that the county was divided three times in less than forty years. The first break formed Granville and present-day Vance and Orange Counties. The second break, in 1758, placed Enfield, at that time the county seat, in the new county of Halifax. By 1760, there were sufficient people to create a town—Tarboro, or Tarborough, or Tarrburg, as it was sometimes spelled. The third break, the creation of Nash County, occurred amid the turmoil of the Revolutionary War.

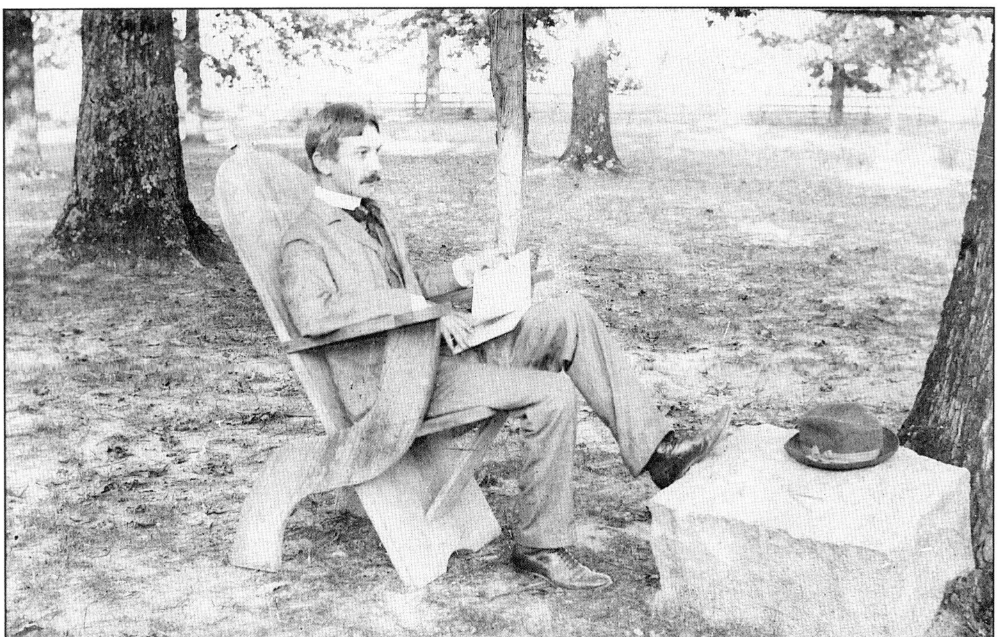

(Above) A town citizen spends a pleasant afternoon reading on the Town Common. This image was made by local photographer Sidney Rufus Alley, who worked in Tarboro between 1880 and 1920. Many photographs in this book are from the S.R. Alley holdings in the Janie Allsbrook Room of the Edgecombe County Memorial Library. (ECML)

In 1763 Tarboro became the county seat of Edgecombe County. Situated along a colonial road and a navigable river, the area became a popular trading center. During and after the Revolution the area was active in the effort to form a new nation, and two companies of Minutemen were raised here. Three area residents distinguished themselves as soldiers in the war. Henry Irwin Toole, who was among the first to accept a commission in the Continental Army, fought at Brandywine. Jonas Johnston gave an inspirational speech in Tarborough, raised volunteers, and led a company of Minutemen to the Battle of Moore's Creek. Toole's cousin, Henry Irwin, was killed at Germantown. Late in the war Cornwallis marched through this area, stopping in Halifax, before his defeat at Yorktown. Local militia attacked the British in a brief skirmish as they crossed Swift Creek.

In 1787 the North Carolina General Assembly met in Tarboro as the town vied to become the state capital. In 1790, when the first national census was taken, Edgecombe County had a population of 10,255. In 1791 President Washington toured the United States and visited a tavern in Tarboro. Less than half a century later, the county boasted the second textile mill in the state, Rocky Mount Mills, and a prominent private academy, Tarboro Academy, which lasted for over seventy-five years.

By 1850, Edgecombe County led the nation in cotton production and the population had increased to 17,189. Southern agricultural specialist Edmund Ruffin of Virginia made a special trip to Edgecombe County in 1854 to visit the Panola and Strabane Plantations. The county again saw its borders change as a new county was formed to honor an Edgecombe County native, Louis D. Wilson, who died in the Mexican War.

With the coming of the railroad, the county's population grew, its agricultural production increased, and communities like Battleboro and Sharpsburg developed. James Smith Battle helped to develop part of the Wilmington and Weldon Railroad through Edgecombe County during the 1840s. In 1860 his son William sent a spur line to Tarboro which changed the town's economy and brought the War Between the States into town.

After the War and Reconstruction, the area prospered as never before, partially due to new rail lines coming in. As numerous mills and factories competed for laborers, the population almost doubled between 1860 and 1910. Rocky Mount was incorporated in Edgecombe County in 1867. A move of the boundary line with Nash County later divided the town at the railroad tracks. In 1870 Edgecombe County had almost 23,000 residents, with 1,300 living in Tarboro. The county remained active in state and national politics, electing several African-Americans to the General Assembly. At the turn of the century an Edgecombe County African-American who was sent to the United States Congress became the last African-American to be sent from a Southern state until the 1990s. The county also gave the state two governors, in 1860 and 1892, and a lieutenant governor in 1912.

As technological developments affected industry and commerce in the late 1800s, the focus of life

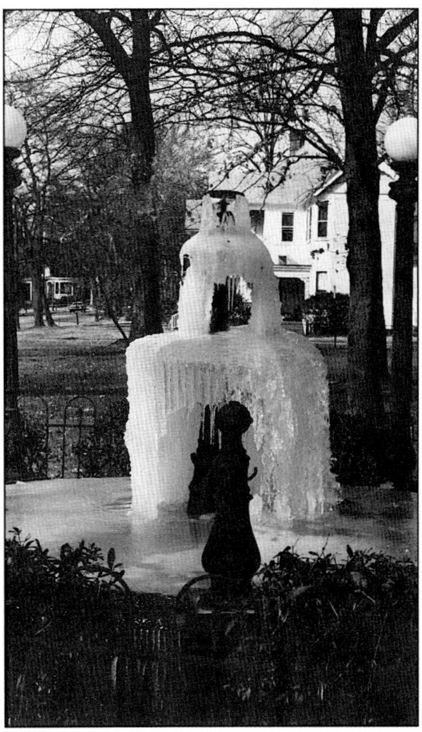

(Left) The United Daughters of the Confederacy installed this fountain in 1910 as a monument to Henry Lawson Wyatt, a Tarboro citizen who was killed in the War Between the States. The fountain is on the Town Common at Main Street. (BBH)

moved from river communities to train depots and mill villages like Runnymede. People began to move from farms to small towns. Pinetops and Macclesfield were created, and the Carolina Telephone and Telegraph Company built the first four-story building in Tarboro. The new century brought a housing boom in Rocky Mount, Tarboro, and many other county communities. The 1910 census reported over 32,000 in Edgecombe County, with 4,000 of those in Tarboro. The county had a total of seventy-five schools; forty for whites and thirty-five for blacks. A 1910 business directory listed the following businesses in the county: five corn mills, dozens of cotton gins, six cotton seed oil mills, four sawmills, three hotels in Tarboro, three hotels in Rocky Mount, four fish/oyster dealers, six brick companies, five textile mills, a fertilizer factory, an iron works, and a coffin plant.

World War I brought many changes to the area. The state's first county health department opened in 1919 in Edgecombe County. The year before, the Tarboro established its own milk company to reduce infant mortality. The county continued to grow and prosper in the 1920s.

During the Depression of the 1930s, many families struggled to survive. Numerous Work Project Administration programs not only created jobs for area citizens, but left long-standing tributes to the work of those involved. City Lake in Rocky Mount, ball parks in both Tarboro and Rocky Mount, a Farmers Curb Market in Rocky Mount, a new county agriculture building, a water treatment plant, an annex to the county courthouse, and the community swimming pool in Tarboro were all projects of President Roosevelt's alphabet agencies that benefited the residents. Although Tarboro had electricity since 1899, much of the county did not receive electric power until 1937, when the Edgecombe-Martin Electric Membership Corporation was established. In 1940 the population was just under 50,000 for the county. Tarboro was at 7,000 when Rocky Mount topped 25,000 people, quite a jump since 1890, when Rocky Mount's population was just over 800. The county presently occupies about 550 square miles in the northern coastal plain of North Carolina, and although agriculture is still an economic force, industry has continued to help the area develop.

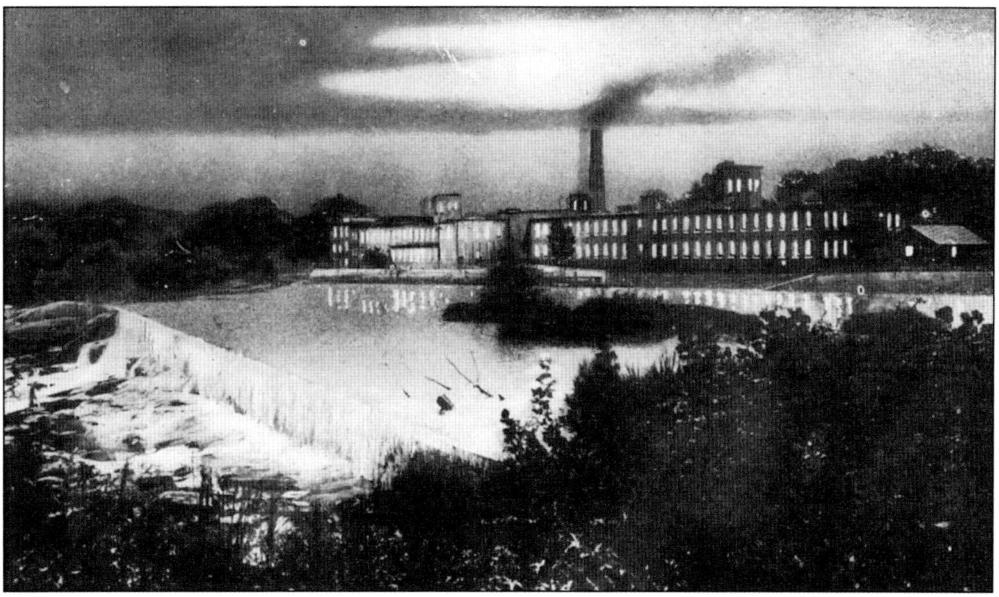

(Above) The second oldest textile mill in North Carolina, Rocky Mount Mills is located at the Falls of the Tar River in Rocky Mount. Started in 1818 by Joel Battle, the mill was later purchased by James Smith Battle (his cousin) and managed by William Smith Battle. The Battles owned all of the land around the mill, which for most of the 1800s was in Edgecombe County. Battle Park now makes it possible for Edgecombe County residents and visitors to view this area. This postcard dates from the turn of the century. (ECUSC DeVisconti Papers)

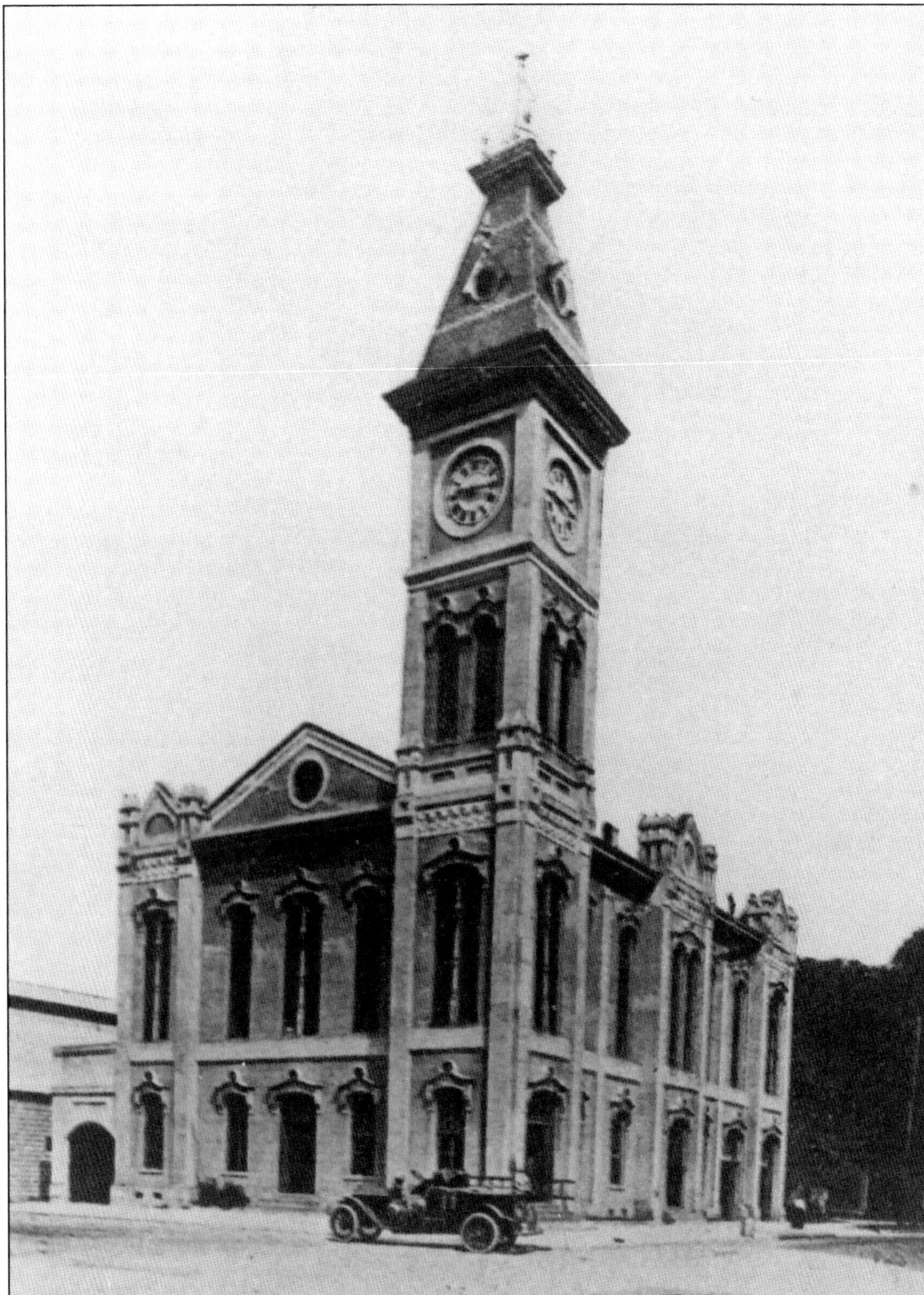

Tarboro Town Hall, located on the corner of Main Street and Church Street, was constructed in 1895 by local carpenters, including George Matthewson. It housed the city administrative offices and the Tarboro Police and Fire Departments. On the second floor was the Opera House, which was used for most community programs. The clock tower was the highest structure in town. The building was demolished in 1962. (BBH)

One

TARBORO AND PRINCEVILLE

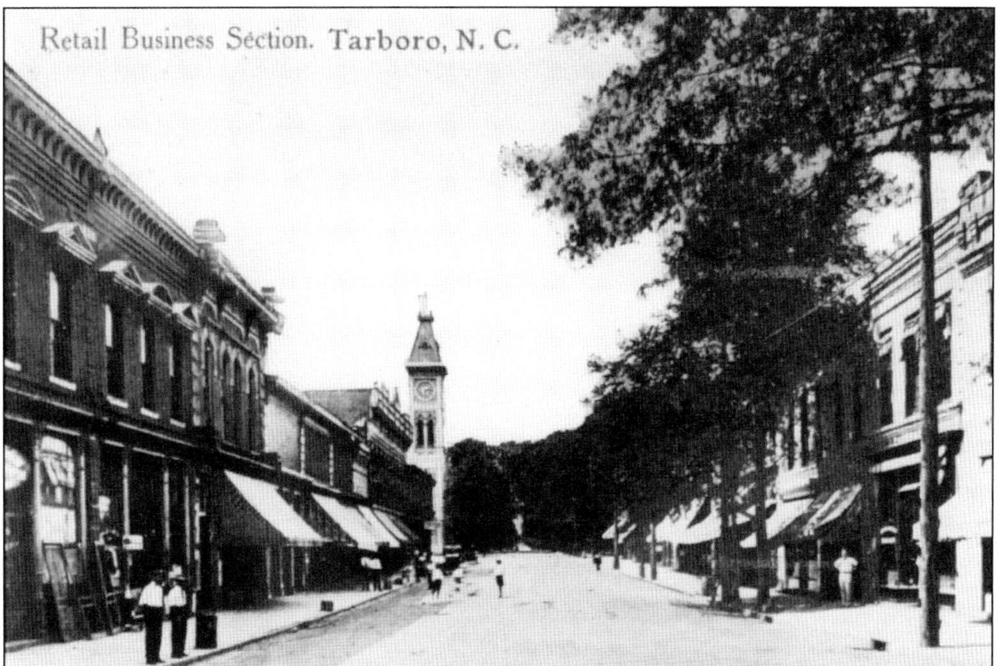

Tarboro was very busy in the 1890s. County citizens could shop in one of over thirty general stores, two hardware stores, three drugstores, and fourteen grocery stores. Undertakers, furniture makers, a tailor, and a jeweler also offered their services in Tarboro. This view of Main Street was taken around 1898. (ECUSC DeVisconti Papers)

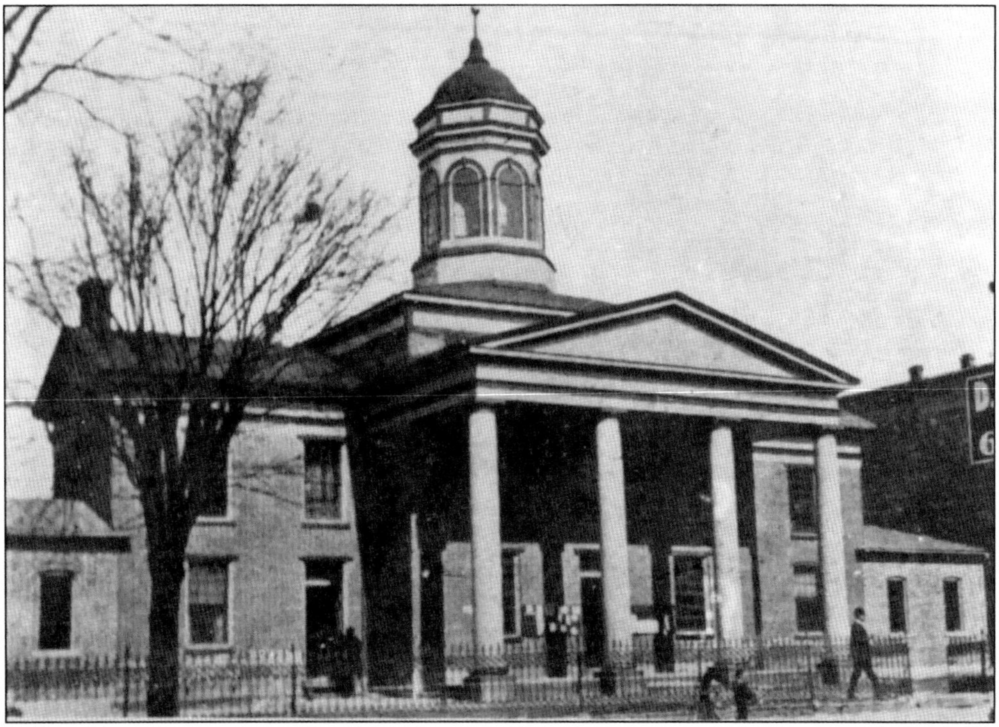

The Edgecombe County Courthouse, located on the corner of Main and St. James Streets, was constructed in 1835, remodeled in 1912, and served the county until 1964. This was the third courthouse to serve Edgecombe County. The first one, in Enfield, became a part of Halifax when the county was divided in 1758. Use of the second courthouse ended in 1835. (BBH)

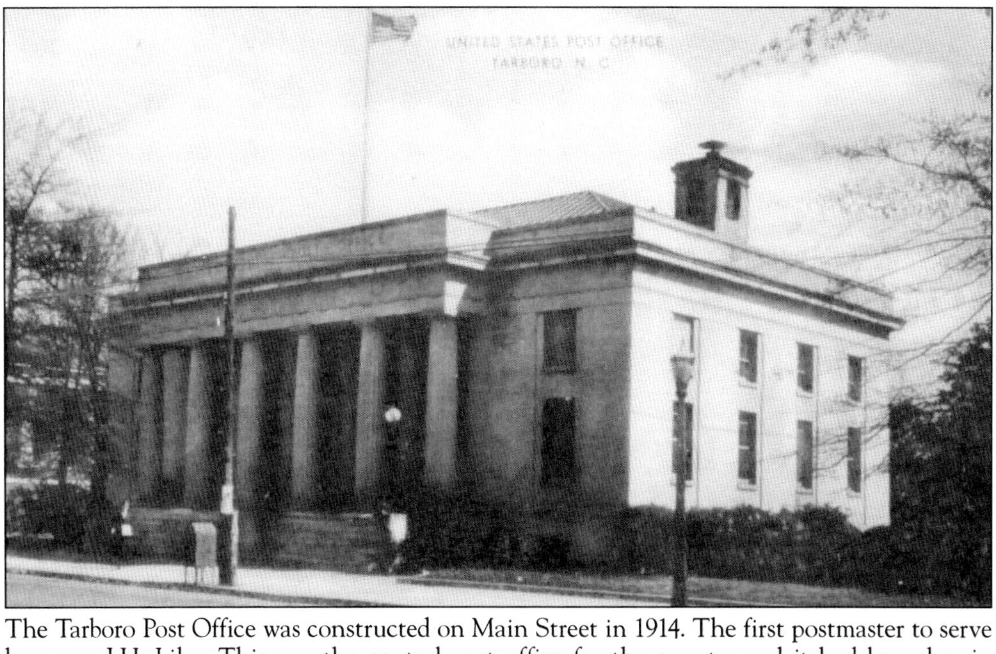

The Tarboro Post Office was constructed on Main Street in 1914. The first postmaster to serve here was J.H. Liles. This was the central post office for the county, and it had branches in Battleboro, Conetoe, Pinetops, Macclesfield, Speed, and Whitakers. (BBH)

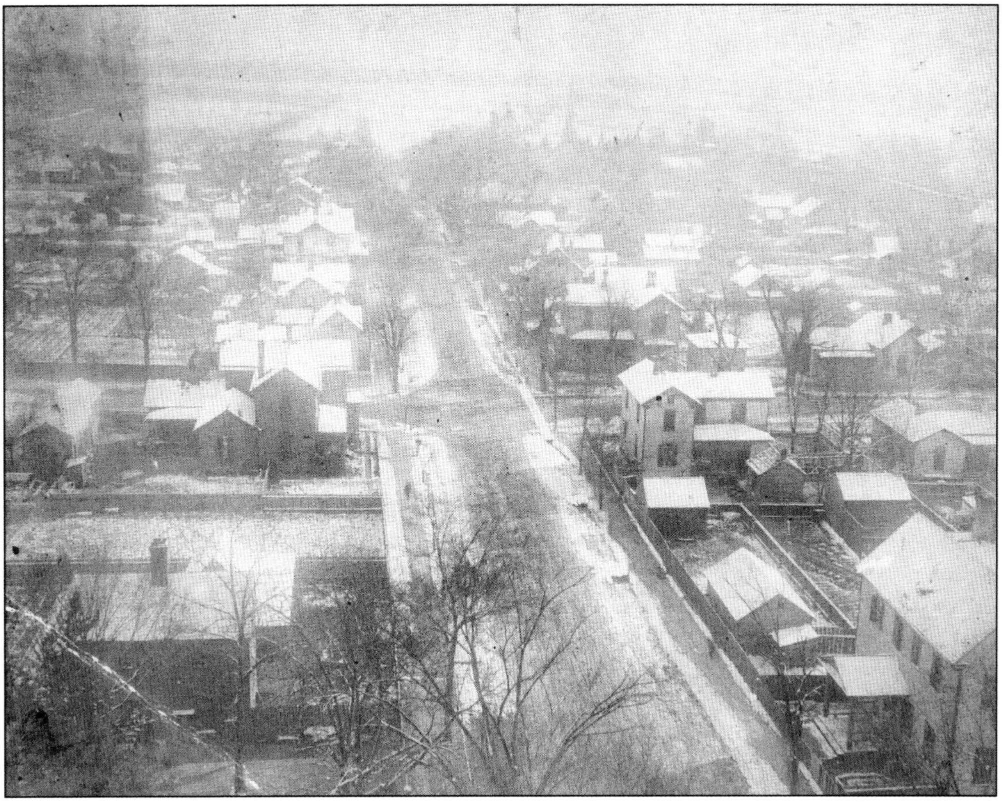

This view of east Tarboro was taken looking down Church Street from the top of the Town Hall about 1899. The photographer was J.P. Keech. (ECML)

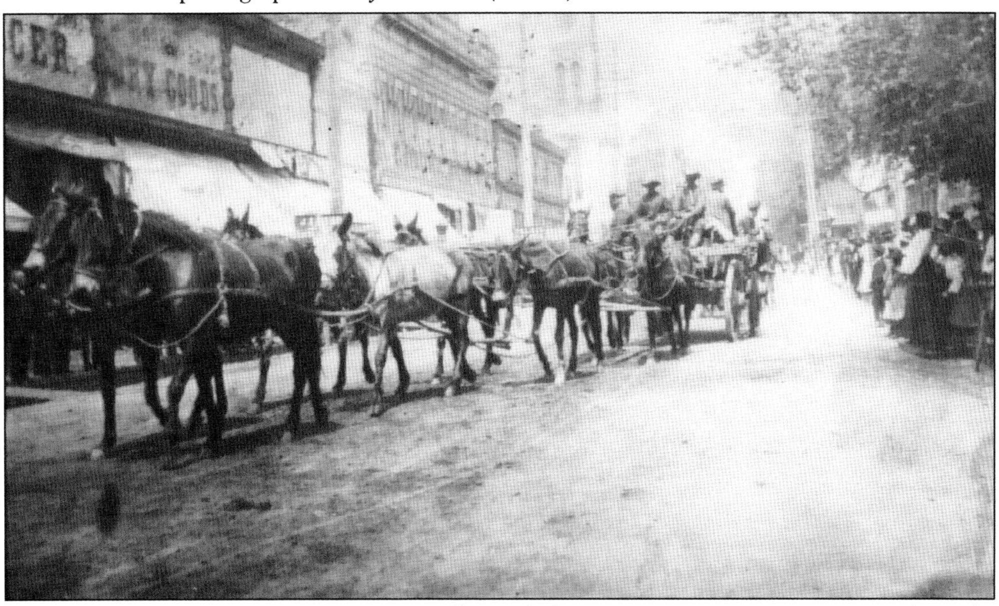

Around the turn of the century wagons still traveled on Main Street transporting goods to the river docks to be shipped downriver. This wagon came through during the time of the Spanish-American War. (BBH)

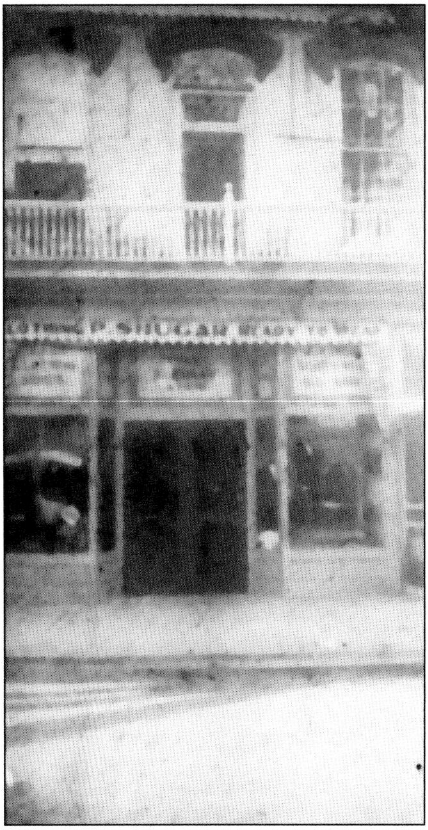

Philip Shugar immigrated to the United States from Lithuania in 1911, at the age of seventeen. He opened Hub Department Stores in Manteo and Elizabeth City, and in 1917 came to Tarboro and opened a third store called Shugar's Department Store. The Tarboro business remained in the family for over seventy-five years, relocating after it was destroyed by fire in 1950. Other well-known Tarboro clothing stores were Adlers (still operating), which sold women's clothing from the 1920s onwards, and Rosenbaum's, which was founded by Julius Rosenbaum in the late nineteenth century and sold men's and women's ready-to-wear clothing as well as dry goods. (BBH)

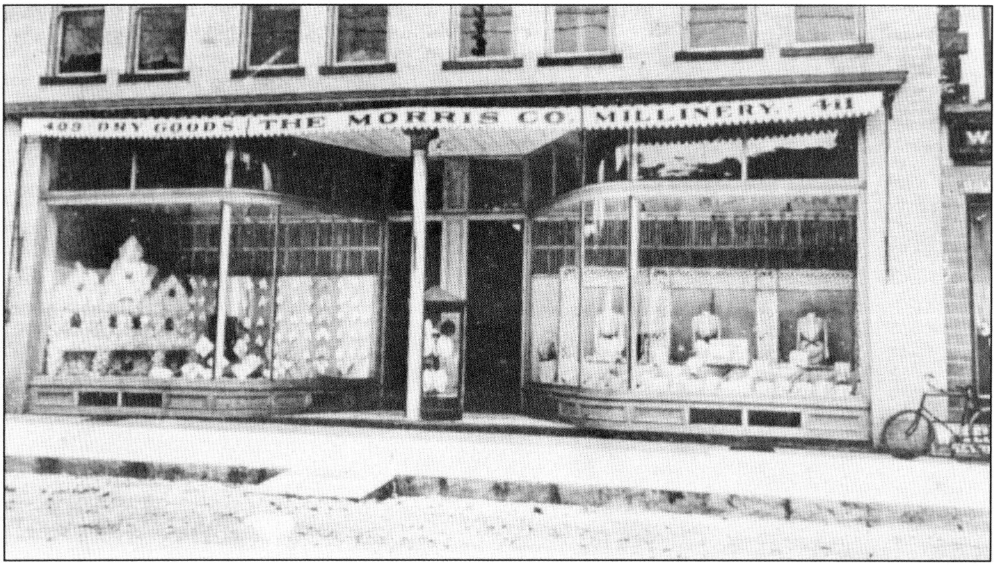

The Morris brothers opened a general store on the 400 block of Main Street in Tarboro around 1870. The business soon expanded, and by 1896 it was known as the Morris Company and was selling ready-to-wear clothing and shoes. In 1906 D. Morris was operating a dry goods store, but the Morris Company was no longer listed in the business directory. By 1910 D. Morris was out of business. (BBH)

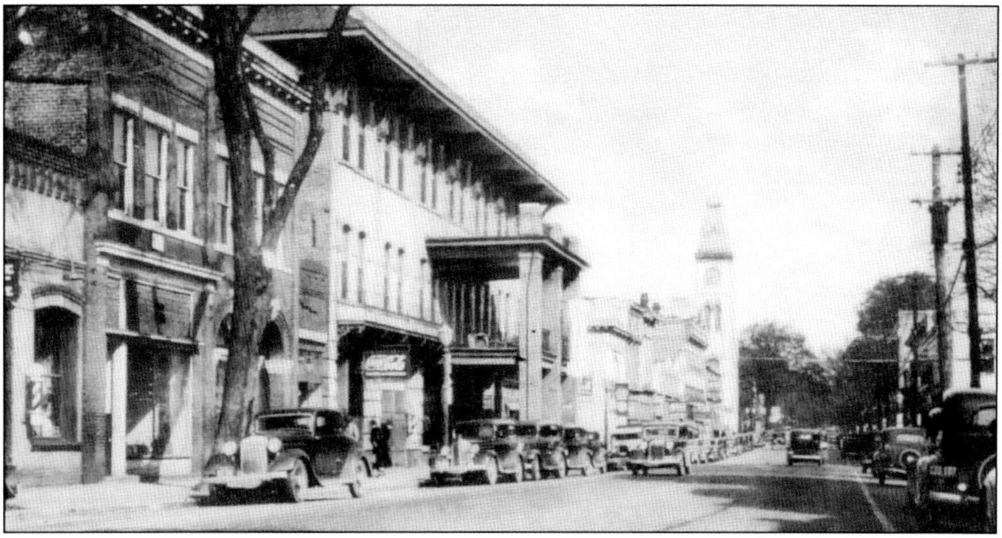

The 1920s saw several new businesses thrive in Tarboro. In 1919, the Colonial Theatre opened under the management of A.M. Smith. Soon after, the Colonial brought the first motion pictures to the area. The 1920s also saw the establishment of several early automobile dealerships. The Enterprise Carriage Company, which started in the 1860s, began selling Oldsmobiles and Buicks under the ownership of Howard S. and William "Thad" Hussey. Zeb Brinson and Milton Moye opened B & M Chevrolet. Zeb Brinson was a local celebrity for a brief time in 1939, when he was kidnapped at gunpoint and ordered to drive out into the country so his captors could take his car. He drove around in circles and was not far from town when he stopped, so the would-be car thieves were caught. (PC Murphy)

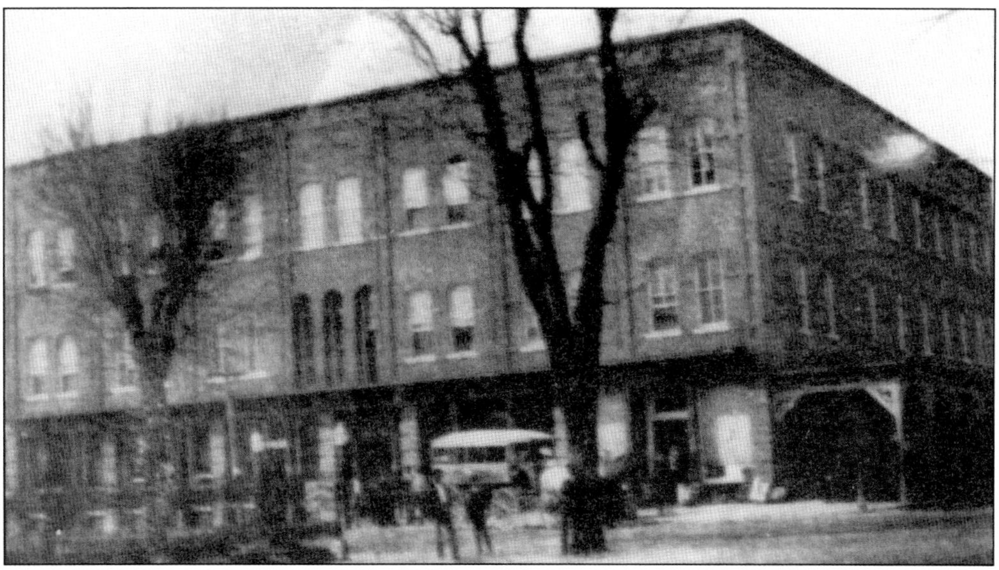

The Farrar Hotel, located across from the courthouse on the corner of Main and St. James Streets, opened in 1887. When it first opened it was considered the best hotel in eastern North Carolina. It was later advertised as "the Worst Hotel in the State." The upper floor contained rooms for rent and the lower floor housed numerous businesses, including a grocery store, a barbershop, and a pool hall. Owen Cicero Farrar was a leading businessman as well as a hotelier, and was one of the founders of Hart Cotton Mill. (BBH)

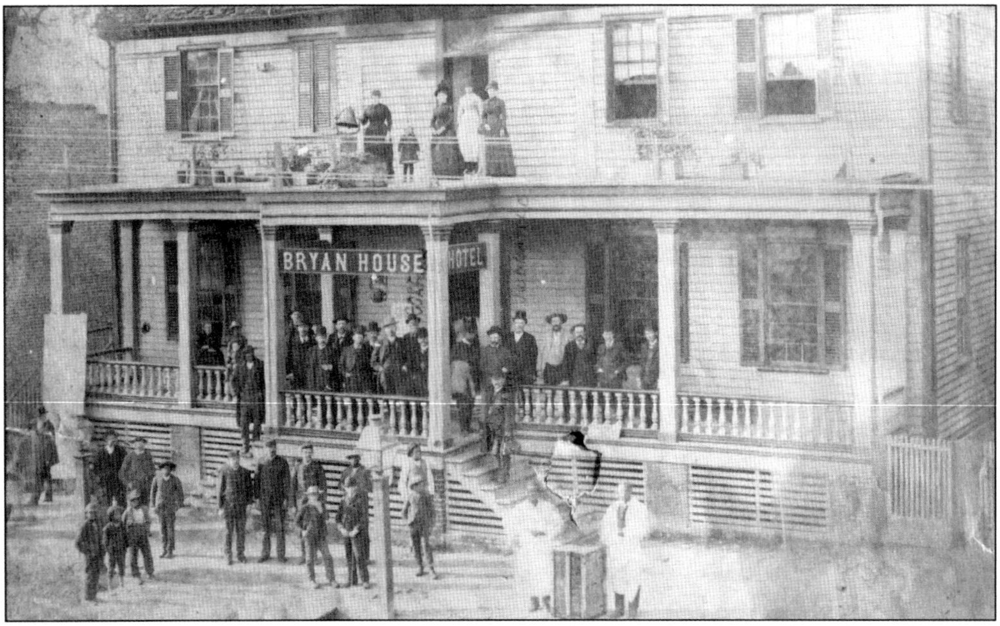

The Bryan House, formerly Mrs. Gregory's Hotel, was the major hotel in Tarboro from the 1830s until it burned in 1897. The dining room also served as the ballroom, with music provided by Frank Johnson's band. Prior to the War Between the States, the hotel hosted monthly dances. Mrs. Gregory had begun the hotel as a tavern for travelers and a boarding house for new residents. A frugal businesswoman, she invested her profits, expanded her hotel, and operated a gristmill in the Conetoe community. (ECML)

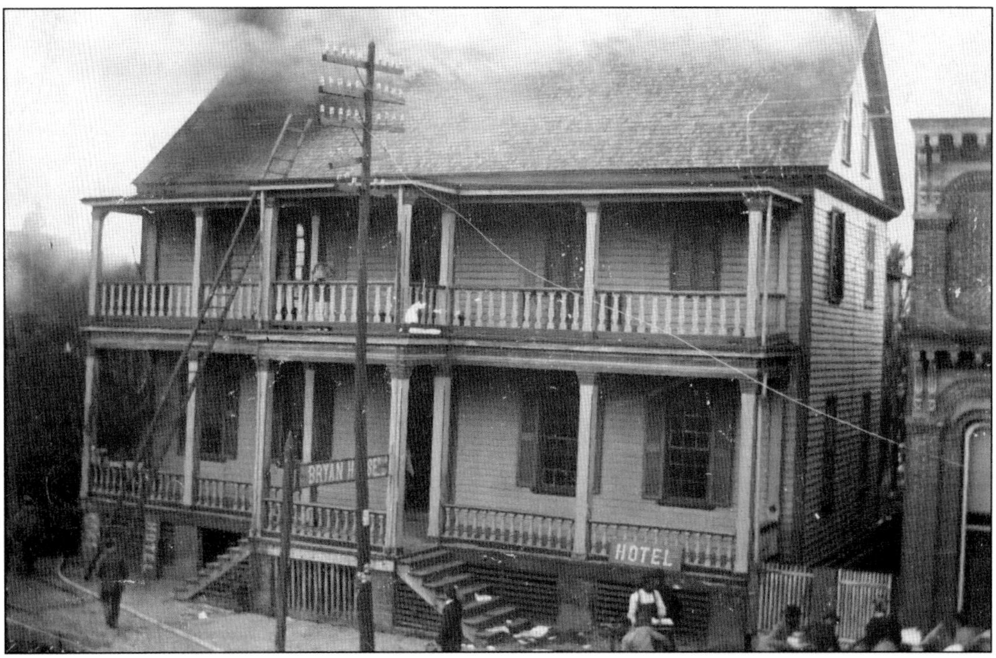

On the morning of November 18, 1897, the Bryan House caught fire, and despite the work of the Tarboro Fire Department a brisk wind spread the flames throughout the 400 block of Main Street. (ECML)

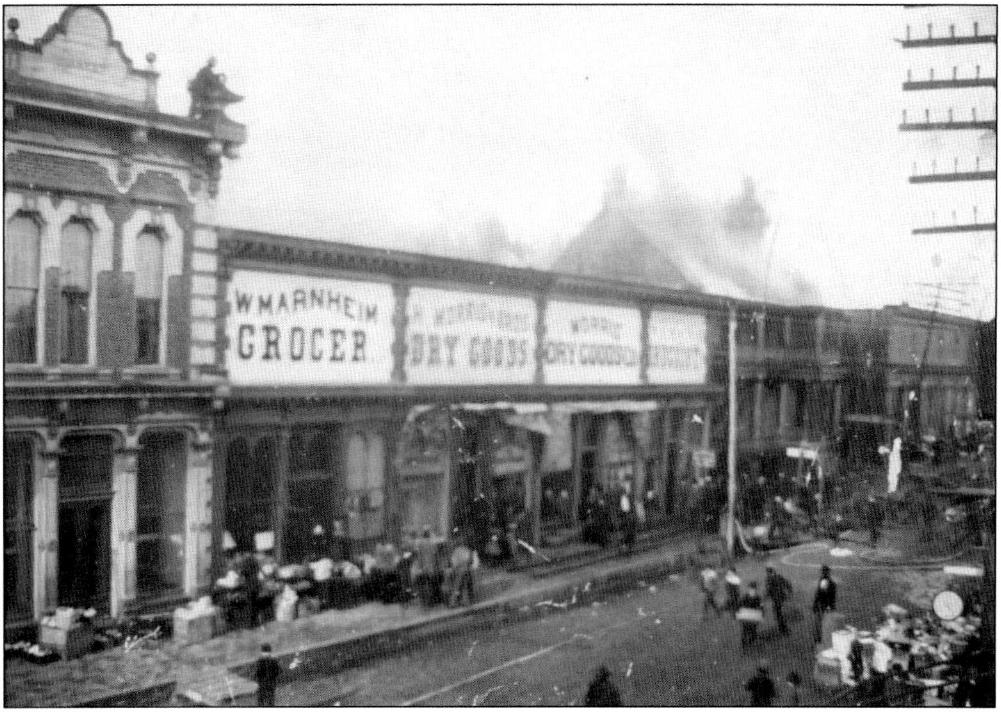

MacNair's store and four other buildings were destroyed by the fire. Although MacNair's store was gone, some of his merchandise was saved by "many ladies who at great personal discomfort, looked after the handling of delicately manufactured articles," according to a letter published in the local paper. (ECML)

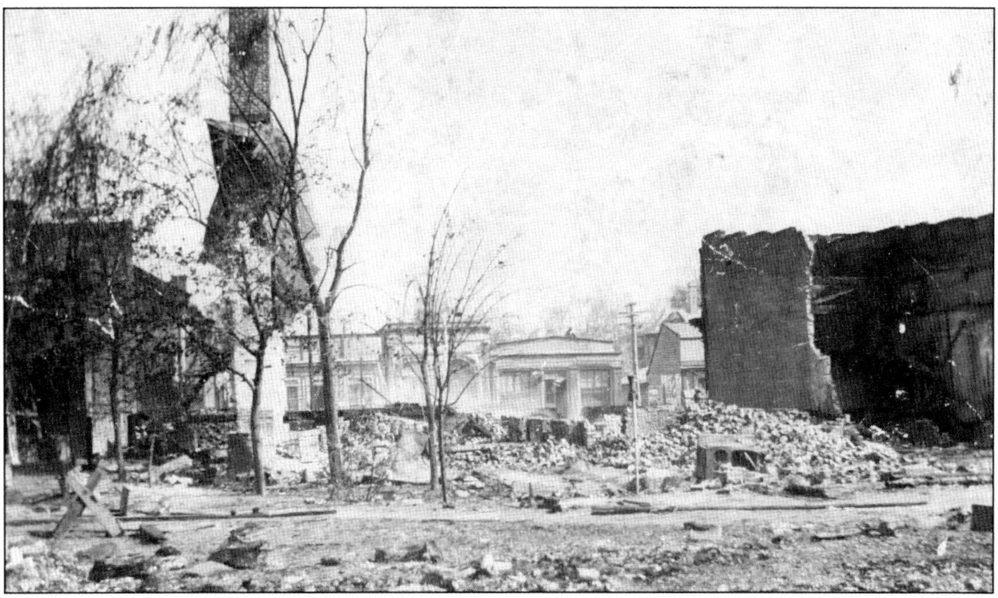

This fire was the first to be photographed in Tarboro. S.R. Alley climbed to the roof of a building across the street from the fire to capture the scene. This image shows Main Street after the fire, which destroyed more than half of the 400 block. S.R. Alley's own studio burned in a later fire. (ECML)

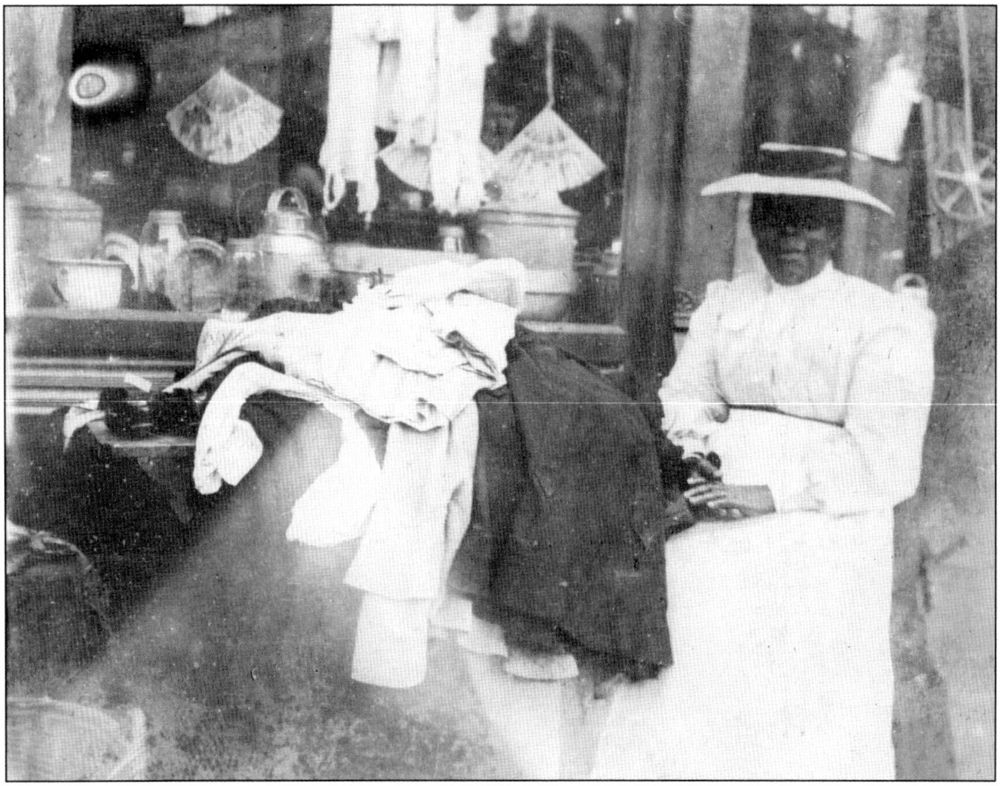

Sarah Shields sold old clothes in front of a shop downtown around 1903. (PC Simmons)

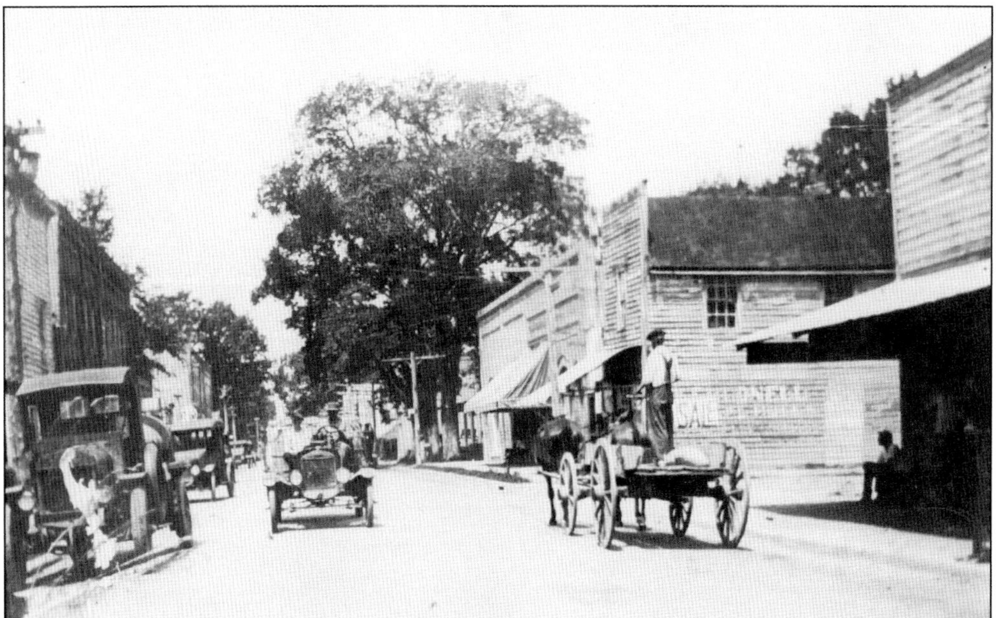

Although most of the retail businesses in Tarboro were on Main Street, residents could find stables, hardware stores, and operations related to farm work and tools on side streets. This view dates from around 1910. (PC Gulley)

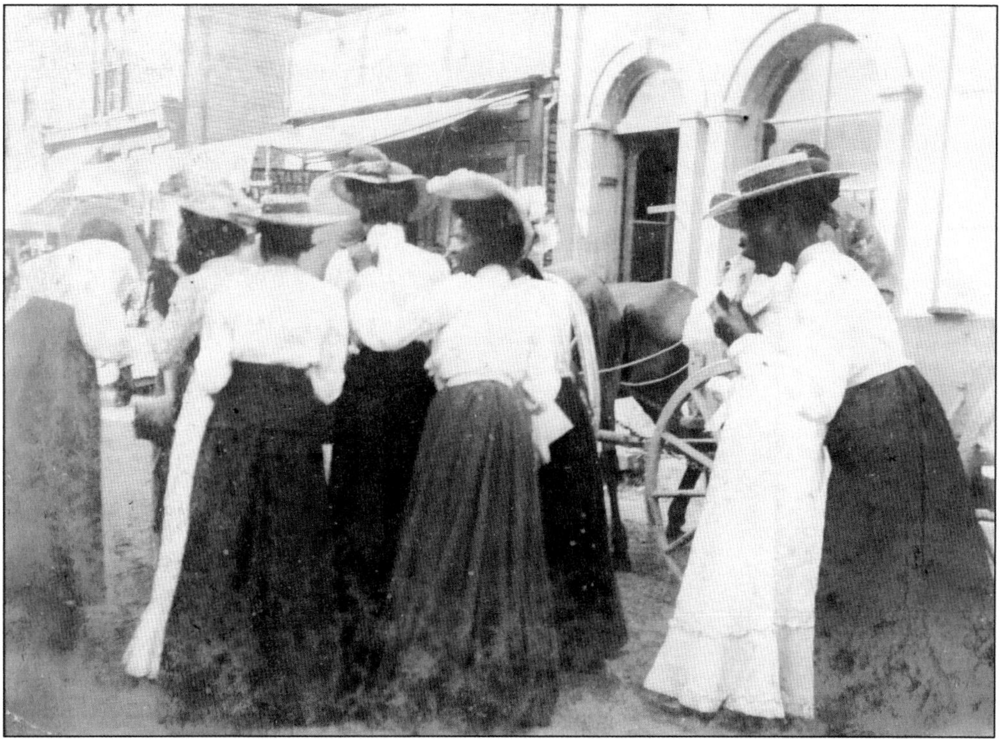

Area families came to Tarboro to shop and to enjoy special events, such as a play at the opera house or a circus. Here a group of women are shopping in 1903. (PC Simmons)

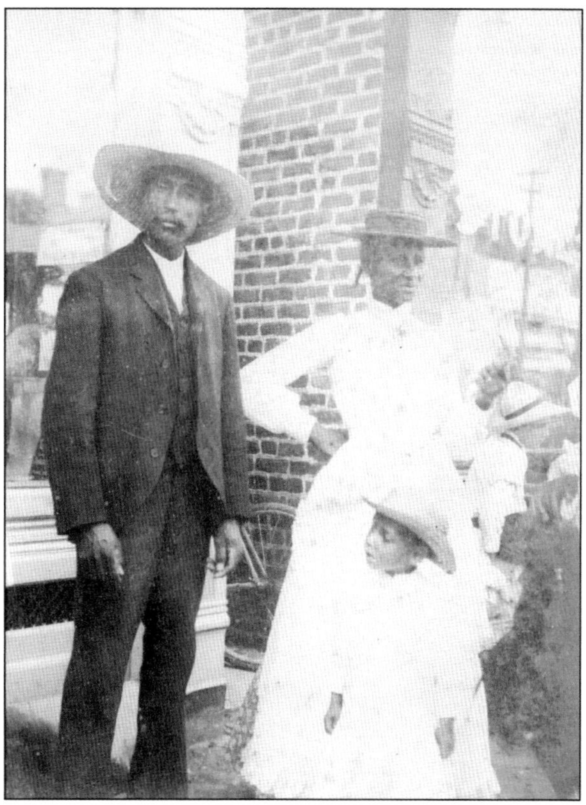

Identified only as Thad, this man enjoys a Saturday afternoon with his wife and daughter in downtown Tarboro in 1907.(PC Simmons)

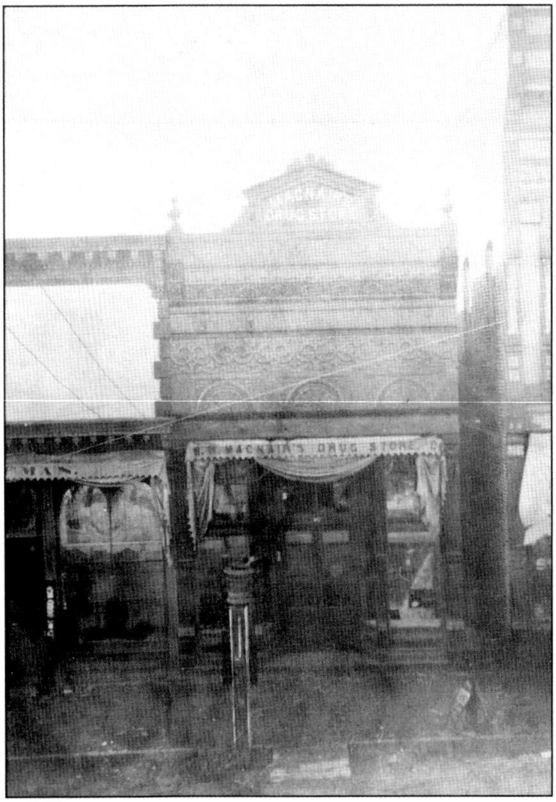

As early as the 1870s the MacNair family had a drugstore in downtown Tarboro. The building was destroyed during the 1897 fire on Main Street. (PC Simmons)

The MacNair family rebuilt the store and continued its operation well into the twentieth century. The store featured a soda fountain in addition to dispensing medicine. (ECML)

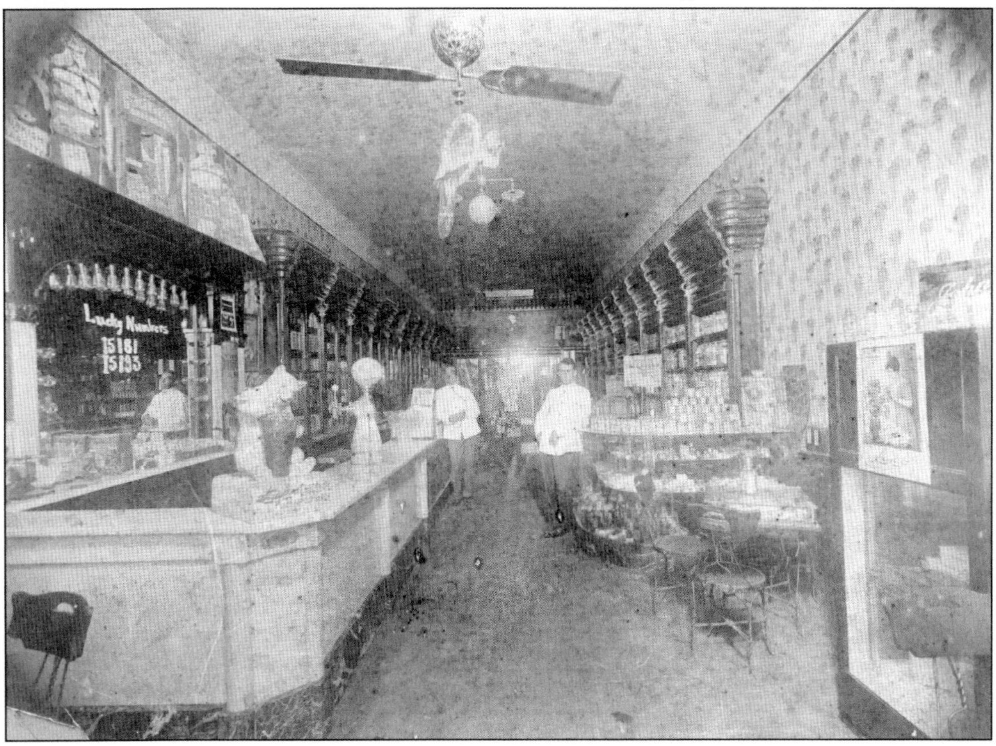

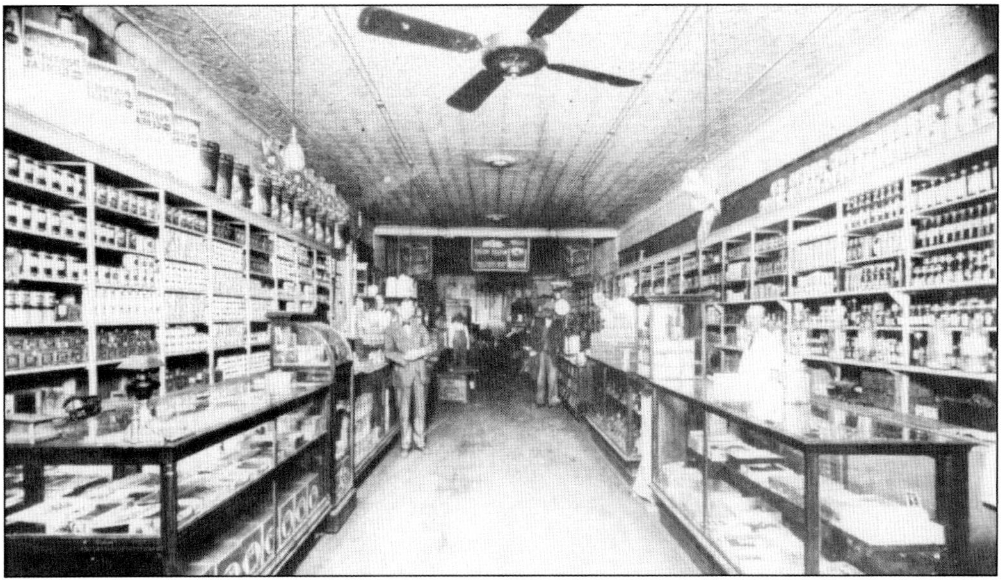

This photograph shows the interior of an unidentified grocery store around the turn of the century. In 1905 the following grocery stores were in business in Tarboro: R.C. Brown & Brothers, T.H. Peters, James Faithful, Camillus Dancey, D. Lichtenstein & Co., Y.D. Garrett, C.B. Keech & Co., Wade Andrews, David Cummings, Howard & Co., and Oates and Liles. Ten years later, in 1915, the list included many of the same names and a few new ones: H.C. Cherry, W.E. Warren, and W.P. Stallings. In the 1920s David Pender added his name to the list when he opened his grocery store in Tarboro. He went on to develop a chain of stores called Colonial Stores across North Carolina and Virginia. (BBH)

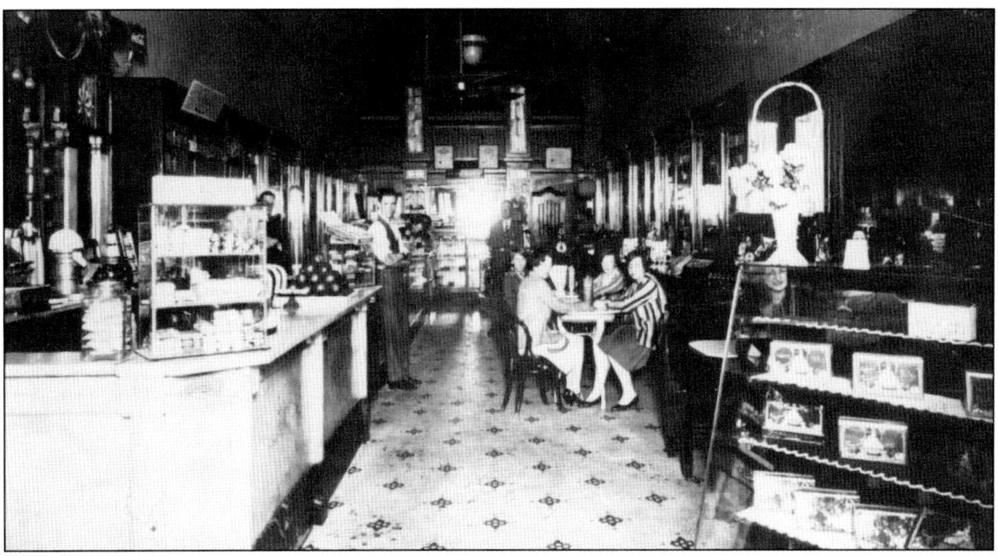

Tarboro had many drugstores prior to World War II. E.V. Zoeller and Dr. L.L. Staton opened Staton and Zoeller near the courthouse on Main Street in 1877. Edgecombe Drug Co., located on the first floor of the Bridgers Building, was founded by the Thigpen brothers but was later sold to J.E. Simmons. Dr. York D. Garrett, one of Tarboro's early black professionals, operated his pharmacy on Main Street in the 1930s. Soda fountains remained popular drugstore attractions well into the 1960s. (ECML)

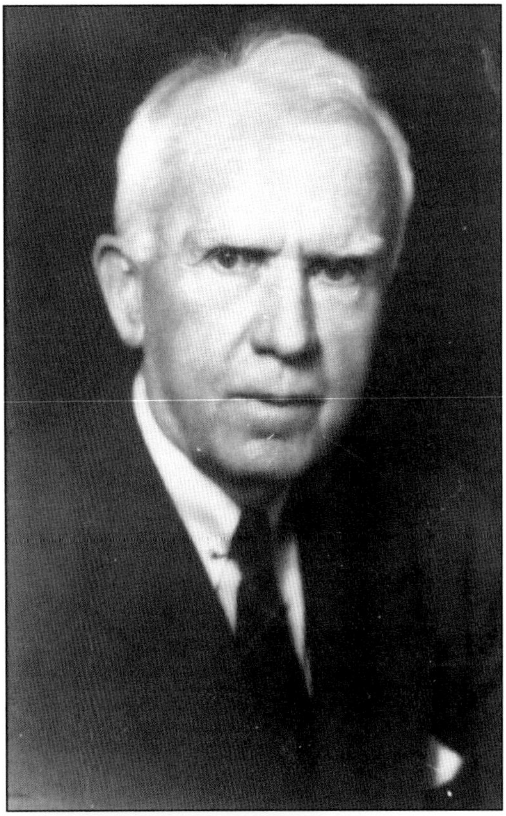

Born in 1876 and raised at "Hilma," Henry Clark Bridgers grew up in a town that was prospering, and he was determined to help the rest of the county to grow. He attended both the University of the South at Sewanee and the University of North Carolina at Chapel Hill. An avid sportsman, Bridgers played on the UNC tennis team and was nationally recognized for his skill at tennis, golf, and shooting. He is credited with introducing golf to Chapel Hill and was instrumental in founding the Hilma Golf Club, one of the first in the state. His career was a busy one: he was president of five area banks and at least ten other businesses over the years. Bridgers died in 1951 and is buried in Calvary Churchyard. (PC H.C. Bridgers family)

The railroad was not just a means of transporting goods to market. Local citizens often took train rides to the coast or to Raleigh for the day. Here D. Russell Clark is among several area youths on a day trip to the coast around 1900. (BBH)

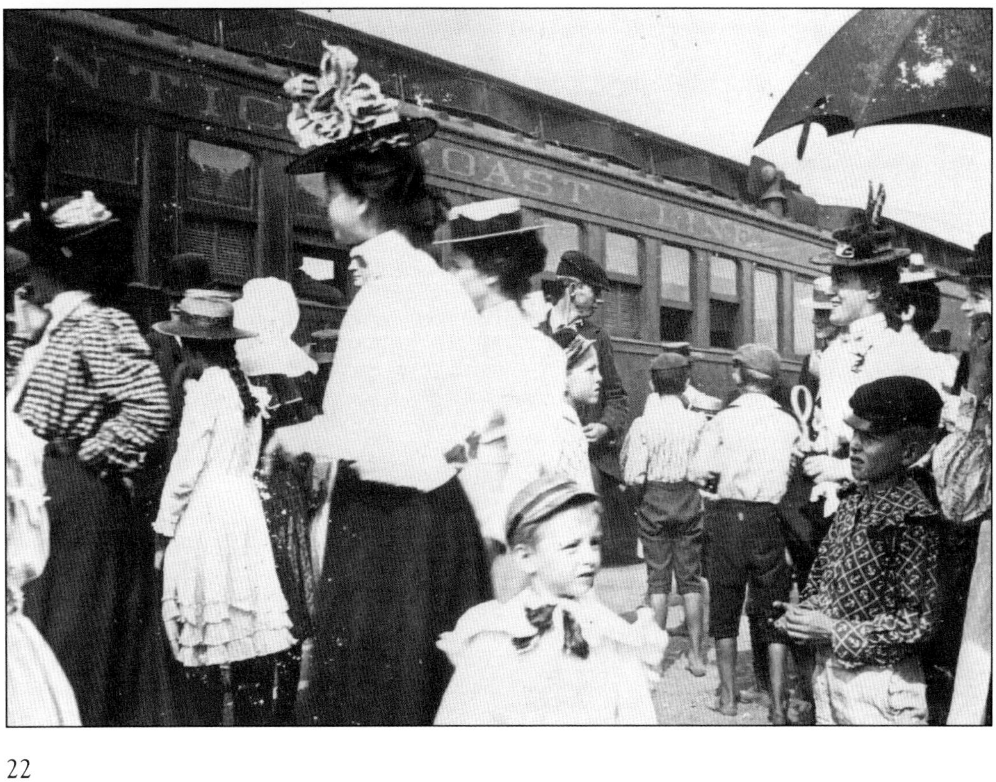

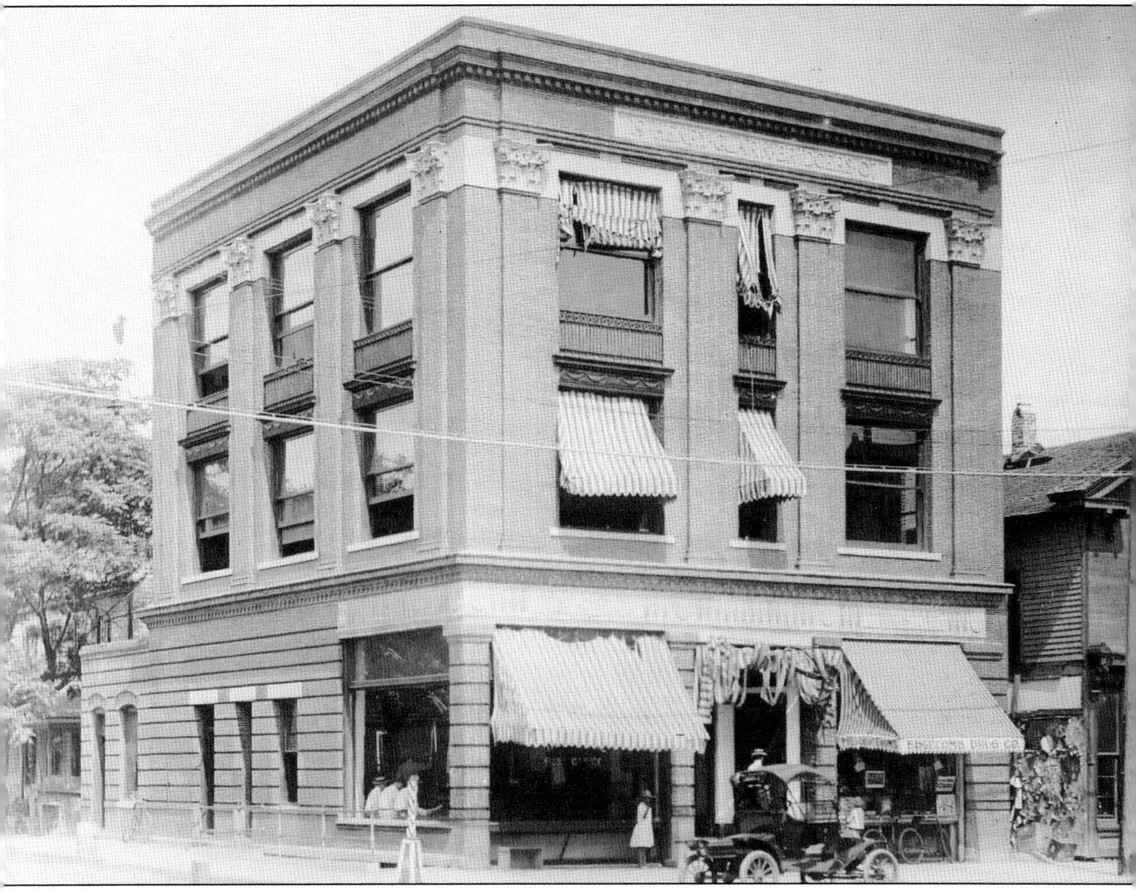

Henry Clark Bridgers constructed this building in 1907 to house the offices of his company, the East Carolina Railway. He is best remembered for running a rail line from Tarboro south to Hookerton in Greene County, providing a trade route for farmers. This line was responsible for the development of the towns of Pinetops and Macclesfield. Located on the corner of Main and Church Streets, the Bridgers Building also housed the post office, a barbershop, and a drugstore. In the1940s WCPS opened here as the community's first radio station. (ECML)

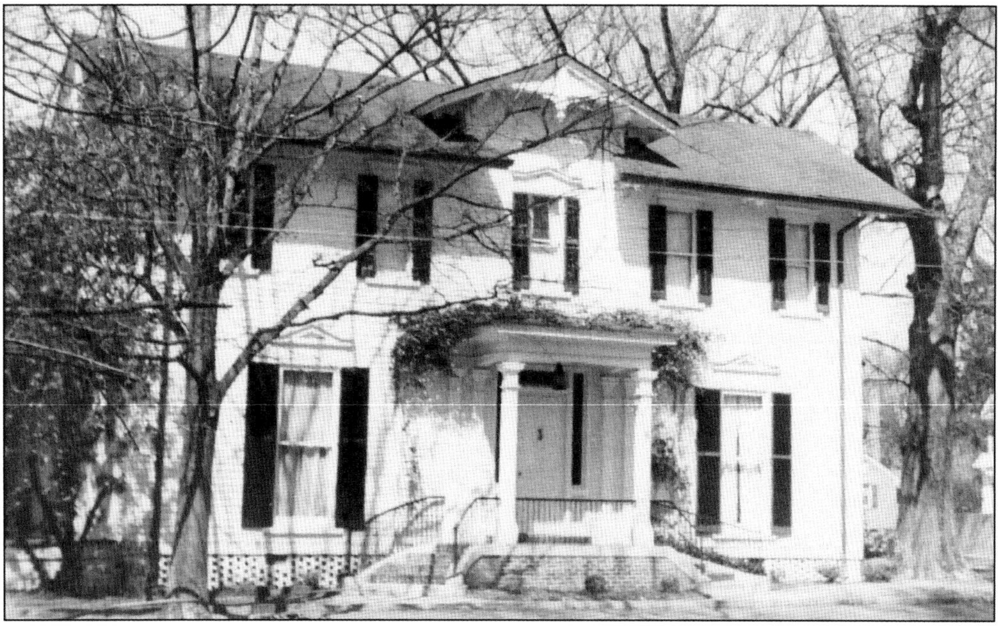

Spencer Cotten is believed to have built this house around 1829. The Reverend Thomas R. Owens lived in the house and operated a private school in the downstairs part for more than thirty years. Reverend Owens was the minister at First Baptist Church from the 1860s until 1880, when he retired. Judge Howard purchased the house in 1860 and enlarged it after the Civil War. (BBH)

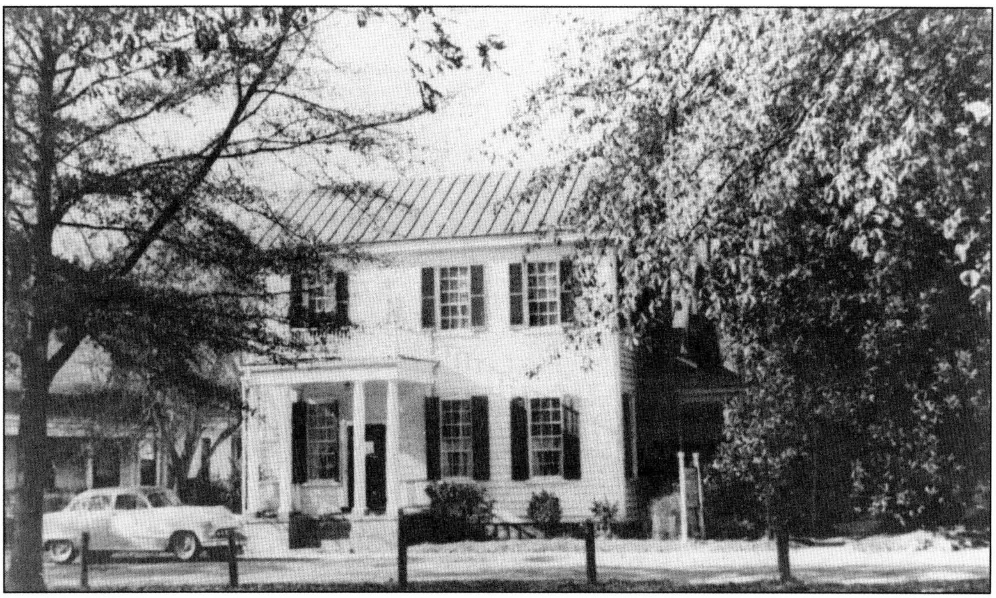

Mrs. DeBerry operated a dining room and antiques shop in the Howell-Sugg-King House on Park Avenue at the Town Common. Part of the house may date to the 1760s when the Howell family, who deeded the land to create Tarboro, lived here. The Sugg family and Coffield King both remodeled the house prior to 1840. Mrs. DeBerry was such a fine cook that her dining room was the most popular place to eat after church on Sundays for many years. A favorite dessert of regular customers was the Caramel Delight. (ECML)

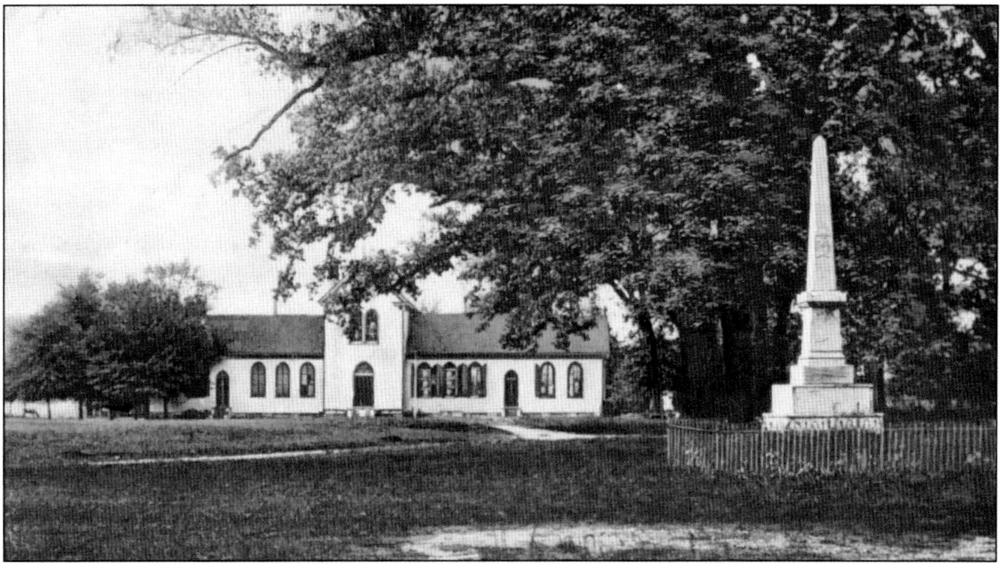

In 1793, the Tarborough Academy was established by an act of the General Assembly. According to records in the Library of Congress, the first trustees were John Leigh, Ethelred Phillips, Amos Johnson, Edward Hall, Jacob Battle, John Ingles, and Blake Baker. Local historical records show that an academy was located on the Town Common in 1813; there has been a school on the Common ever since then. This photograph shows a public school on the west end of the Common around 1915. (PC Murphy)

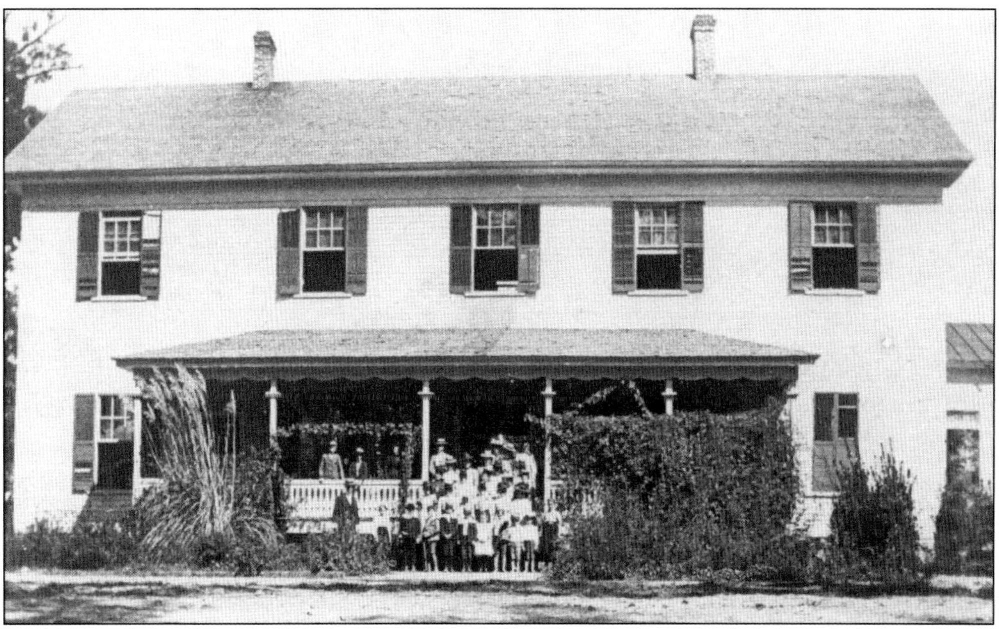

The Tarborough Academy became so popular that by 1820, females were allowed to attend. In 1840 a new building was added on the east end of the Common and the boys and girls were separated. Frank Wilkinson took over the Male Academy as principal. The male campus burned in 1885, but Wilkinson continued to operate a school out of his home. The Female Academy also burned, in 1891, but was renovated. This photograph shows girls outside the dormitory southwest of the Common around 1895. (BBH)

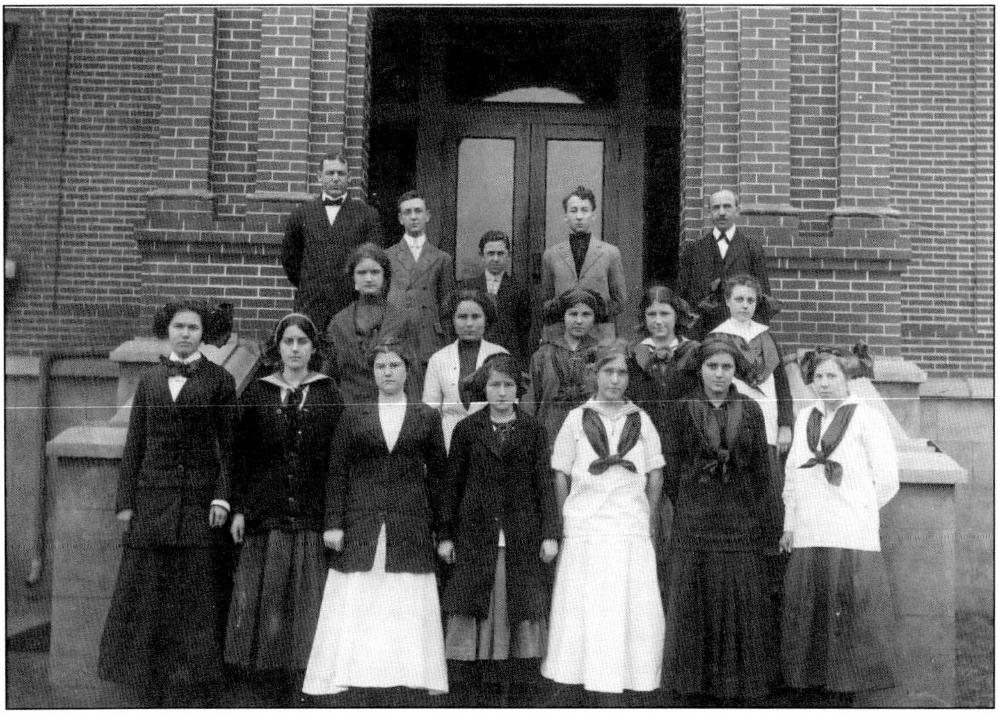

Public schools opened in Edgecombe County during Reconstruction and a new structure was built on the east part of the Town Common. The Tarboro Public School graduating class of 1913 included Hazel Weeks, Sadie Fountain, and Sue Fountain. (PC Fountain)

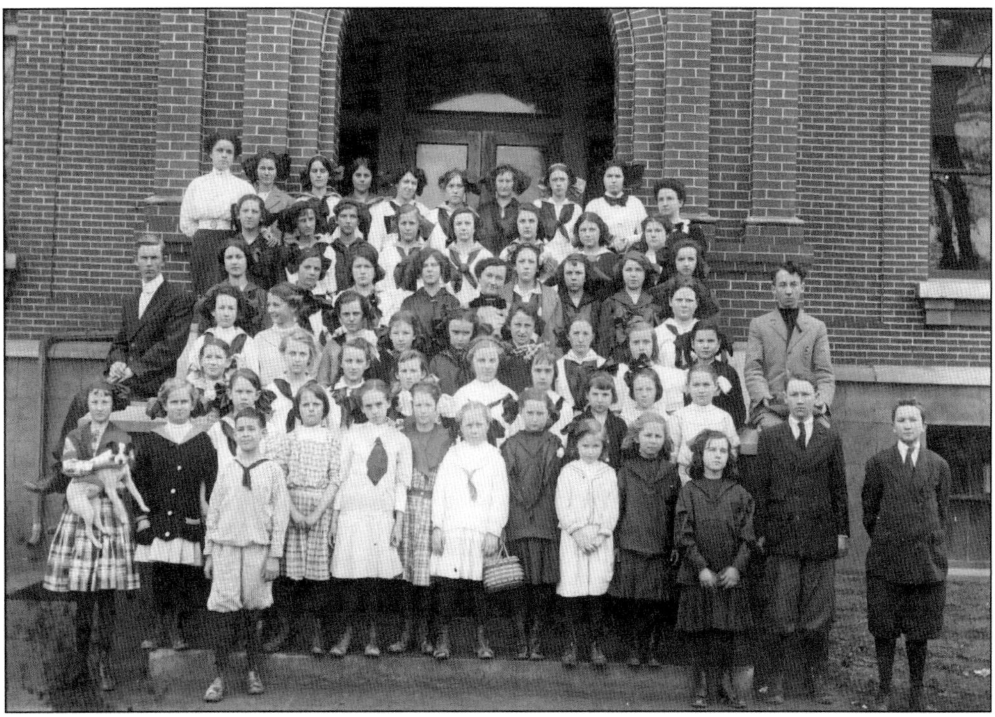

These students also attended the Tarboro Public School in 1913. (PC Fountain)

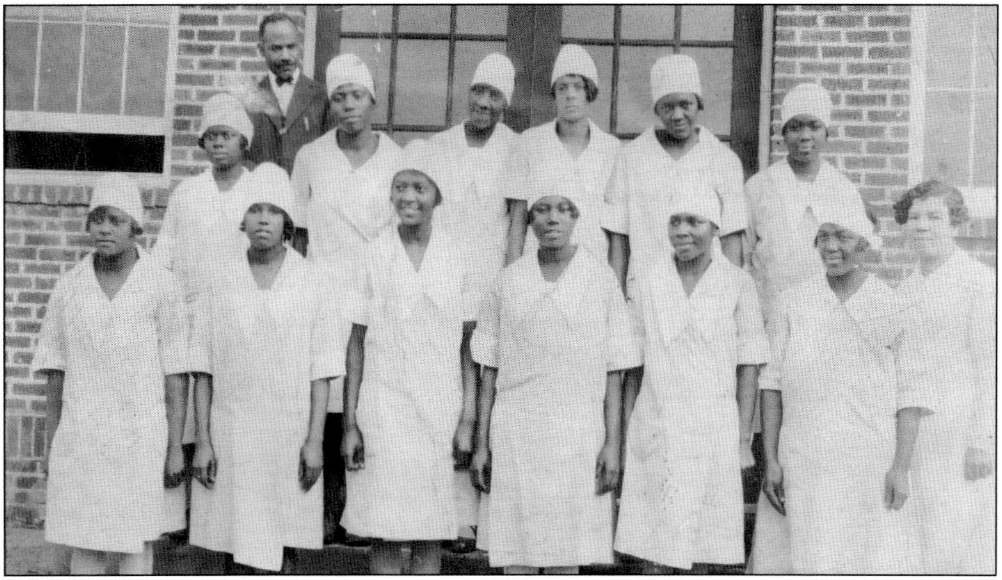

This photograph, taken *c.* 1920, shows a group of Home Economics students at the W.A. Pattillo High School with their teacher, Hazel Scales. The Pattillo School began in 1907 as the Tarboro Colored School. W.A. Pattillo (in the upper left of this photograph) became the principal in 1920, and by 1924 he had expanded the school to include high school grades. Miss Scales later married R.H. Parker and became the first black woman to serve Edgecombe County as a Home Extension Agent. (PC Parker)

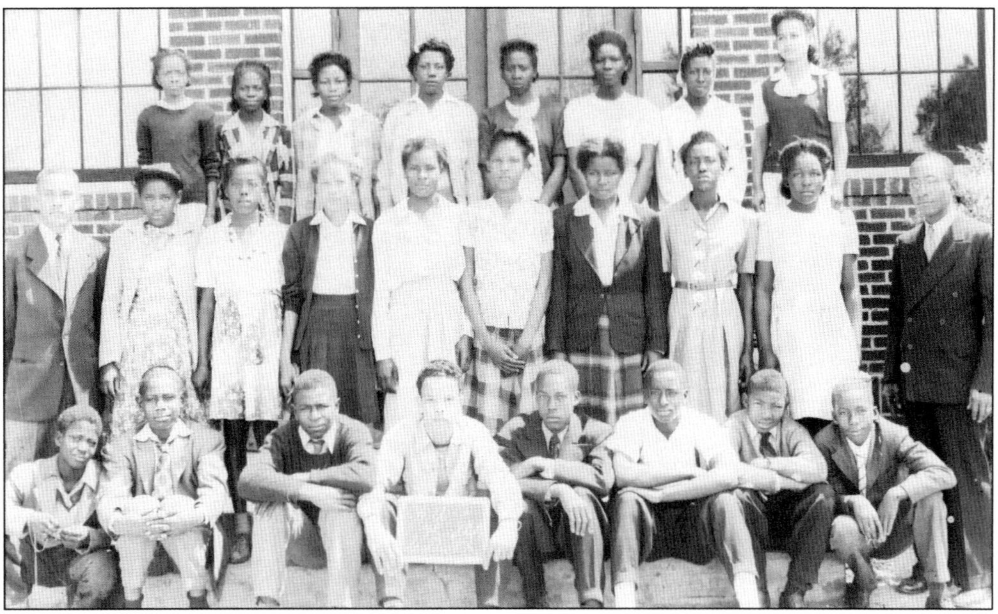

The eighth grade at the W.A. Pattillo School is shown here in 1944. Mr. Matthewson was the history and geography teacher. English, algebra, and health and P.E were among the other courses offered at this time. By 1931 the school had grown so much that a new building was constructed, adding seventeen new classrooms to house the increasing number of students—more than seven hundred in 1931. The school also had a football team and both boys' and girls' basketball. (PC Parker)

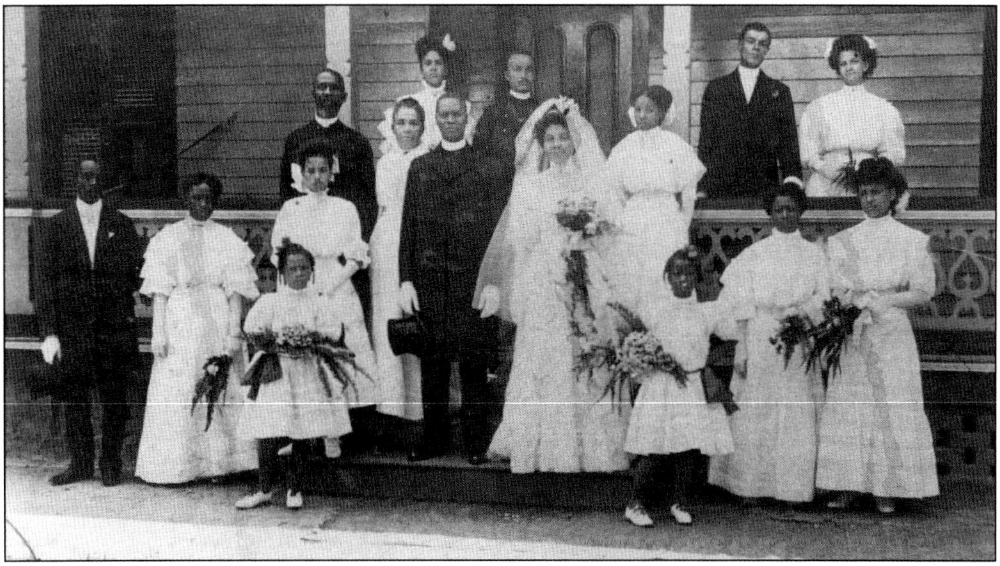

On June 16, 1908, Miss Catharine Perry (July 12, 1884–October 30, 1965) and Milton Moran Weston (October 27, 1871–October 10, 1966) were married. This photograph of the family was made at the home of the bride. The Reverend Milton M. Weston succeeded his father-in-law as rector of St. Luke's Colored Protestant Church. Weston began his career as a minister at St. Philip's Episcopal Church in Elizabeth City. Weston was also principal of the parochial day school sponsored by St. Luke's, and he was assisted by his wife Catharine. (PC Knight)

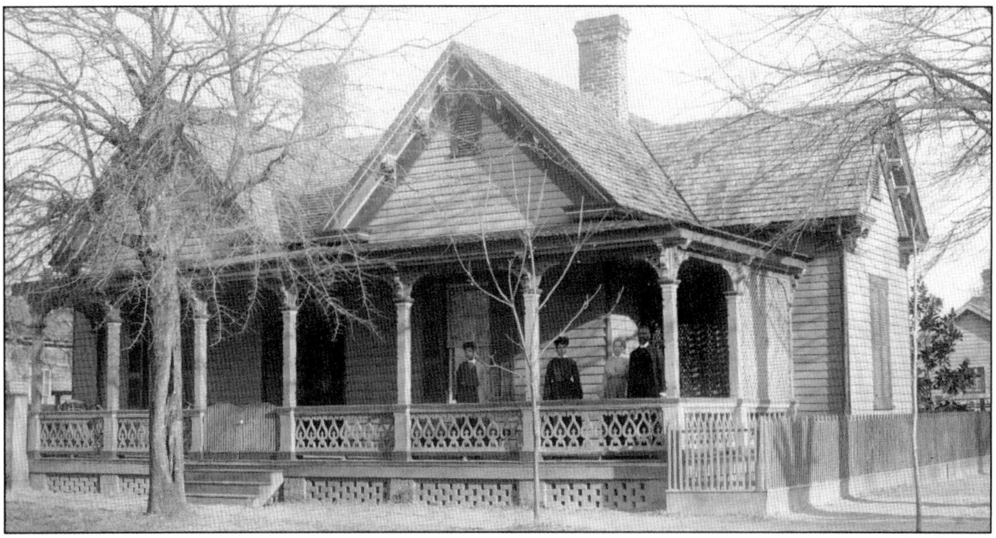

S.R. Alley photographed the Perry family at their residence on East St. James Street in Tarboro around 1890. On the porch are Mary Gertrude Perry, Catharine Cornelia Perry, Mary Pettipher Perry, and the Reverend Doctor John William Perry. Dr. Perry was the first rector of St. Luke's Colored Protestant Church. He was among the first African-American priests trained at St. Augustine's College in Raleigh, and was ordained as deacon in 1881 and to priesthood in 1887. Bishop Cheshire of Tarboro helped to create St. Augustine's College, so African-American congregations like those in Tarboro could have their own ministers. Dr. Perry served as rector of St. Luke's and headmaster of the St. Luke's Parochial School from 1881 until his death on April 14, 1918. (PC Knight)

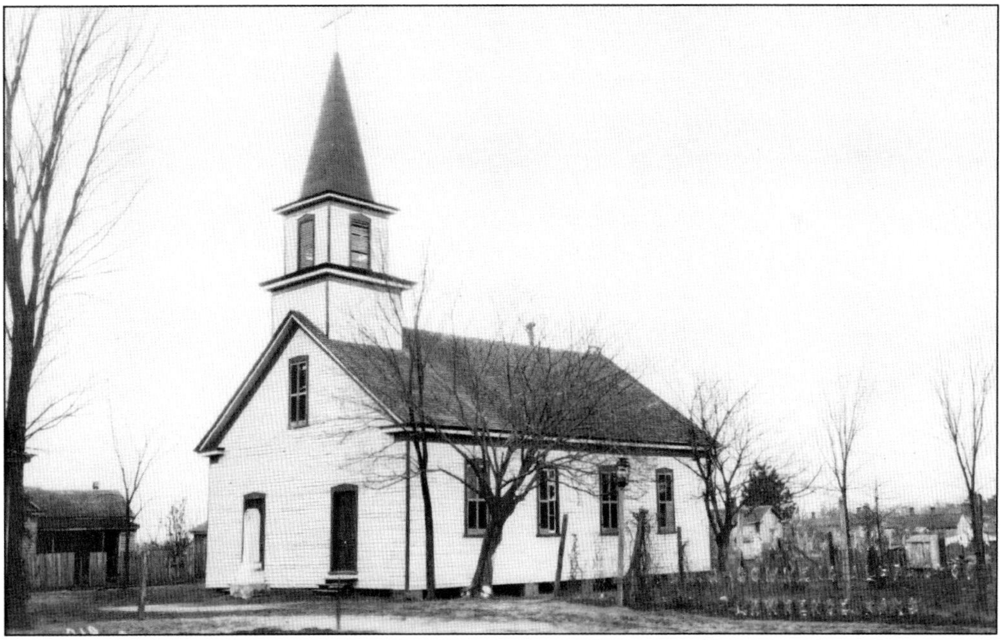

The Mount Zion Primitive Baptist Church in Princeville is the oldest church in the town. A monument in front of the church describes an earlier church, the Radicue Primitive Baptist Church, which was founded by Elder Abraham Wooten and members that came from Otter's Creek, Sparta, and Tyson's Meeting House. (ECML)

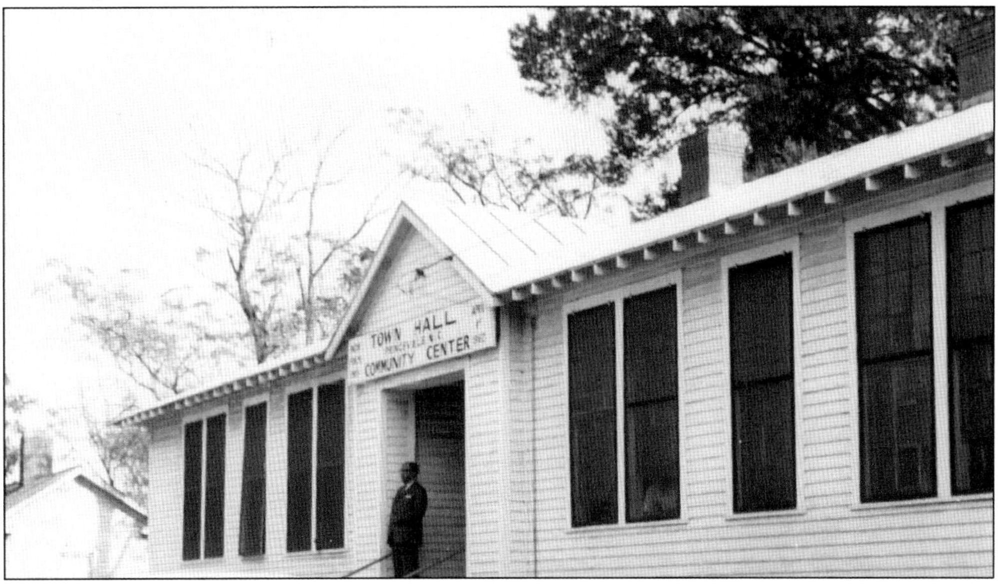

The community that was to become Princeville emerged immediately after the Civil War, when Federal soldiers occupied the area south of the Tar River. The area was originally called Freedom Hill by the former slaves who wanted to stay there after emancipation. The land had not been settled earlier because it was prone to flooding. In 1885 the community became the first incorporated all-black town in the United States. The citizens chose the name Princeville to honor Turner Prince, one of the early inhabitants. In this photograph, Mayor Willie Rayfield Matthewson stands in the doorway of the Princeville Town Hall. (ECML)

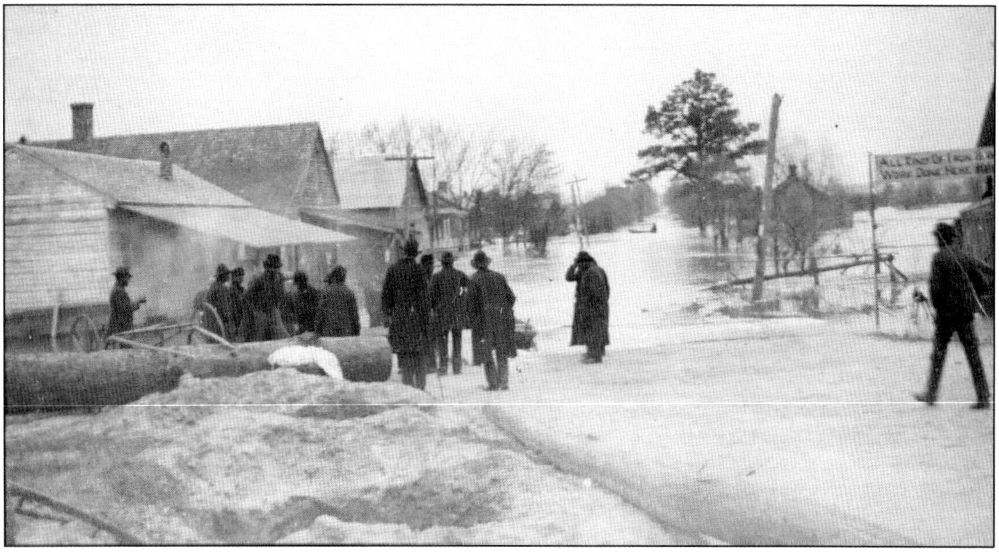

The Tar River has long been prone to floods, averaging at least one severe flood each decade since the 1820s, when records were first kept. The greatest flood on record occurred in July 1919, when water levels were even higher than those recorded during the 1887 flood, which held the previous record. The 1919 flood, shown here, completely devastated the community of Princeville, which was entirely submerged. All residents were evacuated by boat and most lost all of their household possessions. One resident reported going to bed the night before the flood only to awaken the next morning to find water around the bed. The river also flooded on the Tarboro side past Water Street. The flood waters completely covered Bell's Bridge north of town, and the Old Sparta Bridge, 8 miles south of Tarboro. (ECML)

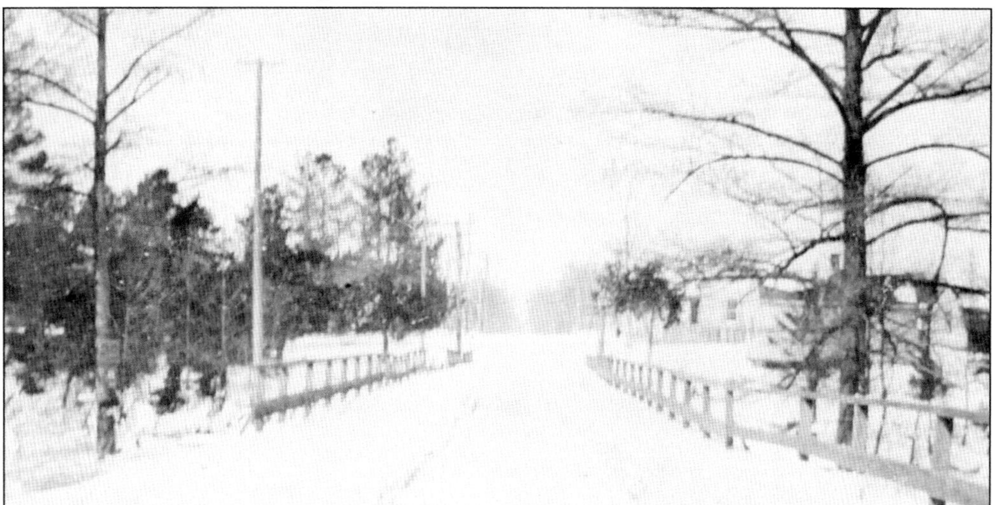

The spring of 1927 brought two severe storms to Edgecombe County. On March 2 a blizzard left 12 inches of snow overnight and created drifts of 7 feet along the railroad tracks, causing train delays. Then, just one month later, on April 2, a tornado came through town destroying many of the trees on the Town Common, knocking out a wall of Hart Cotton Mill, blowing the roof off Mr. Bardin's stables, and destroying several houses. (BBH)

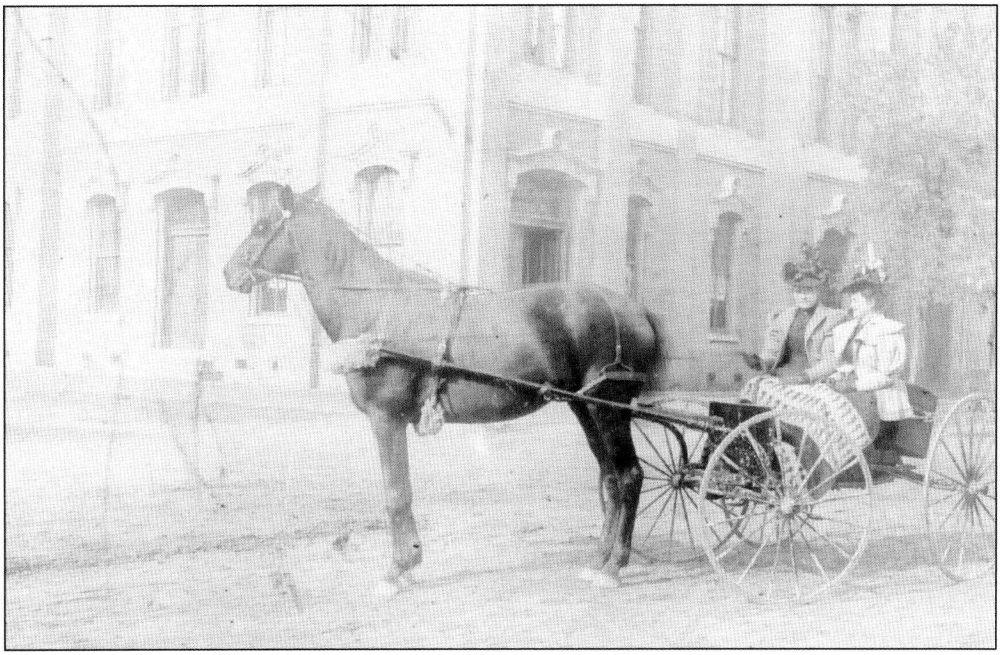

Mrs. Mike Edwards and Frances Coefield visited S.R. Alley around 1905 and had this picture taken in front of the Town Hall. (ECML)

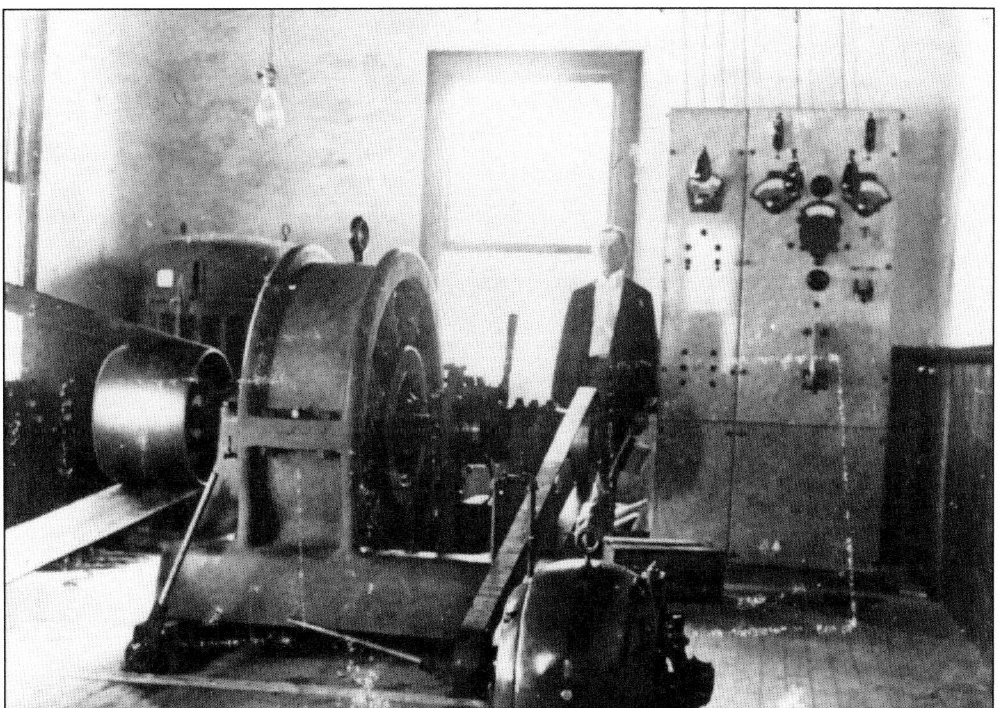

Electricity came to Tarboro in the 1890s. The Hart Cotton Mill was the first to use electric power, and when the day came to throw the switch to light the town and factory, area residents celebrated at a party at the mill. (ECML)

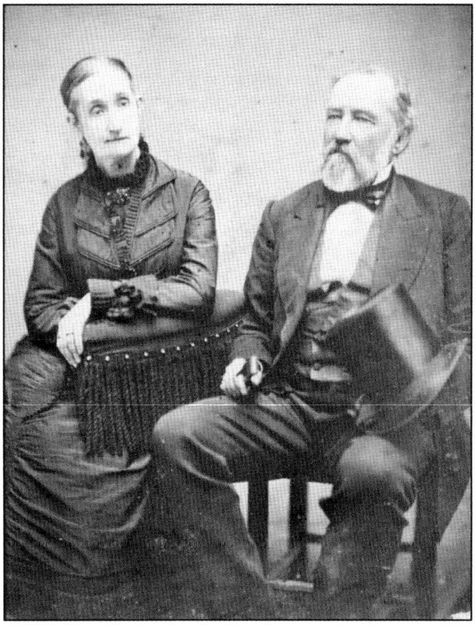

William Smith Battle, born at Coolspring Plantation in 1823, is referred to in one historical source as "Edgecombe's Grand Old Man." The son of Judge James Smith Battle and the great-grandson of Elisha Battle (one of the early commissioners of Tarboro), William Battle attended the Stony Hill and Louisburg Academies before graduating from the University of North Carolina in 1844. He married Elizabeth Mary Dancy, the daughter of Francis L. Dancy, on July 25, 1845. Battle operated a turpentine business before managing the Rocky Mount Mills, a textile mill owned by his father. He also managed the Rocky Mount flour and gristmill. Both mills burned in 1863 during a Yankee raid on Rocky Mount. Although Battle rebuilt both, the textile mill burned again, forcing him into debt. (BBH Gift of Jane D. Church)

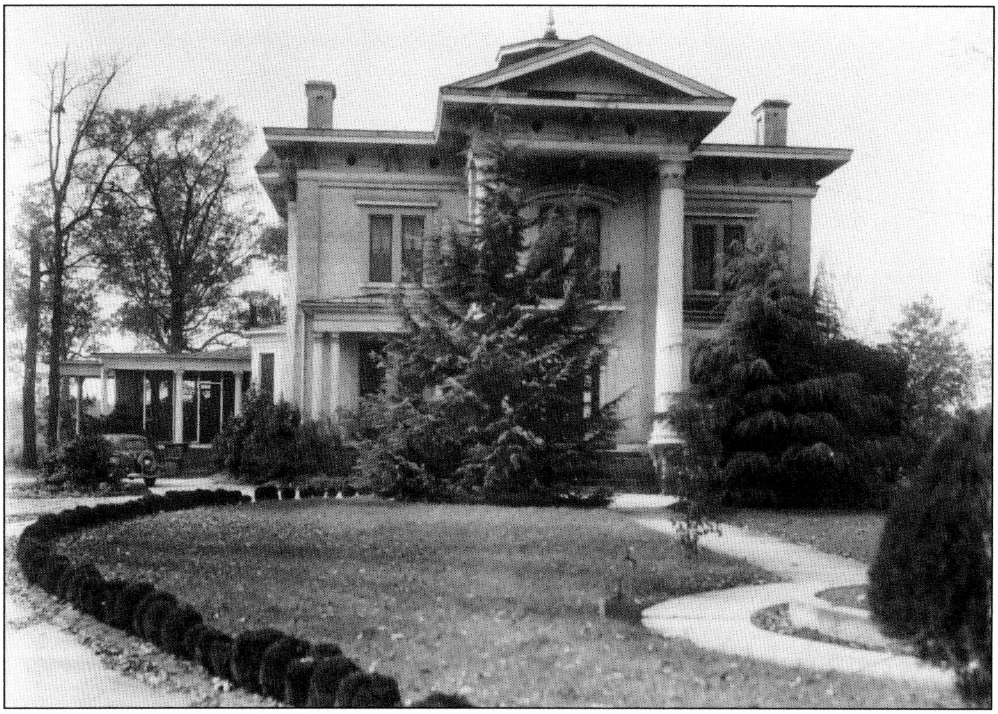

Battle commissioned William Percival, a noted nineteenth-century architect, to construct "The Barracks," a grand home on Albemarle Avenue in Tarboro. When it was completed in 1860 the house was considered the grandest home in the county. It was built of bricks imported from England, and its walls are 2 feet thick. The dramatic interior has massive plaster cornices and coved ceilings, and is rich with detail throughout. When he was forced to give up his home after the panic of 1873, Battle moved his family to "Lone Pine." He and his wife are buried in Calvary Churchyard. (BBH)

Arabella Clark Smith, Captain Wilkinson, John L. Bridgers Jr., the Reverend Walter Smith, and Maria Clark Bourne are shown here in the 1880s. Arabella and Maria, the daughters of Governor Henry Toole Clark, were sisters-in-law of John L. Bridgers Jr. Arabella's husband, the Reverend Walter Smith, operated the Thompson Orphanage in Charlotte. (PC H.C. Bridgers family)

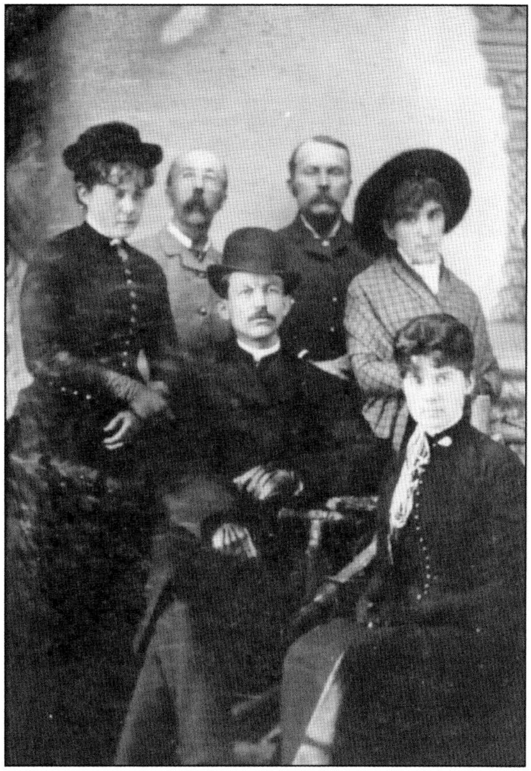

"Hilma," the former home of Governor Henry Toole Clark, was purchased by John Luther Bridgers Jr. and his wife, Laura P. Clark Bridgers, and remodeled around 1900. "Hilma" was located off Wilson Street, near the Hilma Country Club. The house, originally built in an ornate Italian style, is seen here in its Queen Anne phase. Mrs. Bridgers is standing on the porch overlooking the gardens. (PC H.C. Bridgers family)

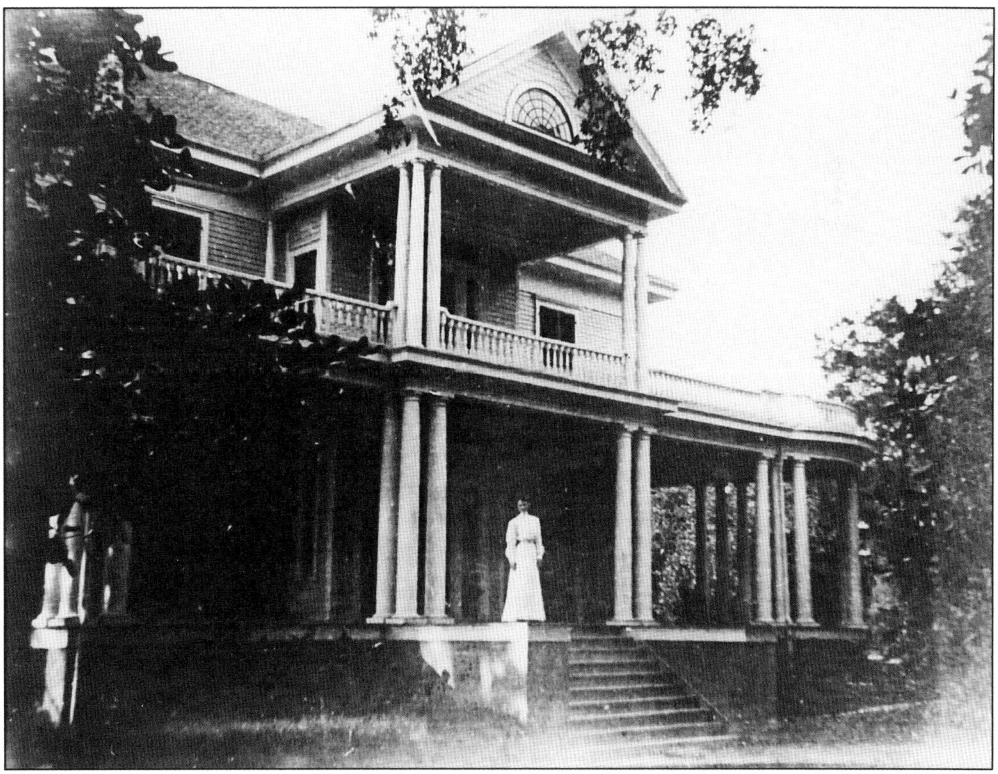

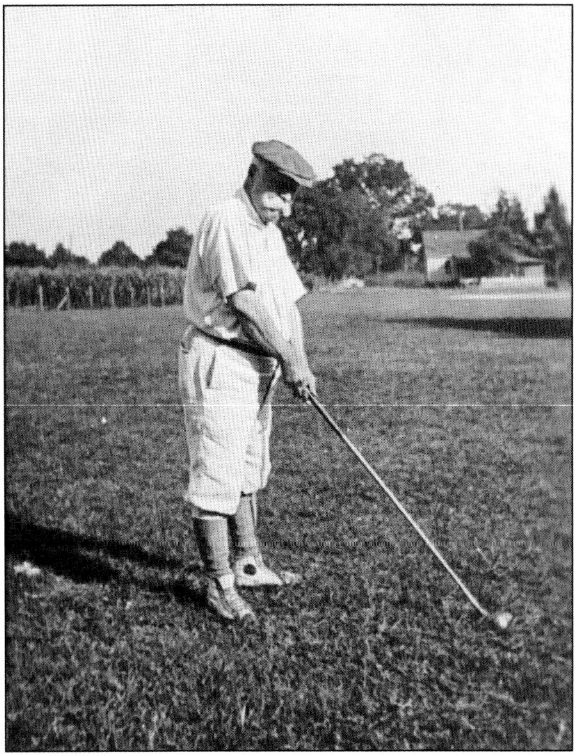

John L. Bridgers Jr. pauses for a moment while playing golf at "Hilma," one of the earliest courses in North Carolina. The fairways were maintained by sheep and goats. "Hilma" was named after the children in the Clark family who originally lived there: Haywood, Irwin, Laura, Maria, and Arabella. Laura married John L. Bridgers Jr. (PC H.C. Bridgers family)

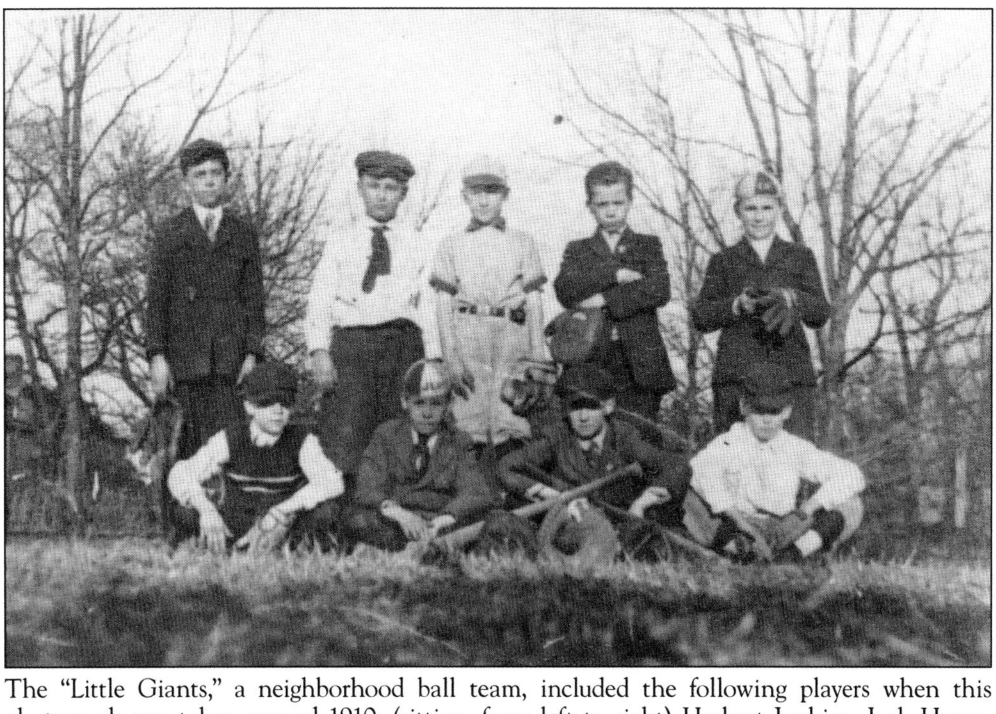

The "Little Giants," a neighborhood ball team, included the following players when this photograph was taken around 1910: (sitting, from left to right) Herbert Jenkins, Jack Herne, Chalmers Marrow, and Francis Jenkins; (standing, from left to right) Buck Fountain, Ed Simmons, Nash Johnston, Jim Woodley, and Cliff Ruffin. (PC Marrow)

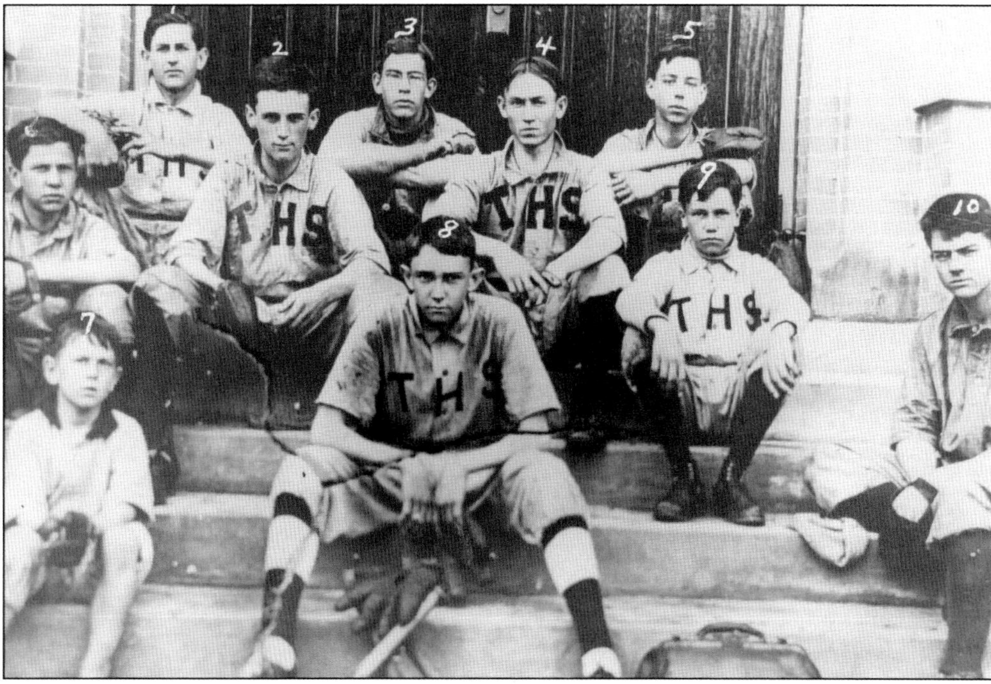

In 1910 the Tarboro High School baseball team had a record of 8–2, making it the area champion. The players are as follows: #1 Fitshugh Gammon, outfield; #2 Henry Keehln, first base; #3 Arthur "Pug" Bass, pitcher; #4 Van Anderson, third base; #5 Ellridge Narrow, right field; #6 Dudley Bryan, second base; #7 Gus Bryan, team mascot; #8 William Powell, pitcher and left field; #9 Leroy Teele, field and utility man; and #10 J.T. Johnson, captain and short stop. (PC Marrow)

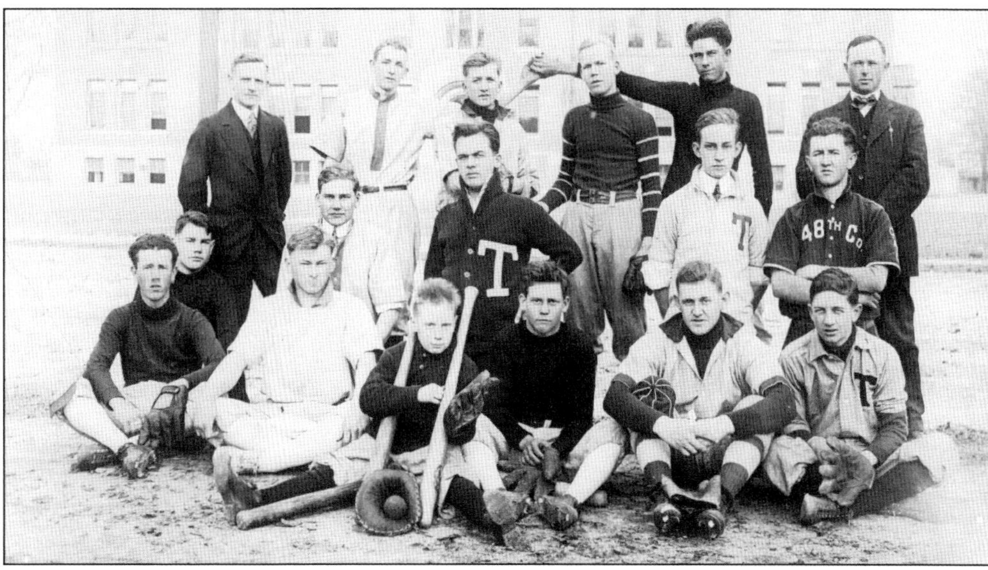

The Tarboro High School baseball team of 1916 is not identified in this yearbook picture, but the top players were nicknamed "Fez" Bunn, "Old B.S." Phelps, "Peanut" Knight, "Napoleon II" Harper, "High Brown" Madra, "Southsea" Norfleet, "Frenchy" Cherry, "Insect" Fly, "Bones" Marrow, "Abraham" Long, and "Henry VIII" Ricks. (BBH)

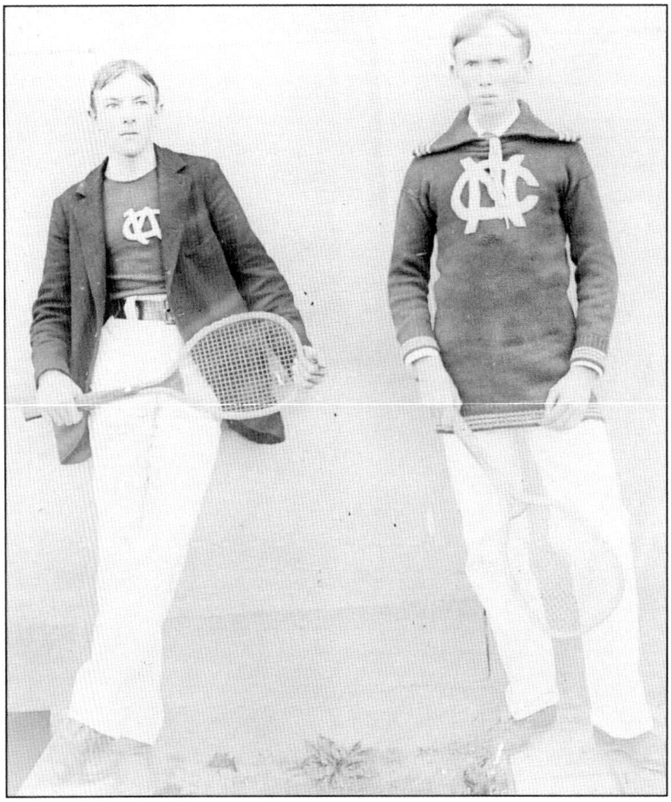

This c. 1890 photograph shows Henry Clark Bridgers Sr. (right) and a teammate on the University of North Carolina-Chapel Hill tennis team. (PC H.C. Bridgers family)

In the 1930s, Tarboreans enjoyed the tennis courts located at "Hillside" on Albemarle Avenue. The neighborhood called Keechtown is in the background. Solomon Pender's house can be seen in the distance. (PC H.C. Bridgers family)

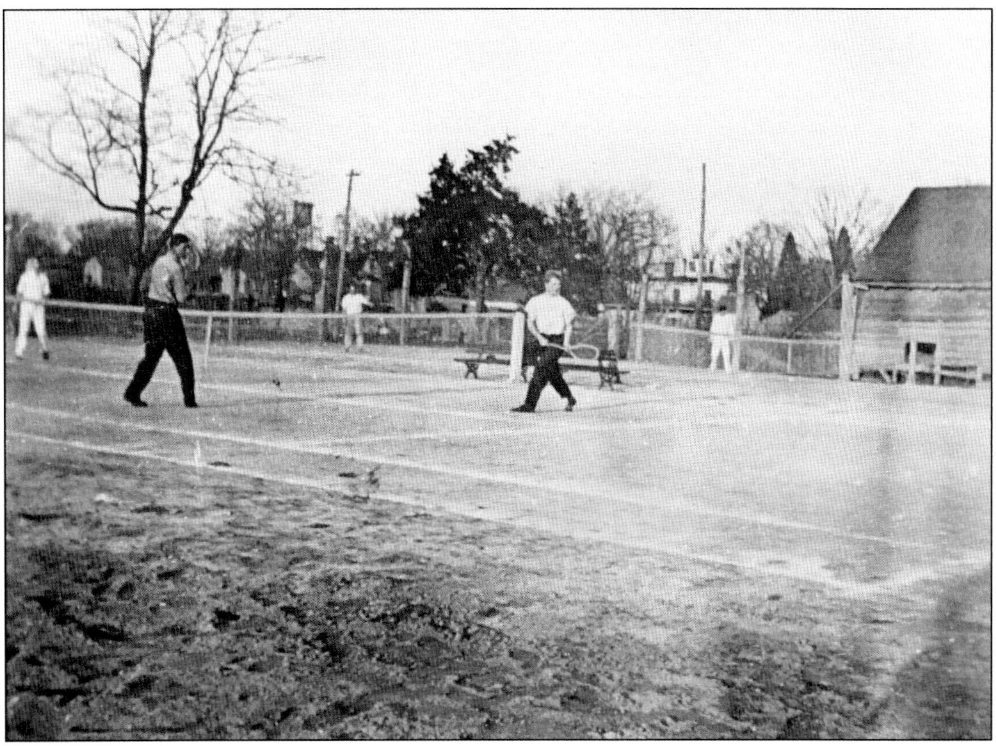

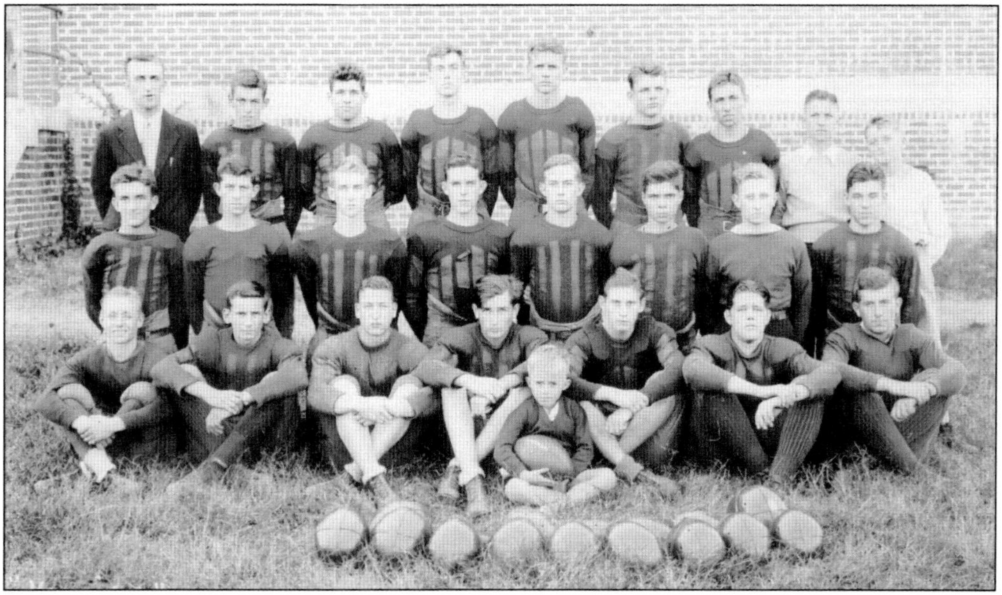

The Tarboro High School football Team in 1931. The players are, from left to right, as follows: (front row) J.C. Taylor, Ralph Whitlark, Bill Adler, Lonnie Wynn, A.D. "Peep" Fowlkes, Tom Mayo, and J.R. Satterthwaite; (middle row) Jack Jenkins, Charles Piller, Dow Pender, James Britt, Rufus Worsley, J.P. Ballard, Robert Knight, and Clarence Olschner; (back row) Coach J.M. Smith, W.A. Hart II, Emile Olschner, George Fountain Jr., Grimes Thomas, Tom Burnette, Jobe Savage, Eugene Brooks, and Eugene Simmons. (ECML)

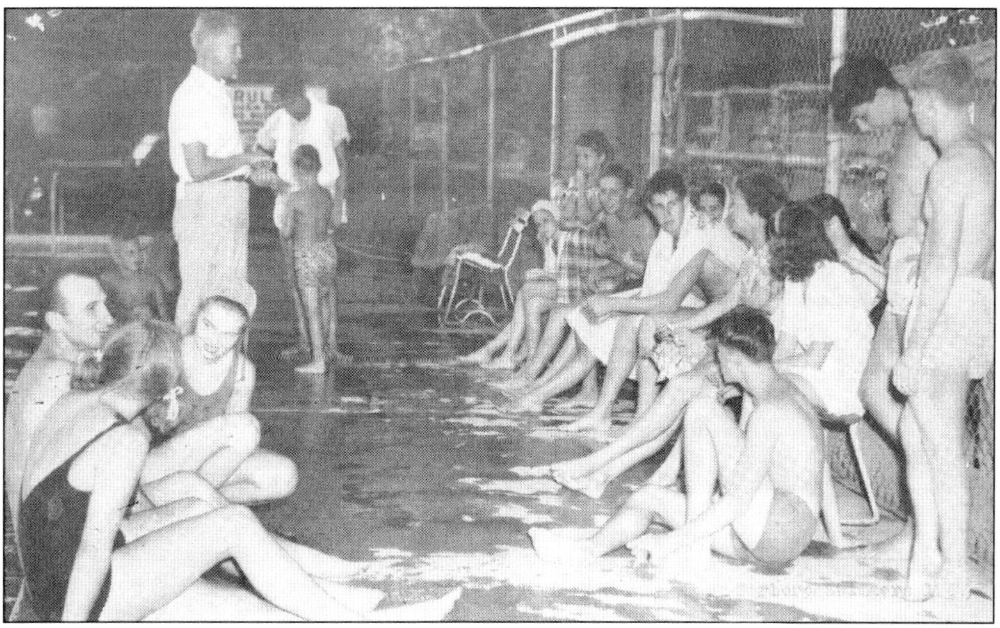

As part of the WPA projects in the 1930s, a community swimming pool was built behind the Blount-Bridgers House, which at that time was called the Community House. The pool was the training site for several award-winning swim teams. In this photograph Peggy Rogers Youngblood, James "Rat" Boykin, Randel Hudson, and Ethel Laughlin are receiving instructions from Coach Willis Casey. (BBH)

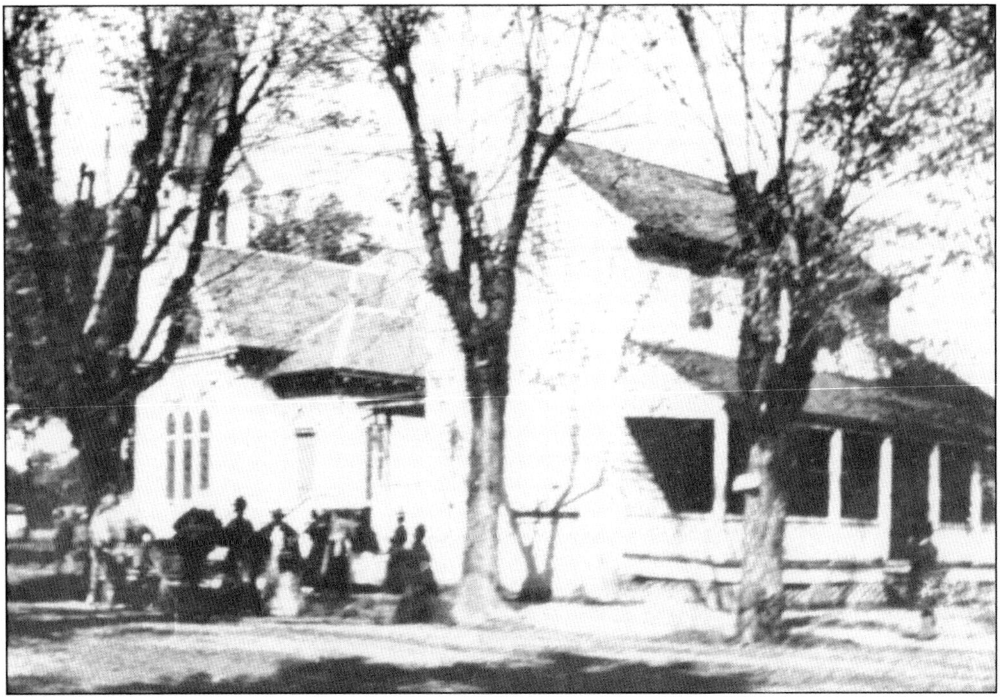

The Baptist church began here in 1819 under the leadership of Elder Joshua Lawrence. During the 1870s the church was located at the corner of Main and East St. John Streets. This image shows the parsonage, which faced East St. John Street. Mr. O.C. Farrar gave the land and financed the building of a new sanctuary. (BBH)

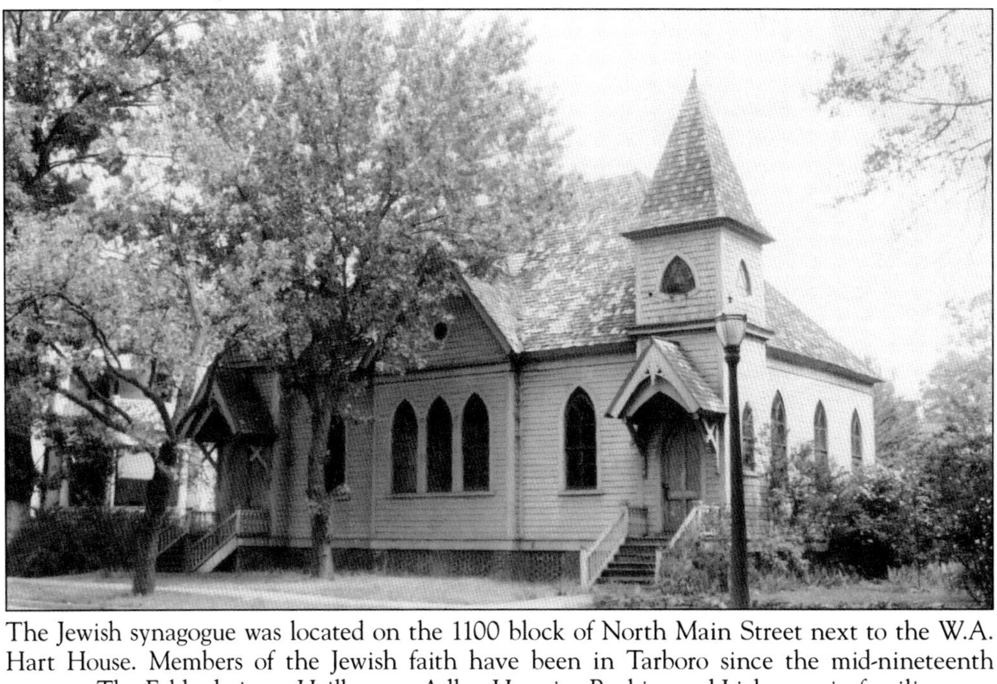

The Jewish synagogue was located on the 1100 block of North Main Street next to the W.A. Hart House. Members of the Jewish faith have been in Tarboro since the mid-nineteenth century. The Feldenheimer, Heilbroner, Adler, Hurwitz, Raskin, and Lichtenstein families were all members of the synagogue. (ECML)

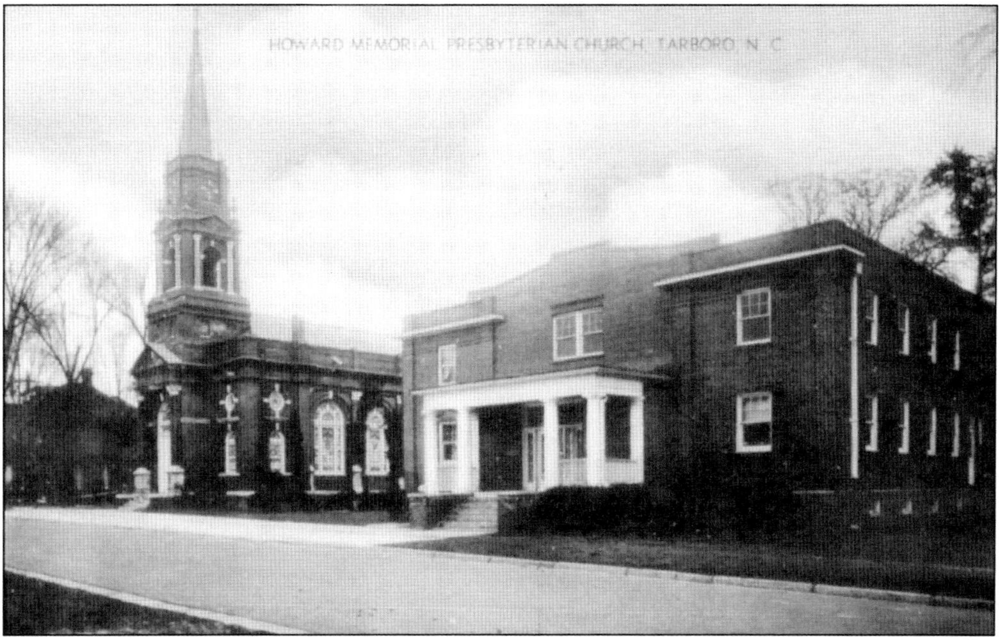

The first church for the Presbyterians was completed in 1874 on St. James Street. It was designed by the "Three Annas": Anna Stamps Howard, Anna MacNair, and Anna Wilkinson, all wives of area businessmen. In 1909 the congregation built this new church, Howard Memorial, and sold the old building to the congregation of the Eastern Star Baptist Church, who moved it on rollers pulled by mules to a site on Wagner and Church Streets. (BBH)

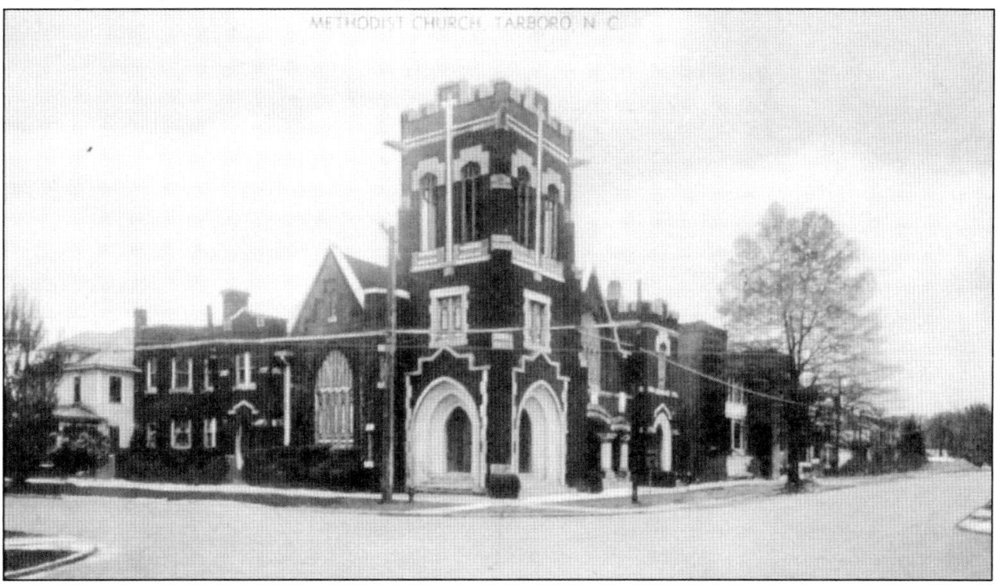

Methodists have been in Edgecombe County since the early eighteenth century. In 1803 Bishop Ashbury visited the new chapel in Tarboro and preached a sermon to a predominately African-American congregation. In 1856, a new structure was dedicated, which burned in 1915. The present structure, shown here on a postcard, was completed in 1918. The church has a stained-glass Tiffany window in memory of F.L. Bond, a prominent cabinetmaker and businessman. (BBH)

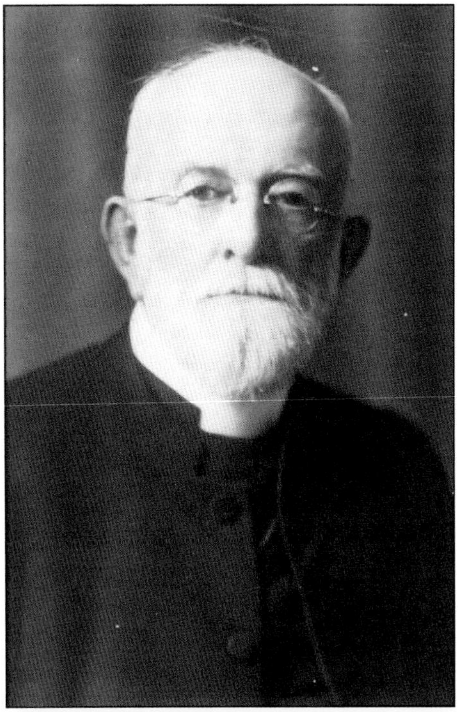

The Reverend Dr. Joseph Blount Cheshire came to Tarboro in 1842 and became rector of the Episcopal church. He married Elizabeth Toole Parker in 1843 and continued at Calvary Church until 1889. His daughter, Katherine Drane, known as Kate, was instrumental in mission churches. His son, Joseph Blount Cheshire Jr. (shown here), studied at Reverend Owen's school, and then at the Tarboro Academy. He graduated from Trinity College in Connecticut and studied law, becoming a lawyer in Tarboro in 1872. In 1876 Mr. Cheshire took holy orders and began to study under his father. He was the rector at St. Peter's in Charlotte for twelve years, and during that time served on the board of trustees of the University of the South. In 1893 he was elected bishop of the Diocese of North Carolina. The Rt. Reverend Cheshire continued to serve the church until his death in 1932. (PC Nash)

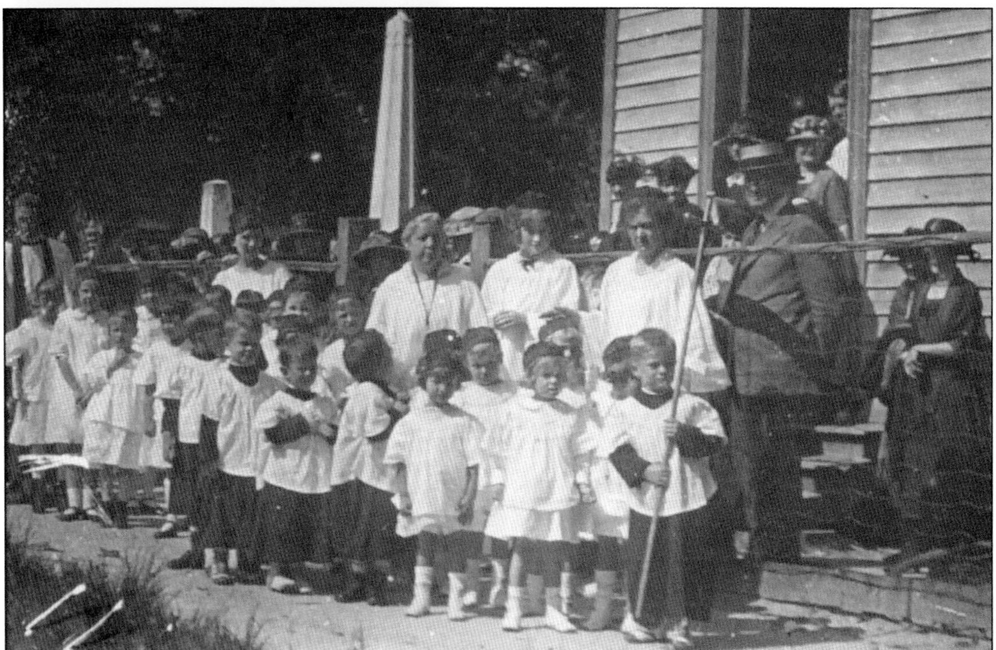

The first Calvary Church was consecrated in 1840. During Reconstruction it became the temporary church for the St. Luke's Colored Protestant Church congregation until their new building was completed. This building was torn down in 1929. The clergyman on the far left is the Reverend S.W. Haley. The other adults include Miss Kate Cheshire, Miss Mamie Bryan, and Mr. Henry Johnston. (ECML)

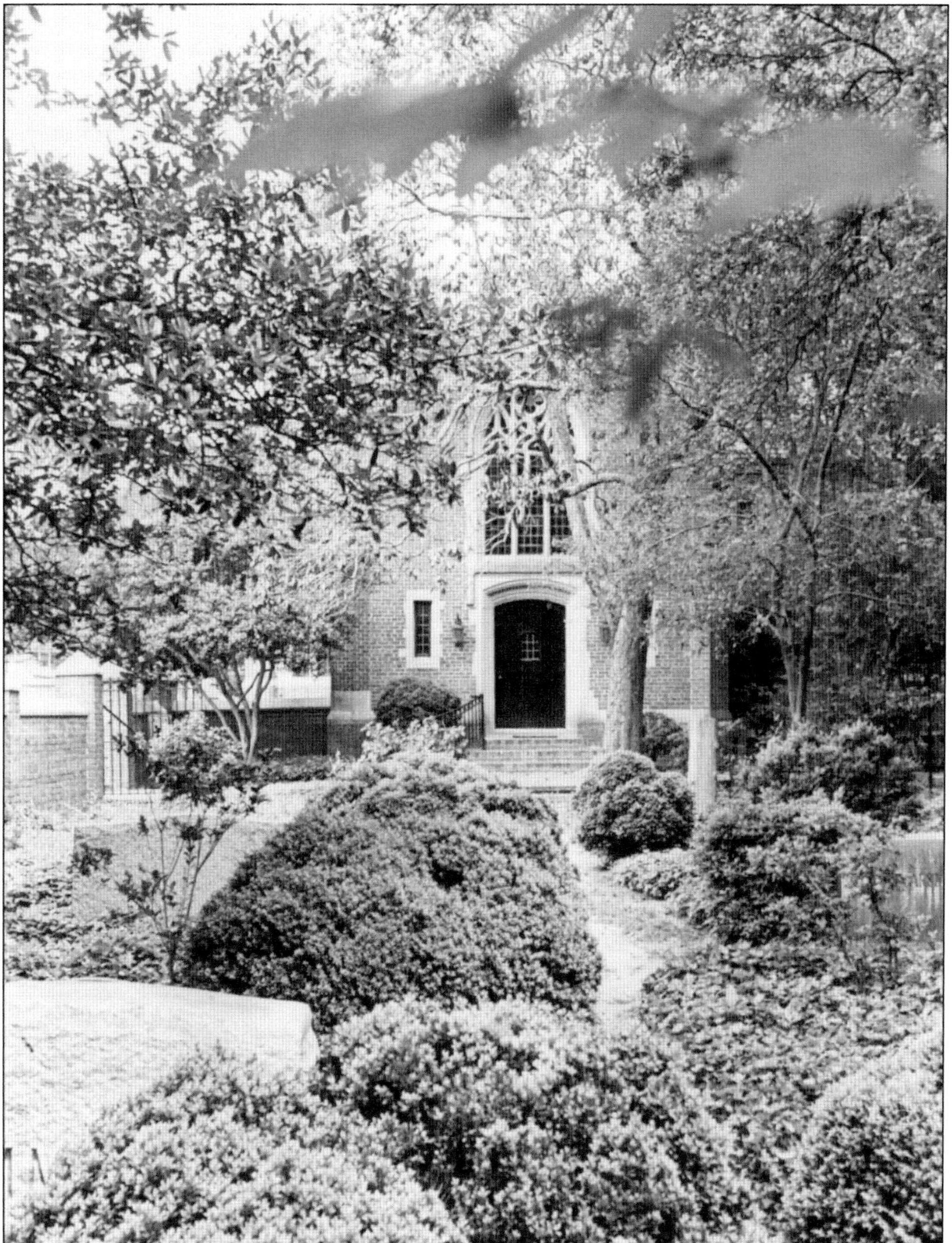

Calvary Church was completed in 1867 after a delay during the Civil War. The churchyard was the joy of Dr. Cheshire, who was a botanist. The grounds include numerous trees from around the world including a cork oak from Spain, several California cedars, a buckeye tree from Ohio, and a Japanese yew tree. According to a church history written by Jaquelin Nash, the rector was told, "Mr. Cheshire, sir, you is doing wrong; you is making this yard so pretty, you is 'ticing folks to die . . ." (p. 24 of *A Goodly Heritage*). Shown here is the entrance to All Saints Chapel, which, with the Cheshire Parish House, was built in 1922. (BBH)

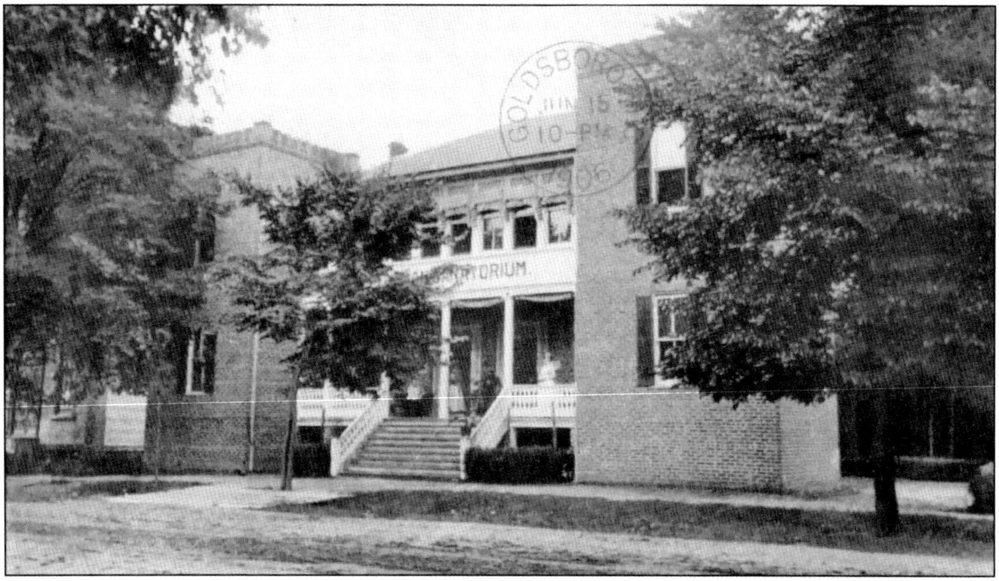

The Pittman Sanatorium was one of the first hospitals in Edgecombe County. Named in honor of Dr. N.J. Pittman, the hospital was built on St. Andrew Street around 1903. At that time, Dr. J.M. Baker was the superintendent, Dr. W.J. Thigpen was the house physician, and Miss Virginia Gray was the superintendent of nurses. (ECML)

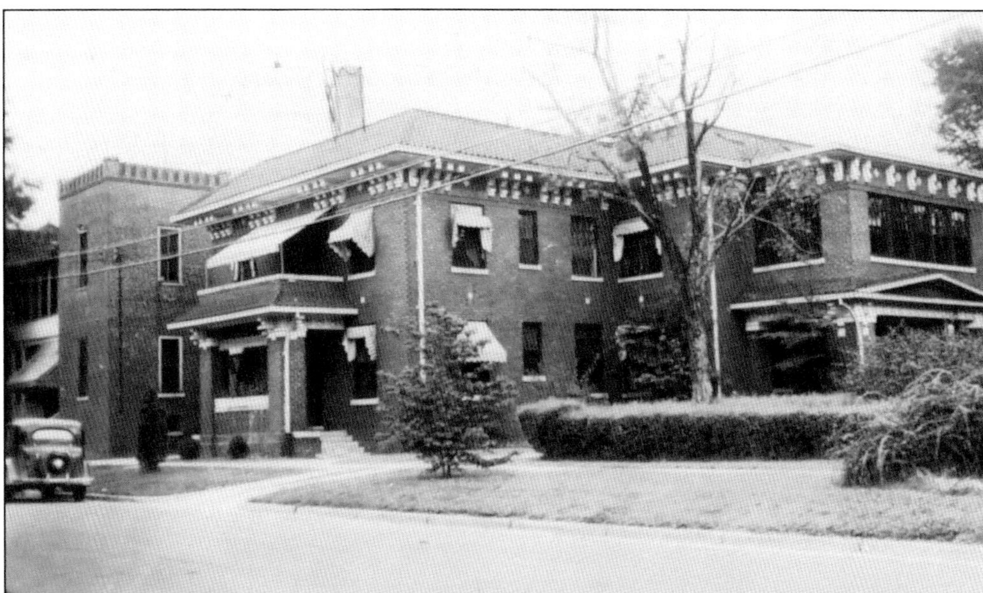

The second hospital in town was Edgecombe General Hospital, located in the 300 block of St. Andrew Street. The hospital remained here until the 1950s, when a new structure was built at the north end of town. (ECML)

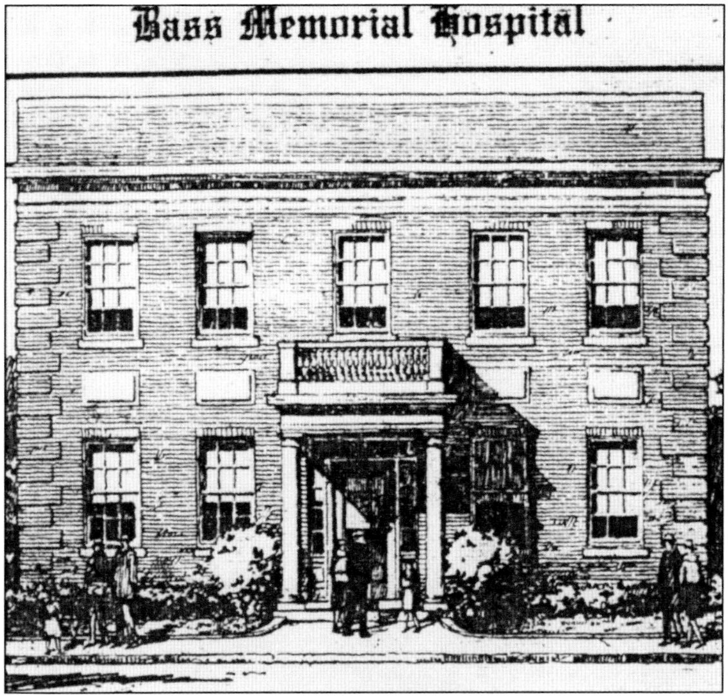

Bass Memorial Hospital opened in 1929 and was dedicated to the memory of Dr. Henry Turner Bass, who died in a shooting on Main Street in 1903. The hospital, located on East St. James Street, was operated by Dr. S.P. Bass. The consulting surgeons were Dr. E.B. Boice and Dr. B.C. Willis of Rocky Mount. (BBH)

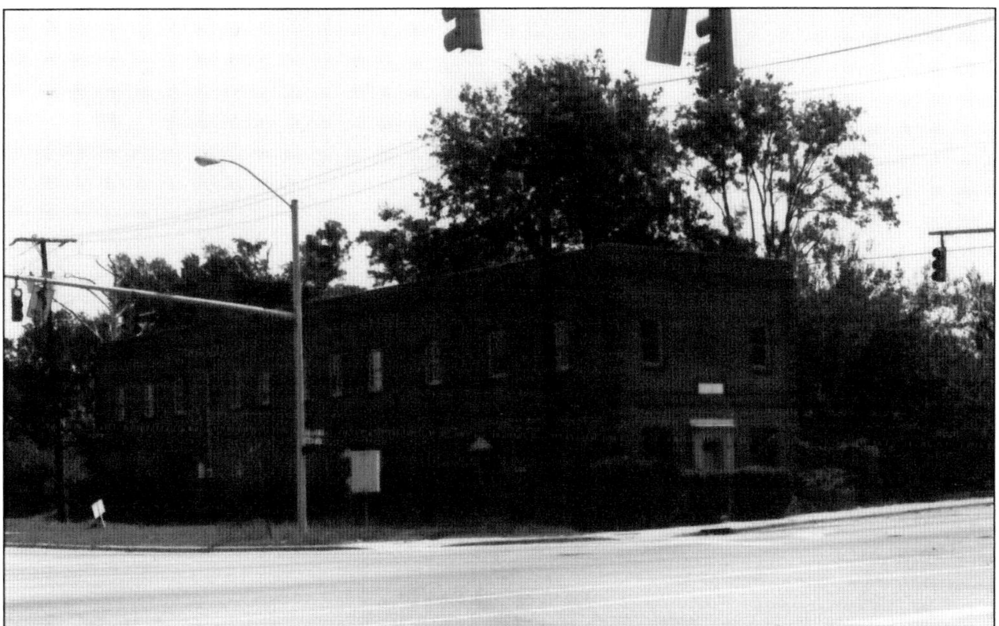

Dr. Milton Quigless, a general surgeon originally from Mississippi, came to Tarboro in 1936 to treat the segregated population of African-Americans in Tarboro and Princeville. Working out of various facilities, Quigless finally managed to open his own hospital at the end of World War II. Patients came from communities within a radius of 200 miles to the hospital, which was located at the end of Main Street beside the river bridge to Princeville. The twenty-six-bed facility continued to operate as a hospital until 1973. At that time Dr. Quigless closed the hospital but continued to keep the clinic open. (PC Quigless)

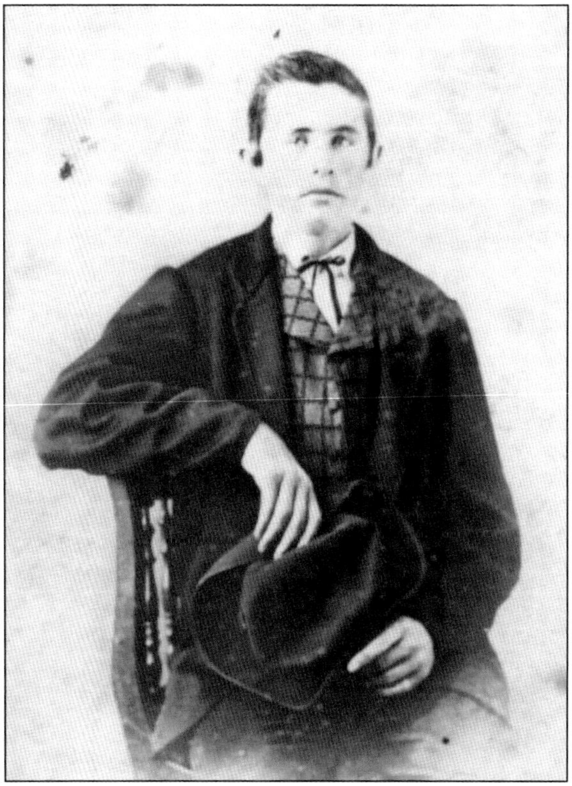

Around 1870, the county boasted numerous physicians. John G. Rives, pictured here, served the Battleboro area. Other doctors in the county included J.W. Jones, Frank Hart, Joseph H. Baker, Reuben Cobb, Donald Williams, W.F. MacNair, A.B. Nobels, Frank Pitt, John Lawrence, J.B. Lewis, John F. Garrett, Ed Thorpe, C.W. Knight, Richard Tilry, W.B. Ricks, P.S. Petway, J.J. Philips, James Lawrence, and John R. Mercer. (BBH)

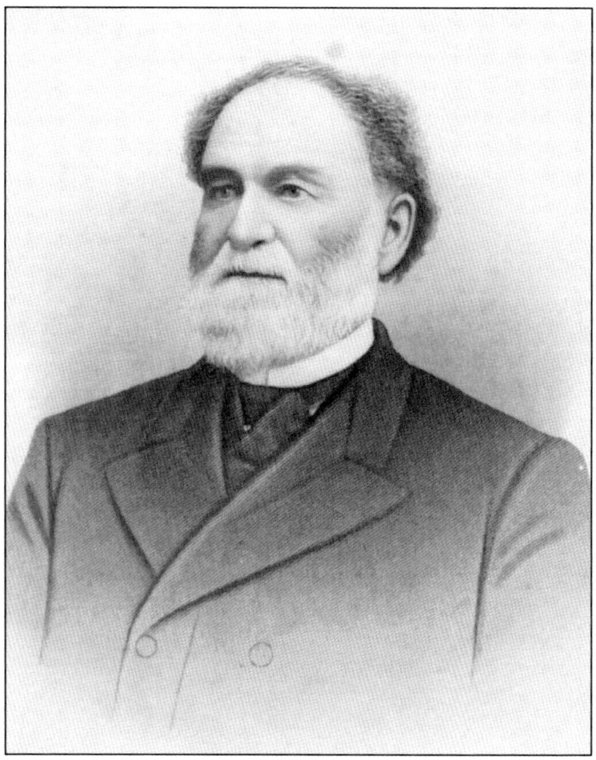

Dr. Newsom J. Pittman served Edgecombe County from the middle of the nineteenth century. Born in Halifax County, he graduated with a MD degree from the University of Pennsylvania in 1839. In 1853 he opened an office of general practice and surgery in Tarboro. He served as president of the North Carolina Medical Society and of the American Medical Society. He also served as a surgeon in the Confederate States Army. His first marriage was to Miss Mary A. Pittman, the daughter of Reddin Pittman, and his second to Mary Eliza Battle, the daughter of James Smith Battle. Dr. Pittman died in 1893 and is buried in Calvary Churchyard. (BBH)

Dr. Lycurgus Lafayette Staton, a co-owner of Staton and Zoeller, a drugstore located on the 400 block of Main Street in Tarboro, was one of the founders of the Pittman Sanatorium, the first hospital in Tarboro. He was also a part owner of Shiloh Mills, the Tar River Steamboat Company, and the Tar River Oil Company. (BBH)

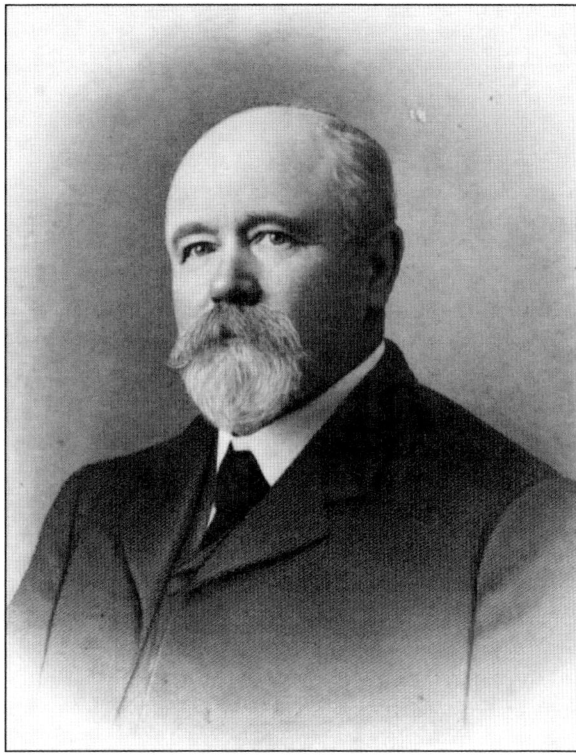

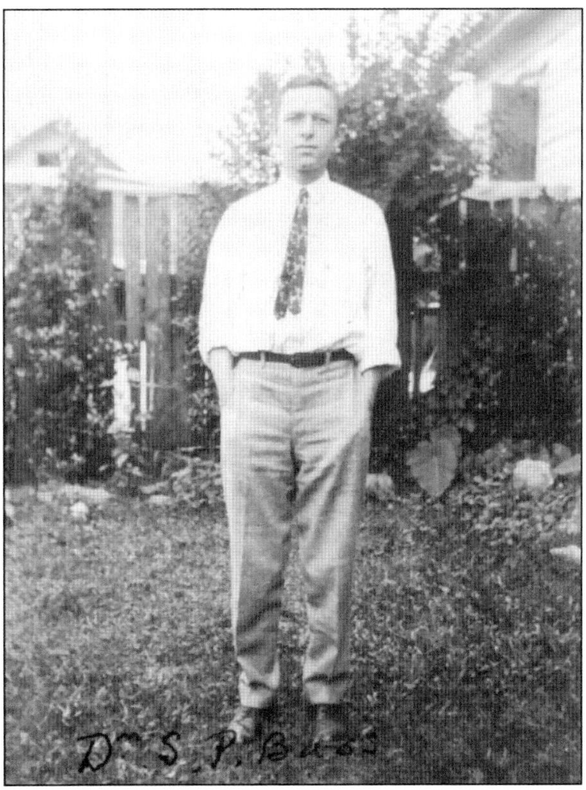

Dr. Spencer P. Bass, born in 1883, was educated by Frank Wilkinson at the Tarboro Academy before going off to the University of Virginia, where he received his medical degree. Dr. Bass returned to Tarboro and set up practice with "obstetrics beings (sic) his biggest line." He opened the Bass Memorial Hospital in 1929, and became the first doctor to practice modern pediatric medicine. Dr. Bass was also chairman of the Pediatrics Section of the North Carolina Medical Association. In his spare time he farmed and wrote interesting history columns for the local newspaper. (PC Simmons)

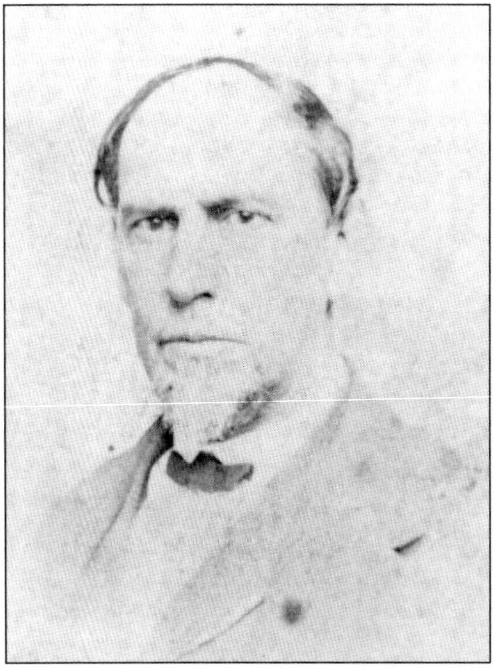

Dr. Augustus Harvey MacNair was born in 1819 into one of the oldest families in the county. After obtaining his medical training, he spent his entire life in Tarboro, serving as the county physician for over forty years. His sons opened the MacNair Drug Company in later years. When he first married, Dr. MacNair took his sixteen-year-old bride to their new home, the former Solomon Pender House. Mrs. MacNair didn't like staying out in the "country," so the house was soon sold. The house is three blocks north of the Town Common. (ECML)

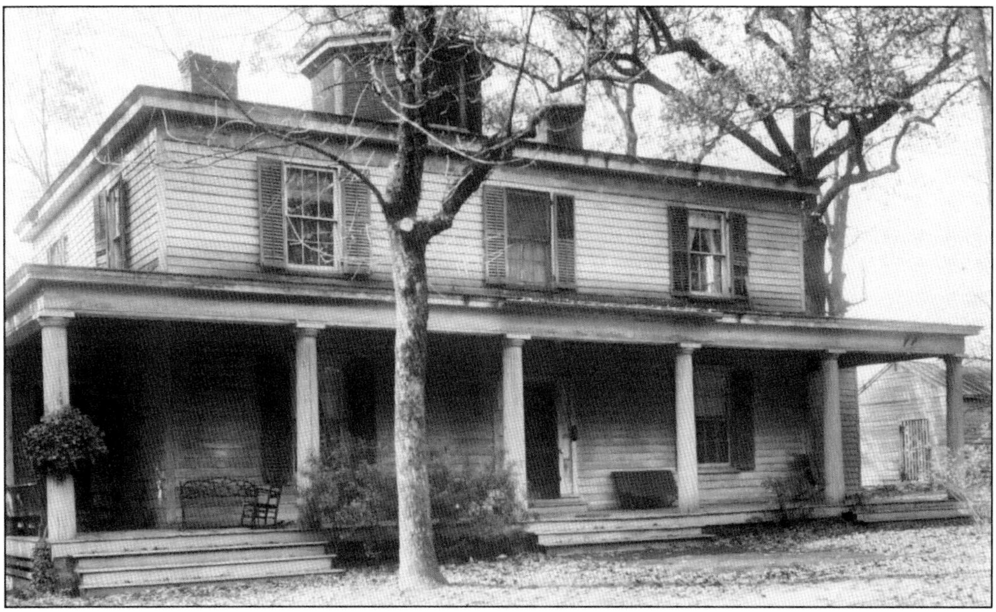

Built by Solomon Pender around 1832, this Greek Revival house is located on land that once formed part of the Thomas Blount estate. The property originally extended from Main Street to Hendricks Creek. Historical records suggest that Pender may have established Pender Hotel (referred to by Pender as Plantation House), which was later called the Edgecombe House. Pender was a merchant and his sons and grandsons operated grocery stores. His daughter Laura married Josiah Pender, a distant cousin, and the couple became blockade runners during the War Between the States. The Solomon Pender House was later home to Dr. Augustus MacNair, to C.C. Lanier, and to Mrs. Richard H. Lewis. It is interesting to note that the cupola is original. (BBH)

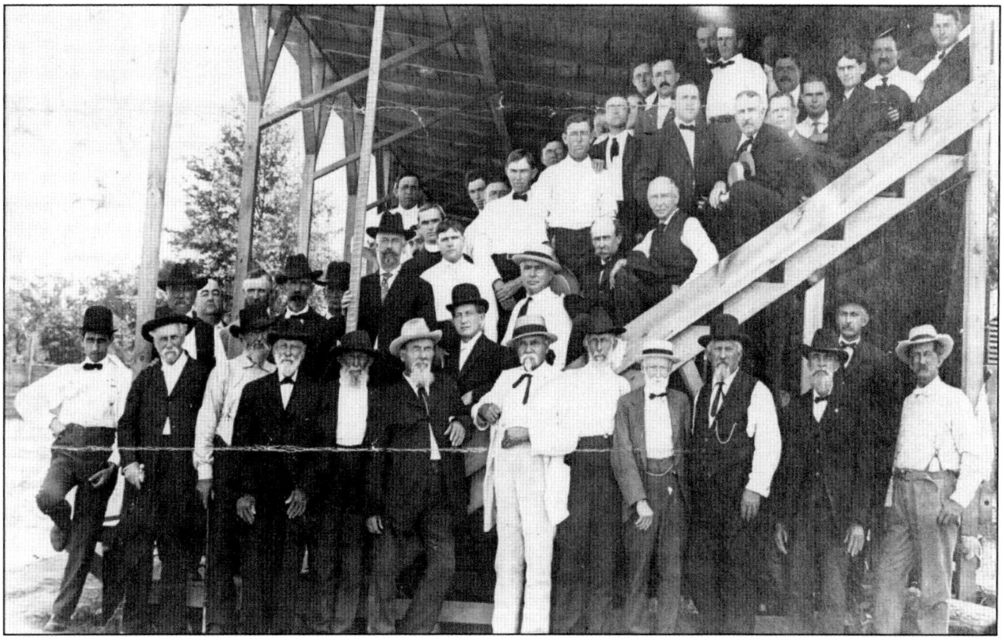

Civic and fraternal groups have been present in Tarboro since the town was established. One of the first Masonic lodges in North Carolina was built in Tarboro. Some of the other groups active prior to World War II were the Woodmen of the World, the Moose, the Kiwanis Club, the Rotary Club, and the American Legion. Women belonged to the Daughters of the American Revolution and the United Daughters of the Confederacy. In the 1870s there was an active temperance society which led to the founding of the Temperance Hall community. The civic group pictured here is gathered on the old fairgrounds. The front row includes veterans of the Civil War. Two people identified in the group are George Howard (fourth from the left) and Dr. Keech (at the very top). (ECML)

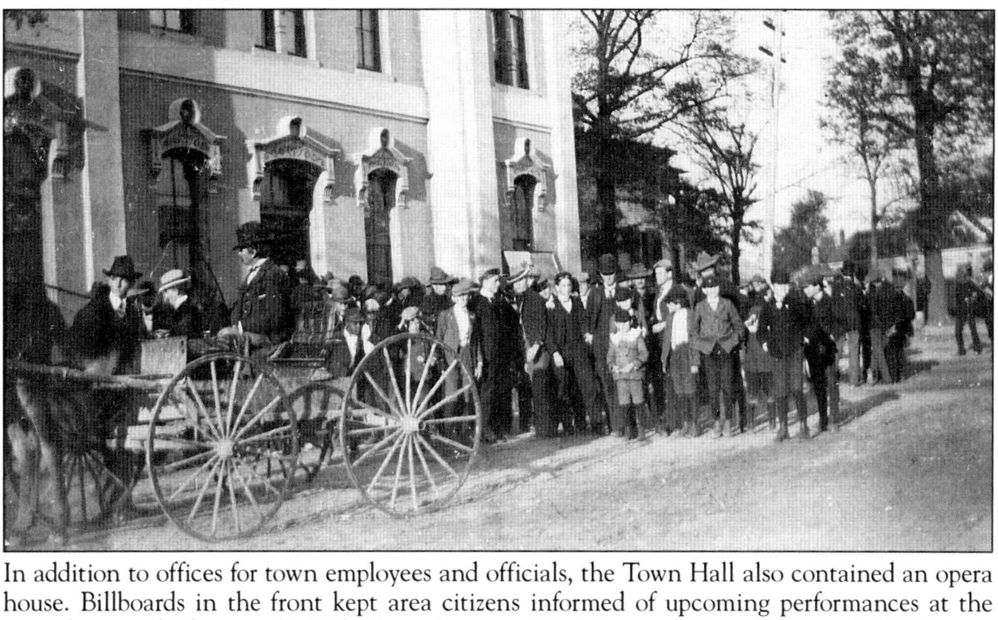

In addition to offices for town employees and officials, the Town Hall also contained an opera house. Billboards in the front kept area citizens informed of upcoming performances at the opera house, which was called "the finest between Washington, DC, and Atlanta." (BBH)

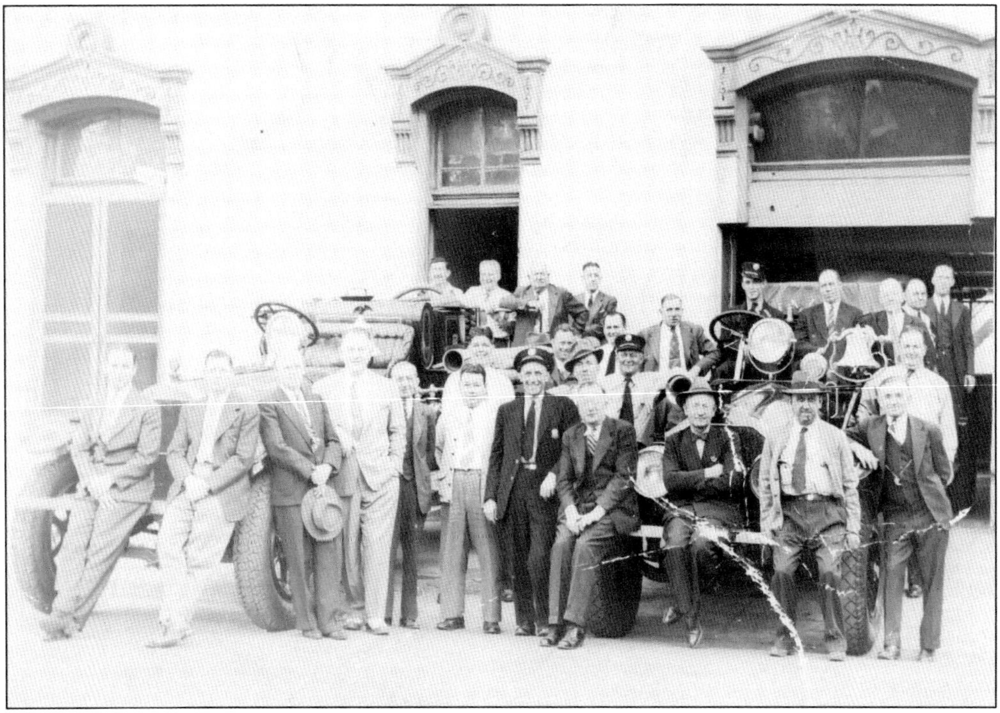

Around 1915 firefighters of the Tarboro Fire Department posed with their new trucks in front of the fire station on the first floor of the Town Hall. Included in the group are Sheriff Ed Bardin, George Earnhardt, W.C. Pitt, T.R. Mayo, and Henry Grey Shelton. (PC Cherry)

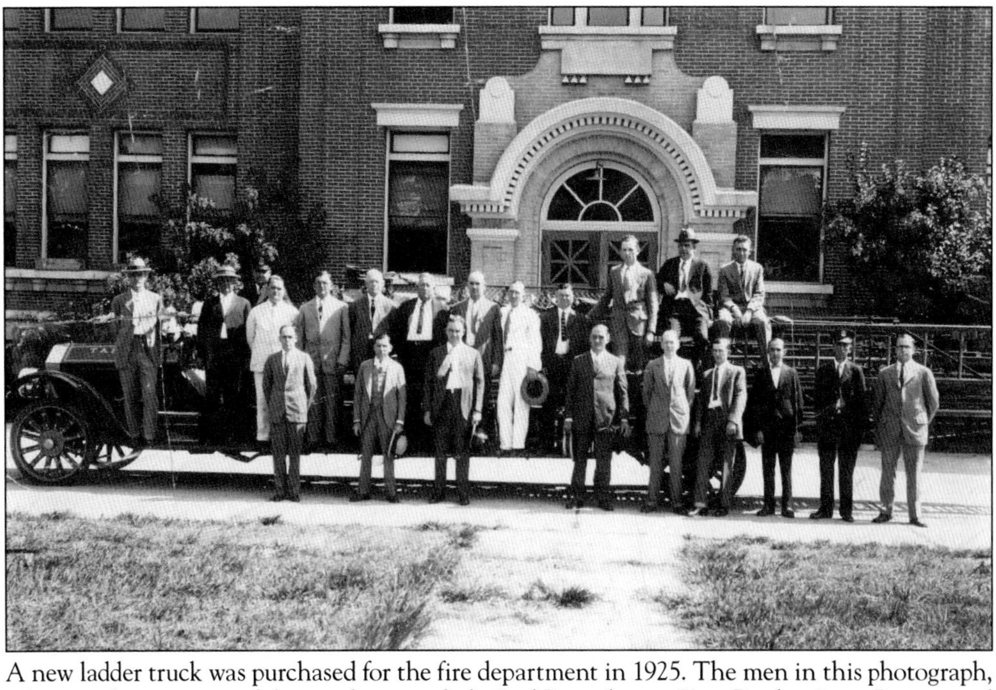

A new ladder truck was purchased for the fire department in 1925. The men in this photograph, taken on the occasion of the purchase, include Carl Rosenbaum, Tom Bardin, Isaac Brown, and John A. Weddell. All of the men were volunteers except for the fire chief. (PC Cherry)

Tarboro has had a police department since the early nineteenth century. Until the early twentieth century, the regular duties of law officers involved arresting offenders, watching the jail, and escorting prisoners to court (or in some cases to a public hanging). In 1917, however, two officers were killed in the line of duty while attempting to arrest a bootlegger. Officers Matt R. Gwatney (top right) and Plummer Ray Riggin (front left) are buried in Greenwood Cemetery under a single headstone. (BBH)

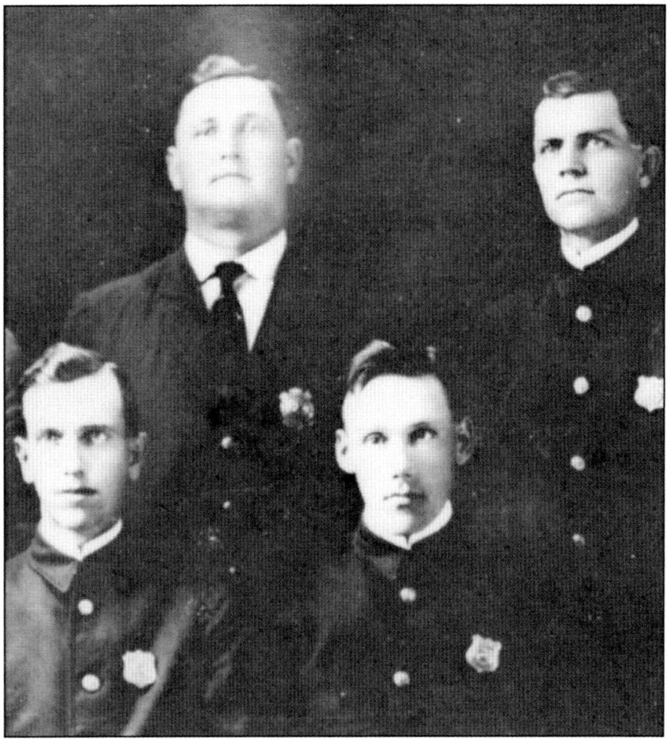

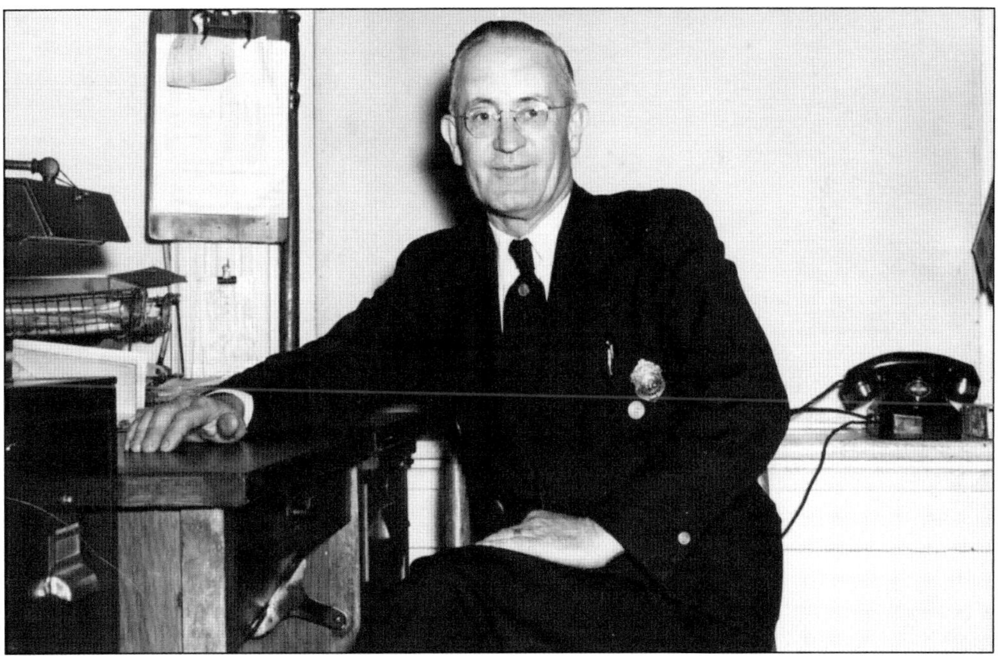

Mr. Worsley was a member of the police department for over twenty years, serving most of that as chief of police. Other chiefs of police in the 1800s were B. Hyatt, H.M. Williams, John Whitaker Cotten, W.H. Knight, and Wood Winsborn. Some of the early sheriffs were Spencer Lee Hart, B.T. Hart, Battle Bryan, W.H. Knight, Joseph Cobb, John R. Staton, and William T. Knight. By 1890 Princeville had its own constable, J.H. Freeman. (BBH)

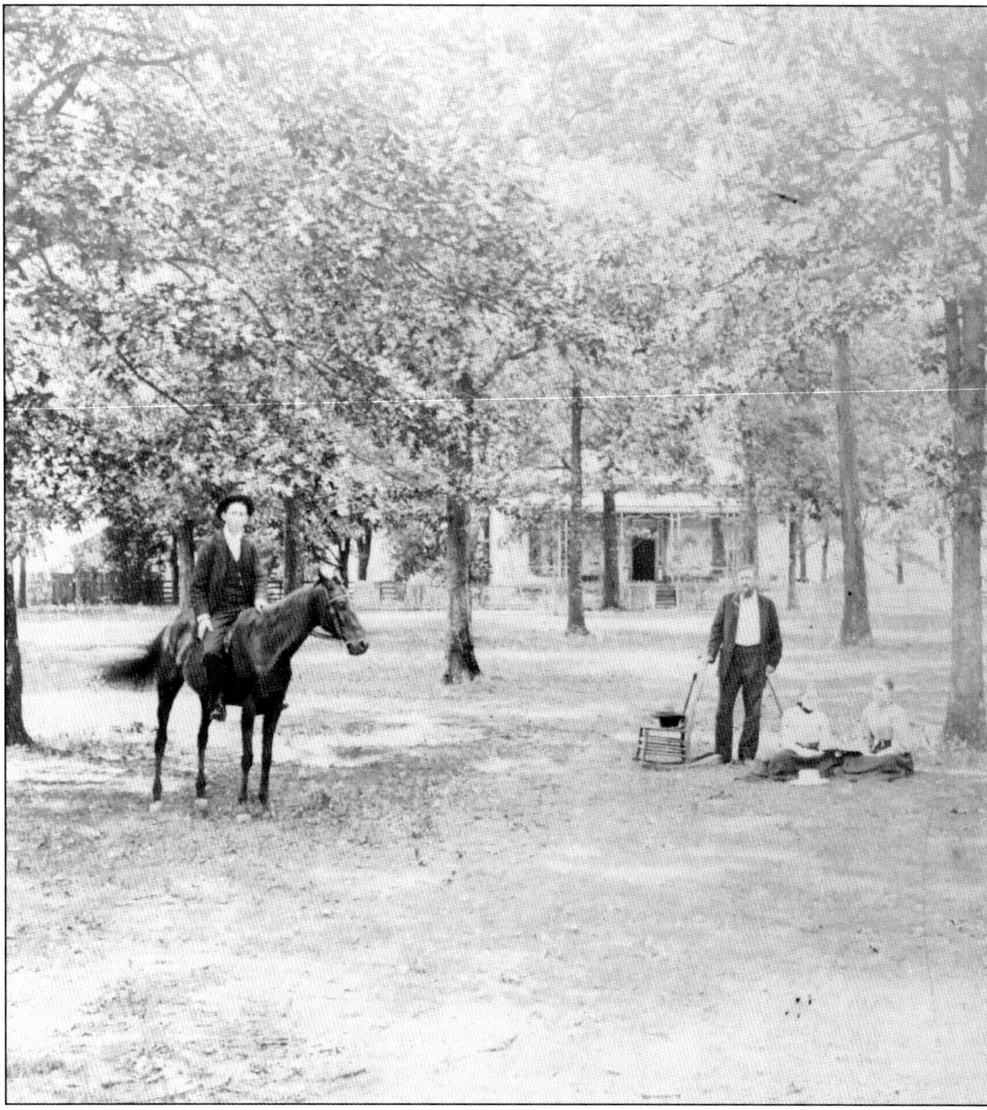

Possibly designed by architect George Lipscombe, "Adelphia" was constructed in 1854 for Dr. Joseph John Garrett. It may be one of the best examples of antebellum cottage architecture in eastern North Carolina. Located north of Pinetops, near the Wiggins Crossroads, the house has been in the Wiggins-Brown family since 1881. This photograph was taken in 1897, two weeks before Mr. Wiggins died. John Lawrence Wiggins is standing, his son, Fred Wiggins, is on the horse, and his daughters, Nannie Elizabeth Wiggins and Octavia Josephine Wiggins, are on the right. (PC Brown)

Two

County Communities

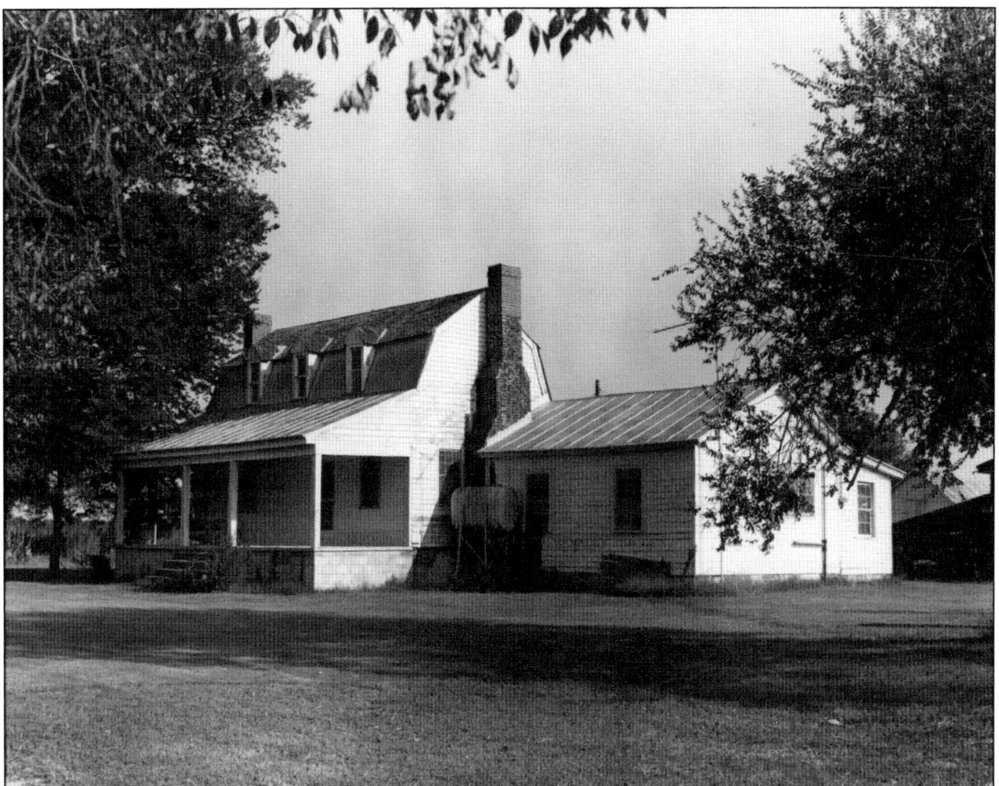

Old Town Plantation was built around 1760 by Samuel Holliman. It is believed to be the oldest house in Edgecombe County. In 1747 Elisha Battle settled in the area and later purchased the house. As the Battle family grew, a larger home, Cool Springs Plantation, was built. That home burned in 1899. Old Town remained in the Battle family for over two centuries. (BBH/NCDAH)

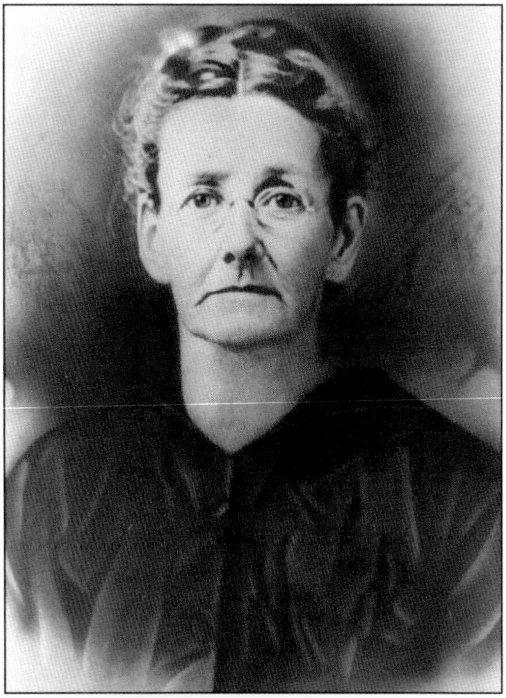

Lena Rivers Andrews was born in 1866 to Levy John Andrews and Mary Rouse Andrews. On August 13, 1884, she married James Edward Harris. The couple had several children, including Viola Harris, who later married Whit Roberson. The Robersons' grandson, Earl Roberson, restored the Wilkinson House. (PC Roberson)

Built by Joshua Wilkinson between 1816 and 1826, this Federal-style home with a double-tiered portico has been restored by Earl Roberson. (BBH)

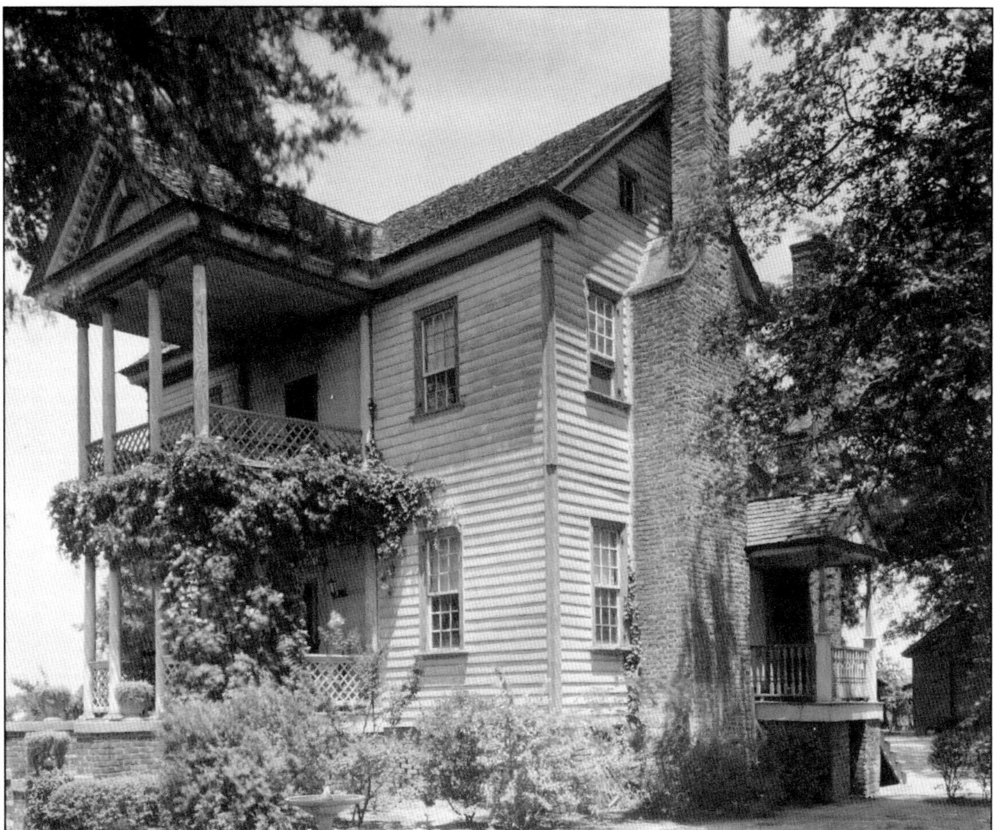

James Edward Harris was born in the early 1860s. He was twenty-two when he married Lena Andrews. He died on April 5, 1901, and is buried on land that was once part of his farm at the junction of Manning and Chinquapin Roads in the Conetoe area. His wife survived him by fifty years, dying on April 4, 1951. She is buried in Greenwood Cemetery in Tarboro. (PC Roberson)

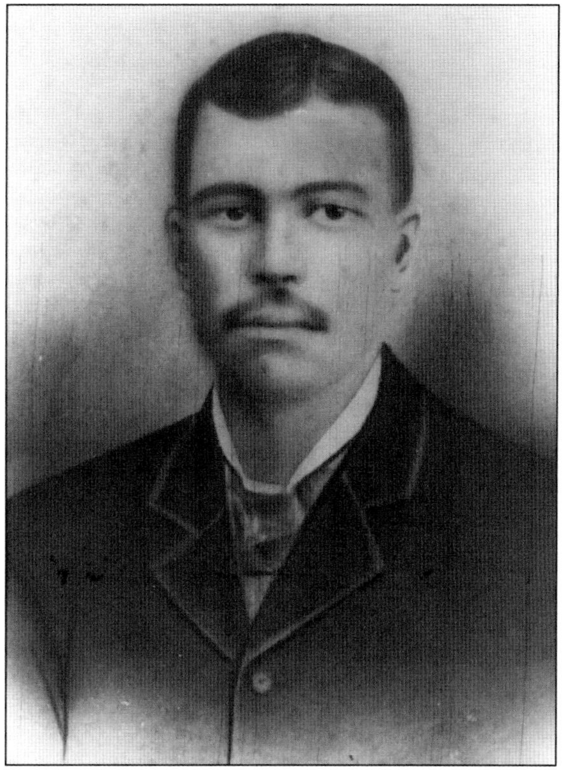

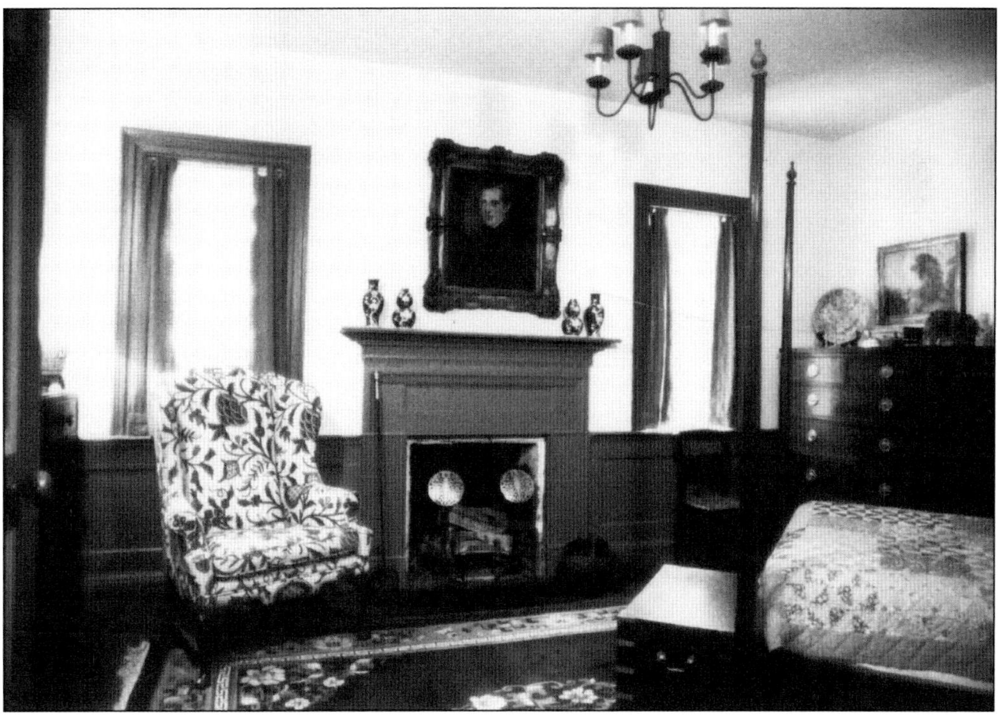

Among the interior features of the Wilkinson-Dozier House are Federal mantels, crown molding, and elaborate details. (BBH)

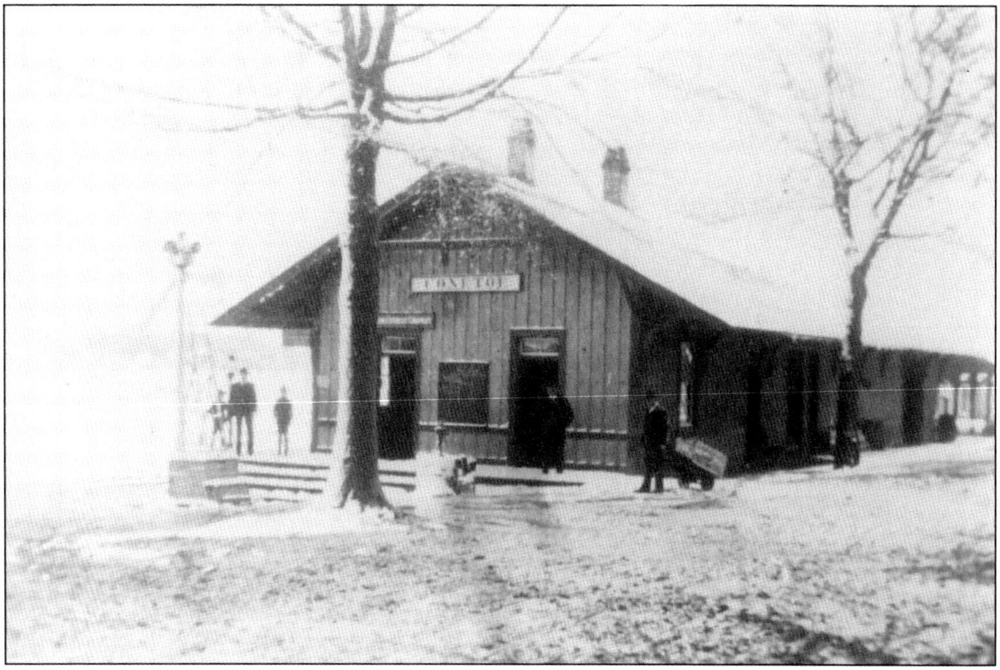

Trains ran from the Conetoe Depot, built in the 1880s, to Tarboro twice a day, carrying mail as well as passengers. In the 1890s the children of Conetoe rode the train to school in Tarboro each day. (PC Worsley)

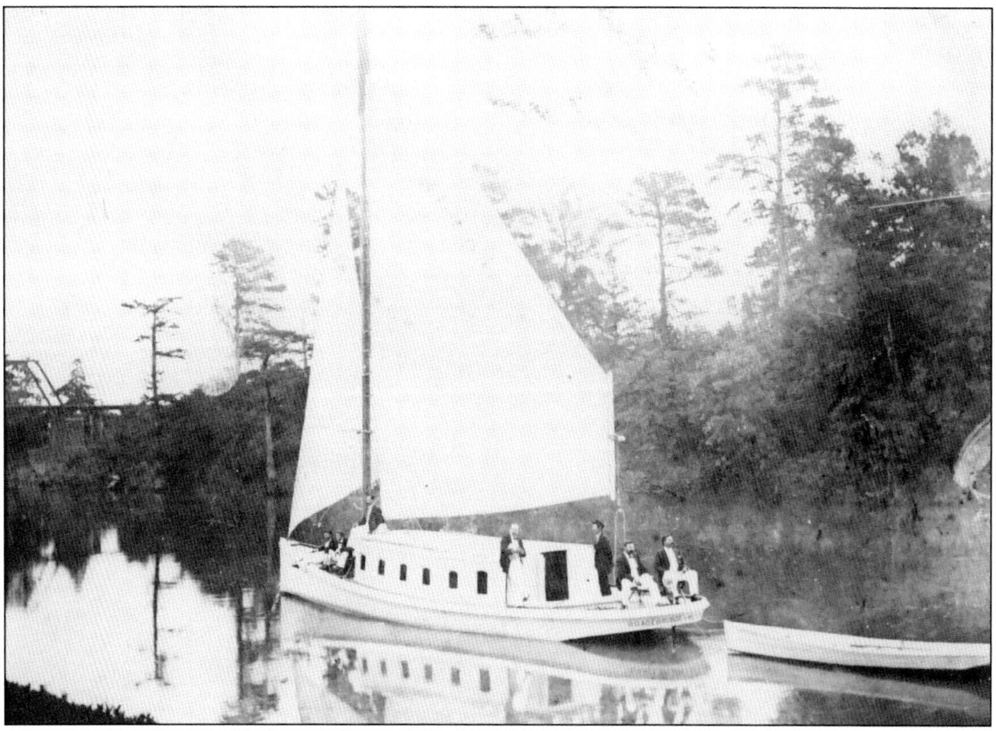

The Carr family named their sailboat *Bracebridge* after the homeplace. This photograph shows Governor Carr's son and friends taking a sail up the river from Old Sparta. (BBH)

Between 1880 and 1926 Calvary Episcopal Church sponsored eleven mission churches throughout the county for people who could not travel into town. Here, the Reverend Bertram E. Brown is standing with a group of children at one of the mission churches. Mr. Brown was assisted by lay readers and teachers Russell Clark, S.S. Nash, John R. Pender Sr., Sallie Dow Pender, and Lela Parker. (ECML)

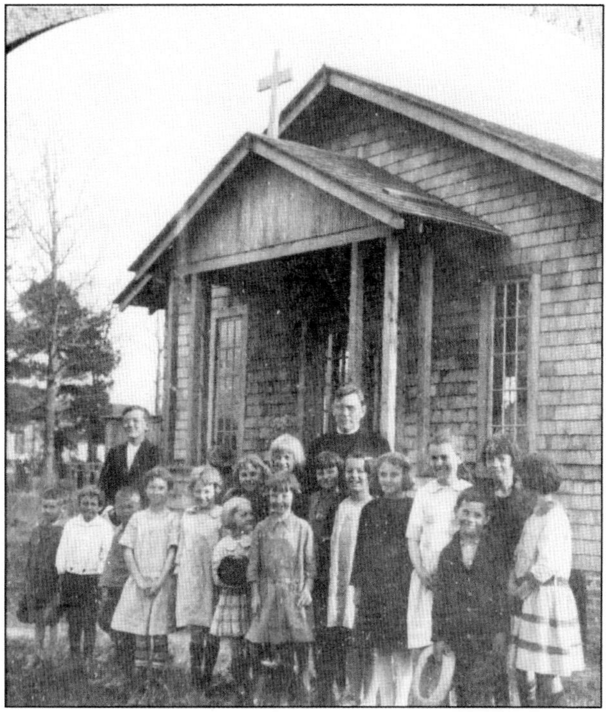

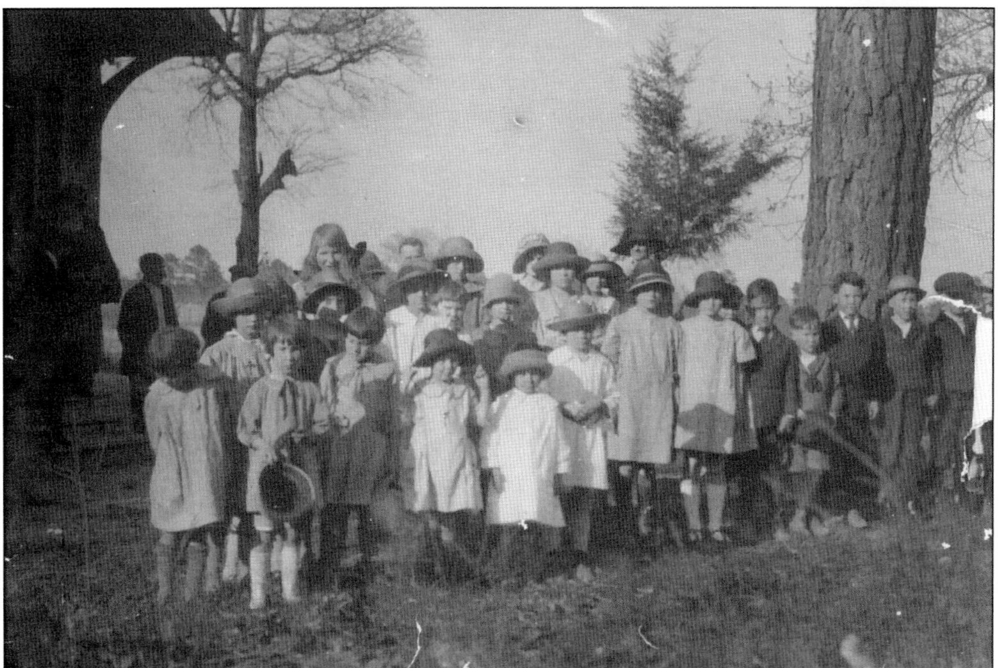

St. Ignatius Episcopal Church in Old Sparta was one of the mission churches of Calvary Church of Tarboro. This photograph, taken in 1925, shows local children gathered in front of the church. While the individual children are not identified, the families of the parish included those of Charlie Edwards, Henry Britt, Albert Anderson, Frank Eagles, Pheston Gray Shelton, and Charlie Forbes. (PC Johnson)

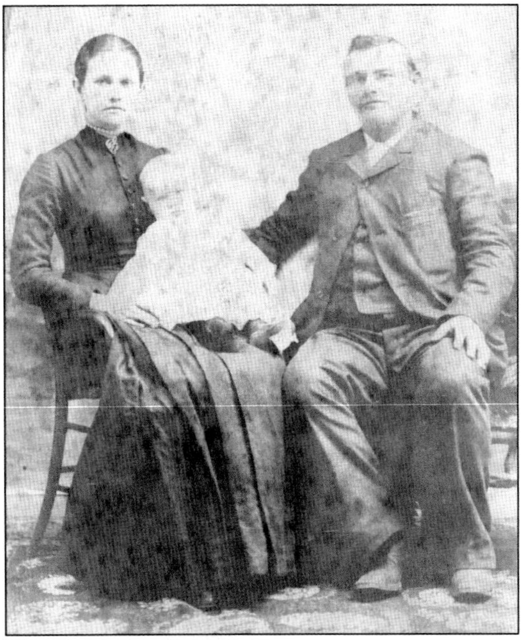

Wright Lawrence Stallings, Emma Rebecca Jenkins (his wife), and Ruth Virginia Stallings (his daughter) visited the studios of S.R. Alley in Tarboro in 1890. A farmer and a magistrate for Old Sparta Township during the 1890s, Stallings also served as sheriff. (PC D. Stallings)

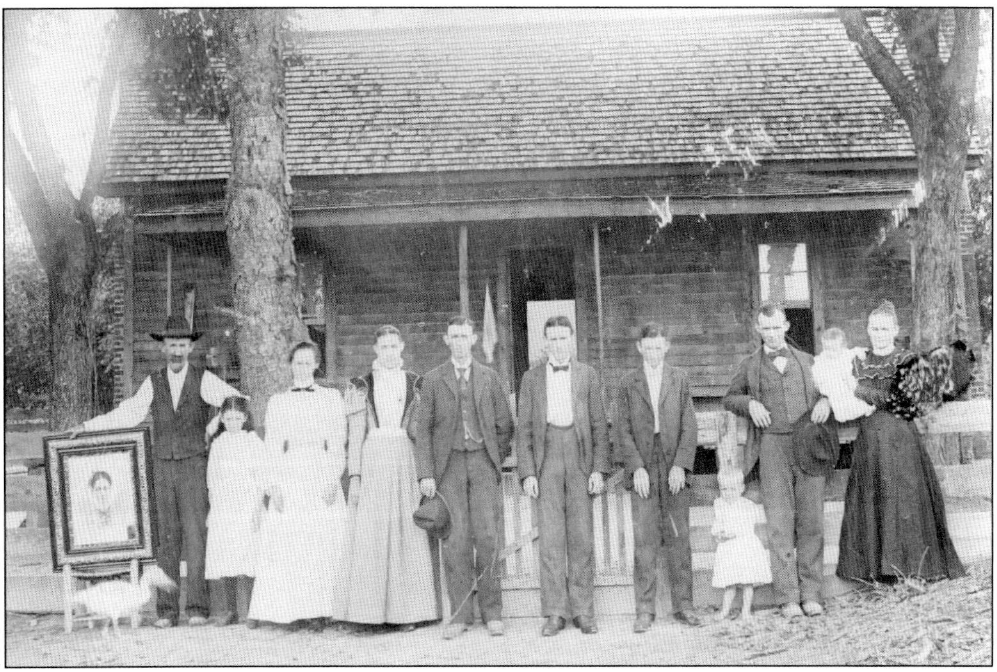

In 1901 Benjamin Pittman had a family picture made on his farm in the Autry Creek Township near Macclesfield. The portrait on the left, held by Benjamin, is of his wife, Elizabeth Phillips Pittman. Included in the picture are the following, from left to right: daughter Mattie Pittman, daughter Susan Pittman, daughter-in-law Janie Forbes Pittman, son Lafayette Pittman, son David James Pittman, son Battle Pittman, grandson Mark Pittman, son William Eddie Pittman, daughter-in-law Delphia Webb Pittman, and grandson Willie Pittman (held by his mother). Most of the family members are buried in the Pittman family cemetery near the house, which is still standing. (PC Reason)

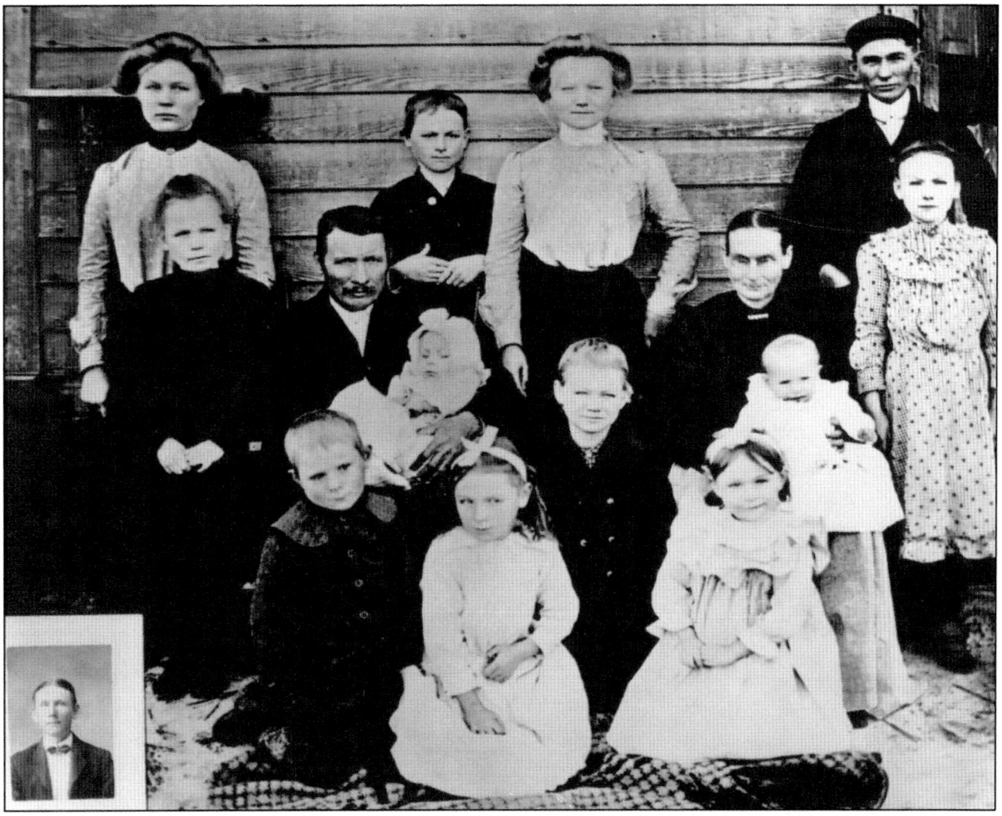

In September 1881 Hiram Webb married Ella Vainwright, who was twenty years old. They had thirteen children over the next twenty years. From left to right are as follows: (front row) oldest son David Payton Webb (in the corner), Thomas Ransom Webb, Leary Webb, and Minnie Ella Webb; (middle row) Ann Eliza Webb, Hiram Webb (holding his youngest son, Buck Ransom Webb), Rufus Webb, Ella Webb (with Pennie Bessie Webb in front of her) and Berthia Webb; (back row) Edith Elizabeth Webb, Collin Webb, Annie Webb, and Joseph Randel Webb. (PC Webb)

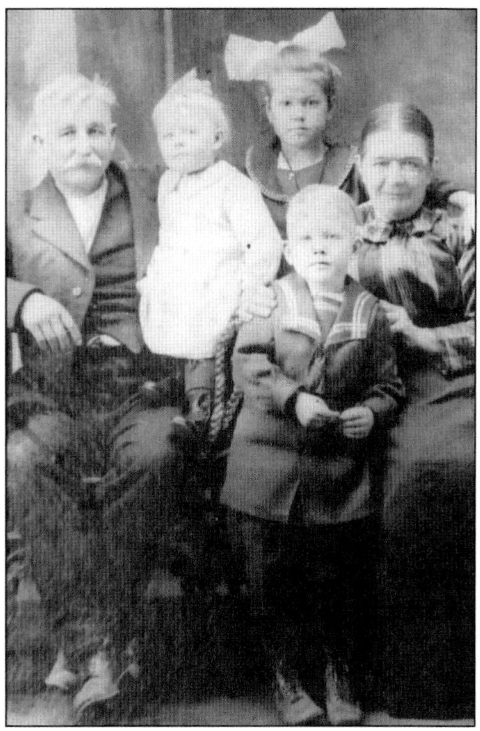

Thomas Christopher Bunting and his second wife, Betsy Ann Warren, were photographed in 1920 with three of their grandchildren. Mamie Lee Bunting is standing in the back, John Thomas Bunting is standing in the front, and Fannie Gold Bunting is standing on her grandfather's lap. Mamie Lee Bunting married John Edward Roberson and had twins, Edward and Earl, in 1935. (PC Roberson)

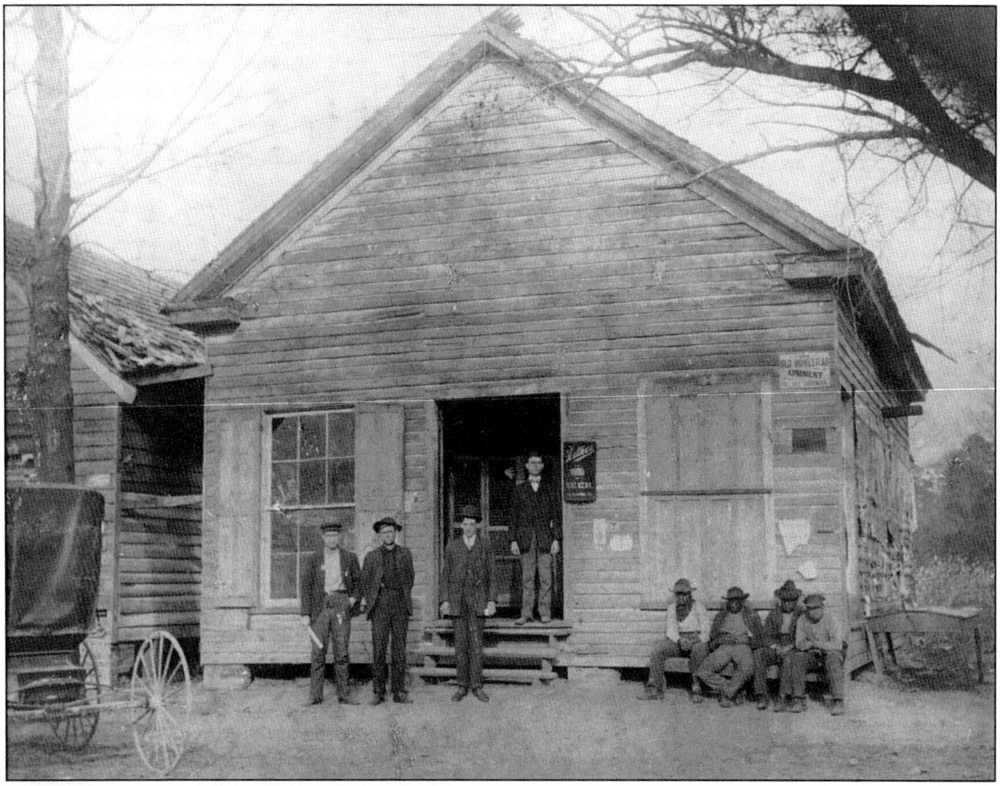

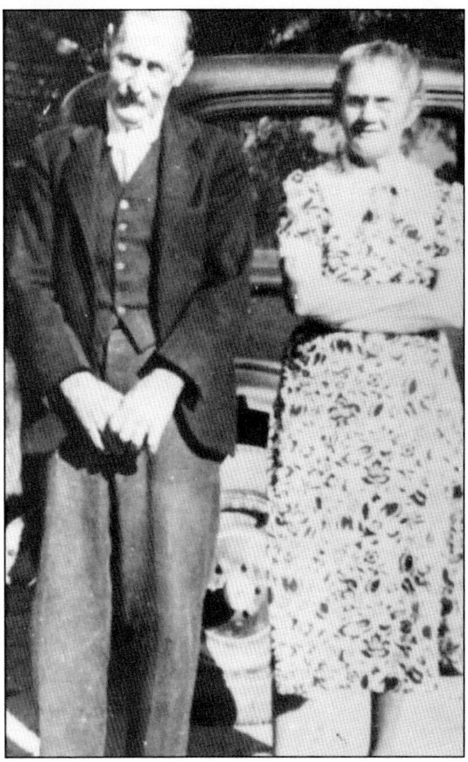

Standing outside the J. Edwards General Store in Old Sparta in 1908 are G.C. Webb, Tom Exum, T.G. Shelton Sr., and Charles Edwards. The men seated are Nathan Thorn, Write Stincle, Drew Mercer, and Brice Cobb. G.C. Webb was Grover Cleveland Webb, better known as "Cheb." He was the last police chief of Old Sparta. (PC Webb)

Charlie Frank Forbes and his wife, Susan Elizabeth Keel Forbes, operated a general store in the Old Sparta community from 1900 until 1930, when this picture was taken. Other general stores in the area included B.F. Eagles, Barns & Williford, B.J. Keech, E.L. Moore, Watson Pitt, and V.B. Sharp. (PC Crisp)

This Federal home was built in the early 1830s for Reddin Pittman Sr. An unusual T-shaped gable roof covers the house, which had three chimneys and a partial basement. The detailed cornice and corner boards have interesting sunburst designs. Old photographs show the porch with a large, scalloped frieze and fancy Victorian elements, all of which were probably added in the 1850s or 1860s. The house was later owned by Dr. Bass. (ECUSC William Elmore Papers)

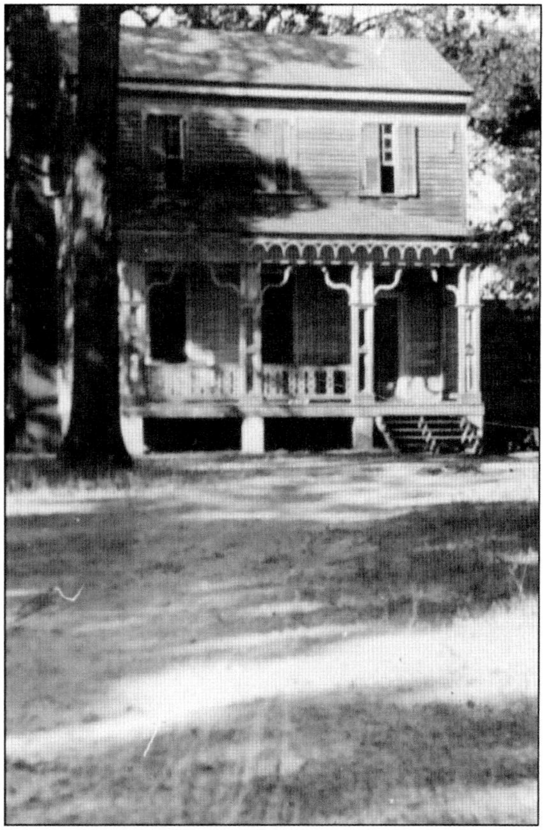

Daniel Powell and Sallie Ann Proctor, both natives of Edgecombe County, were married in 1885. The couple had nine children and named them in alphabetical order. They are, from left to right, as follows: Ada Belinda (Cummings), Claudia Dorinda (Tolston), Effie Fostina (Joyner), Gertha Helen (Goff), Ivey Joseph, Katie Luelnor (Harper), and Marion Napolean. On either side of Daniel and Sallie are Oliver Pervis and Queen Ruby (Goff). (PC Powell)

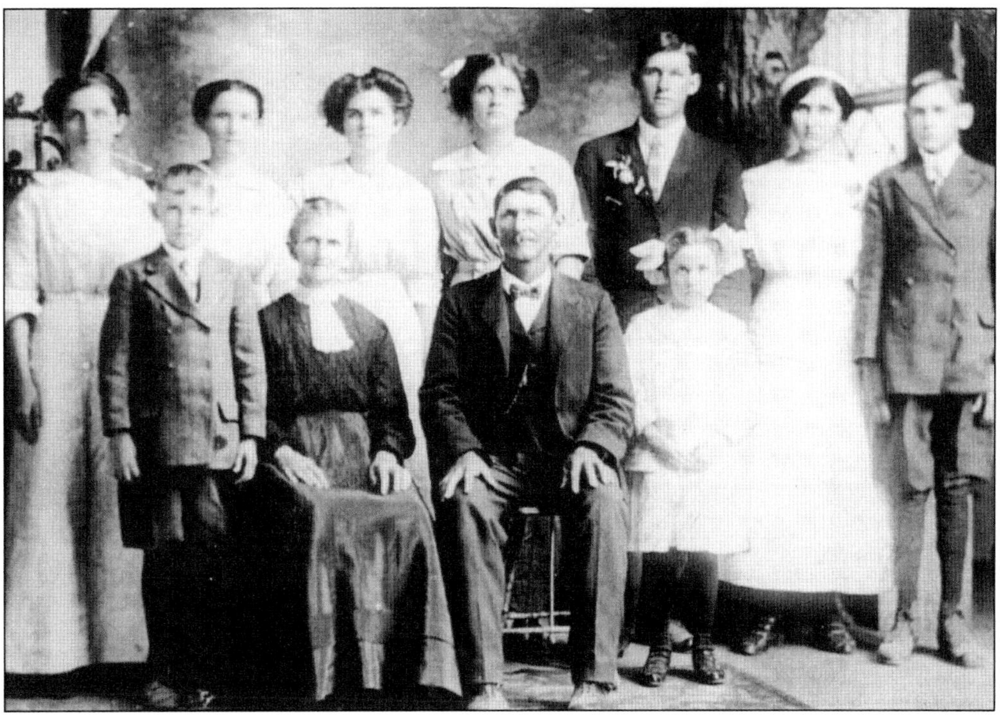

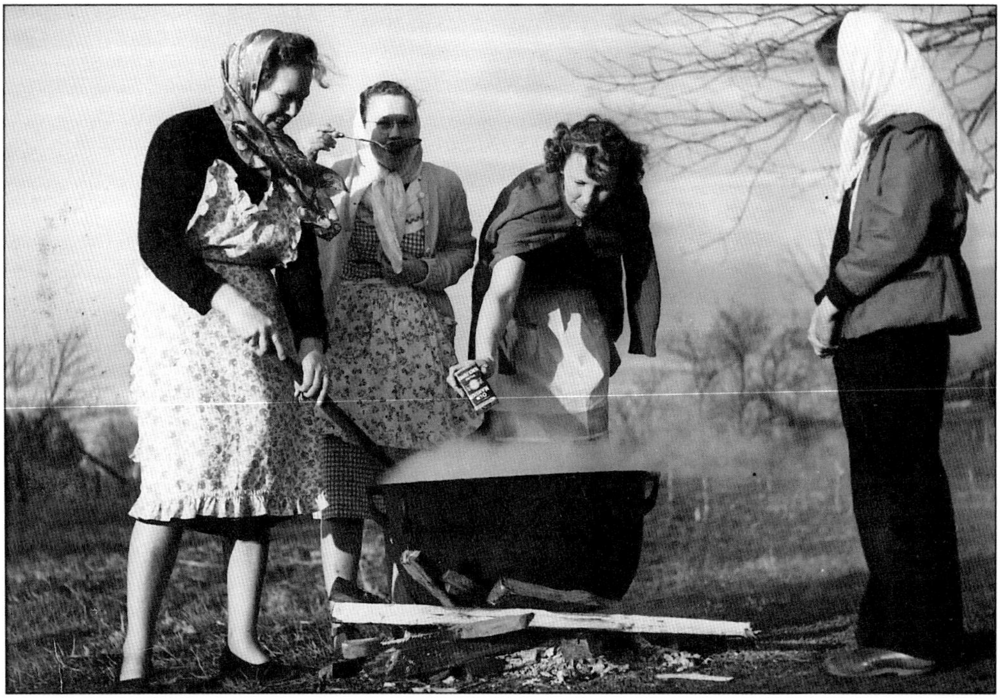

Lela Lewis, Nita Harrell, Sara Burnett, and a neighbor prepare a pot of Brunswick Stew for a stew sale, a traditional area fund-raiser. The Town of Macclesfield used the funds from the stew sale to improve the community. (MAC)

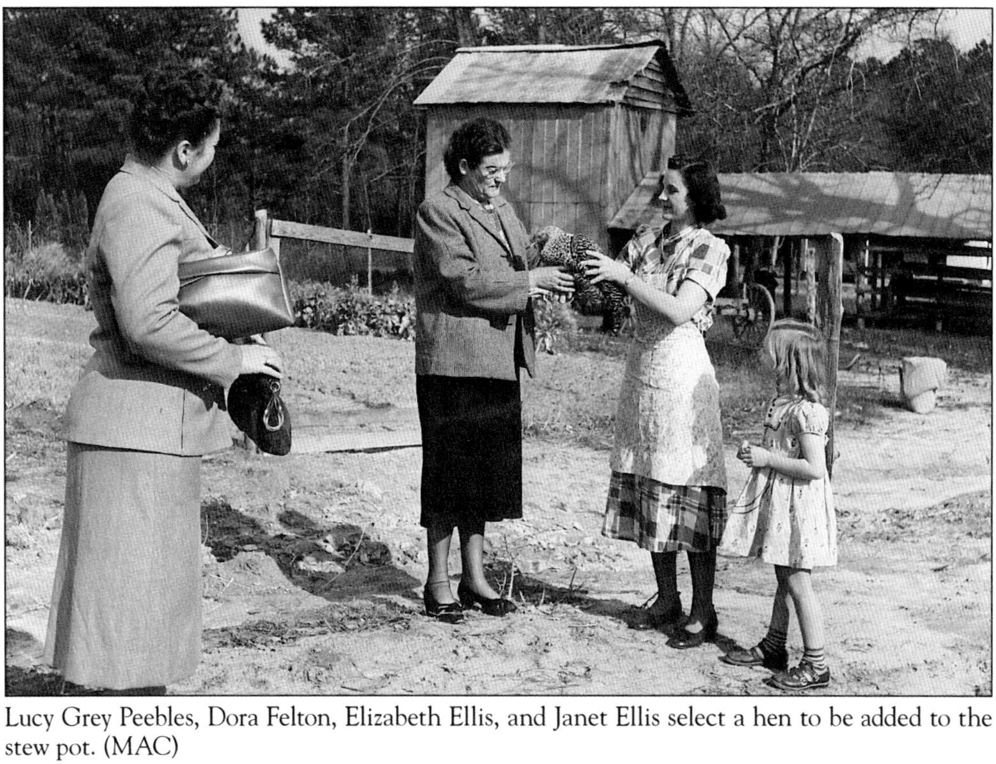

Lucy Grey Peebles, Dora Felton, Elizabeth Ellis, and Janet Ellis select a hen to be added to the stew pot. (MAC)

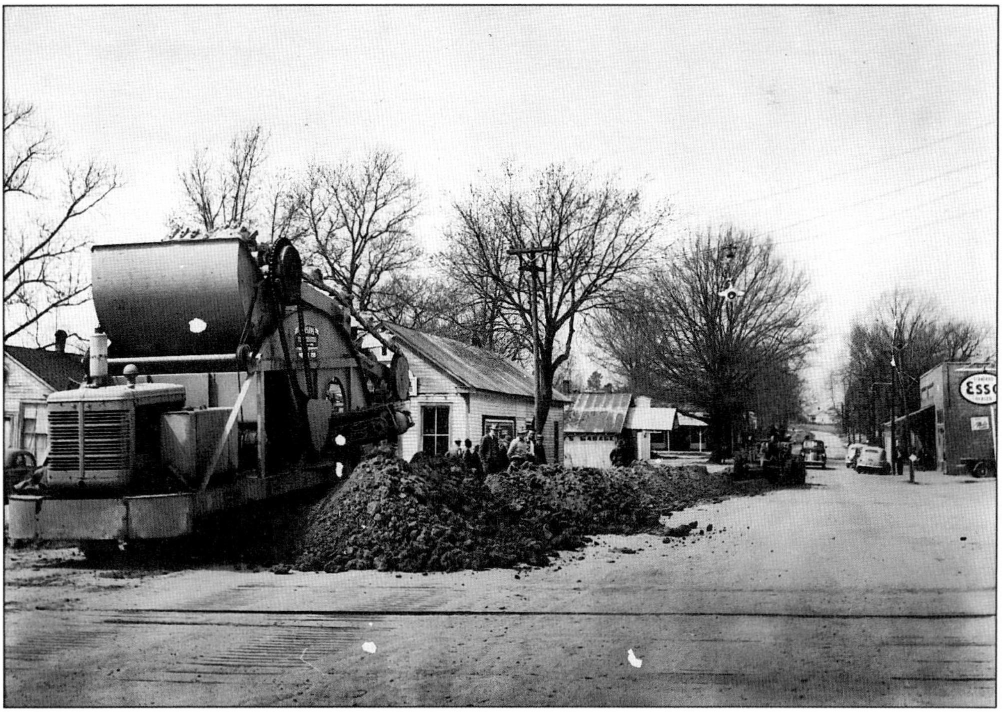

Macclesfield also paved Main Street during its beautification program. (MAC)

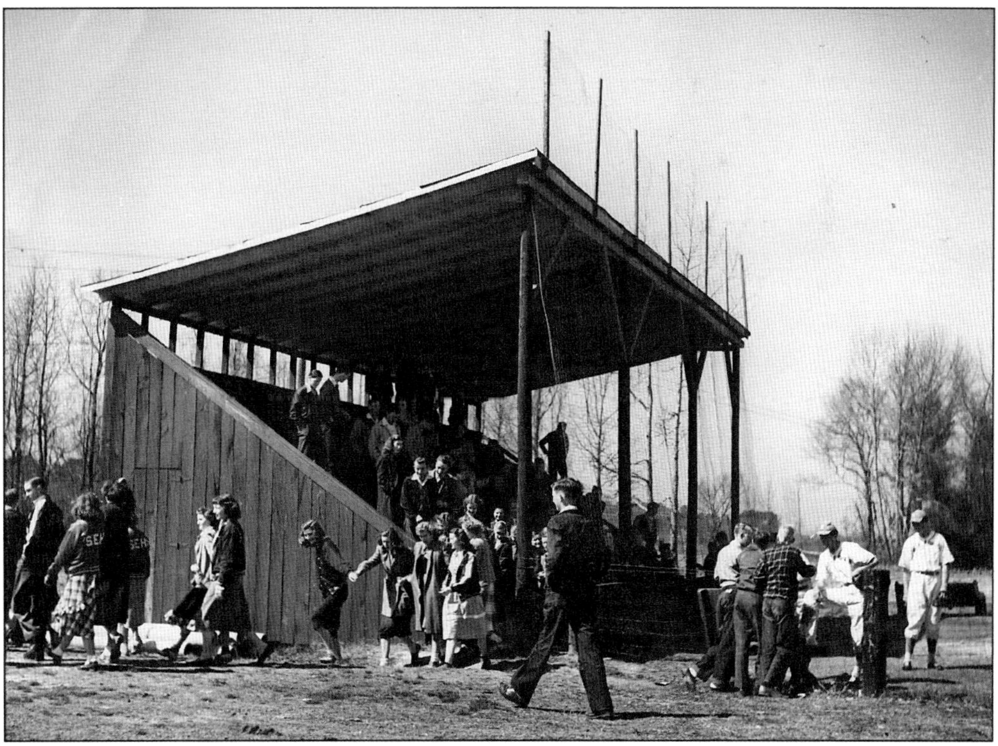

The Town of Macclesfield used the money raised for the beautification project to improve the ballfield used by the high school. (MAC)

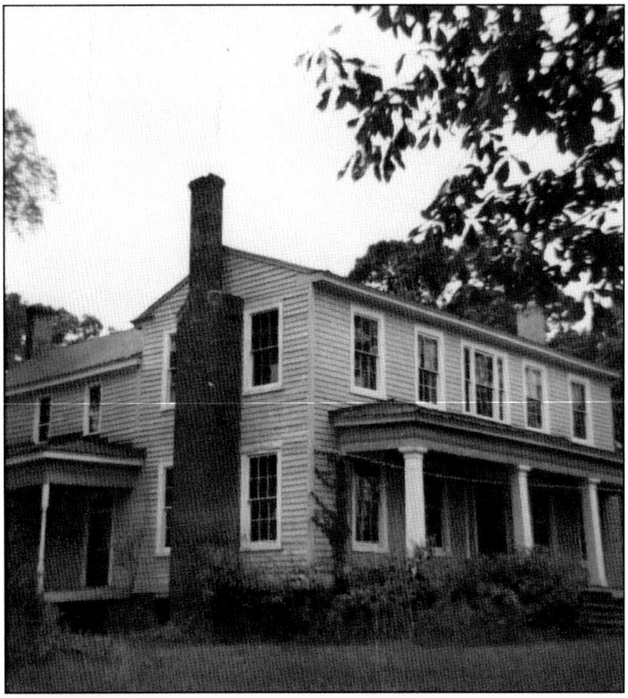

"Mount Moriah," located northeast of Rocky Mount near Battleboro, was constructed about 1827. It served as the home of Dr. James. J. Philips. The homestead also had a school for the plantation children, and at one point it was used as a Masonic lodge. (BBH)

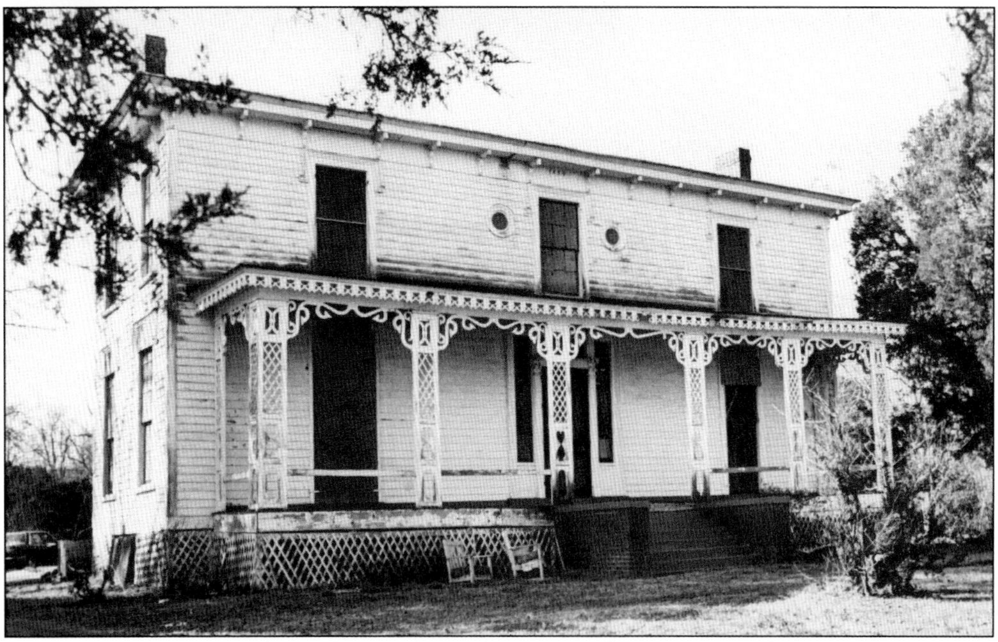

This house, known as "The Cedars," is located near Speight's Chapel. William Ruffin designed the Italianate house for John Francis Speight, the minister of the chapel, and Speight's wife, Emma Lewis. Built around 1859, the house has elaborate Victorian sawn work on the full front porch and an interesting pair of porthole windows flanking the central, second-floor window. Upon the death of the Reverend Speight, his son Richard acquired the home. Richard was a physician and a member of the North Carolina General Assembly. He had a small doctor's office built on the property. (BBH)

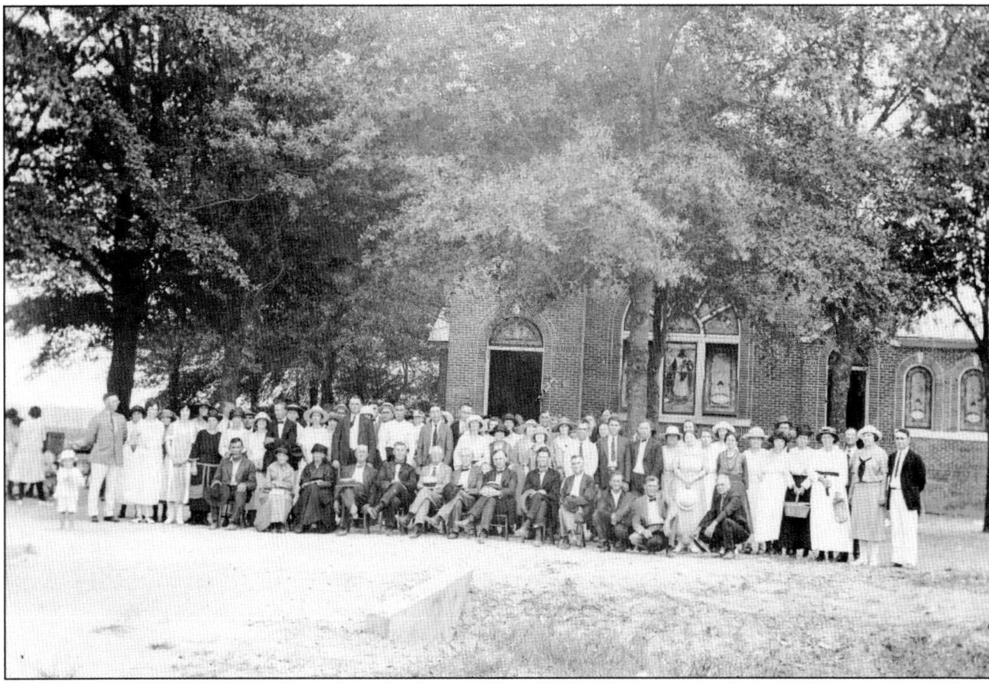

The William and Mary Hart Church was built by Tarboro businessman William A. Hart and named after two of his children. Located in Leggett, the new sanctuary was dedicated in 1924. Hart was the first highway commissioner for eastern North Carolina and he made sure the road between Tarboro and Leggett was paved so folks could get to church. He was also the founder of Hart Mills. (PC Fountain)

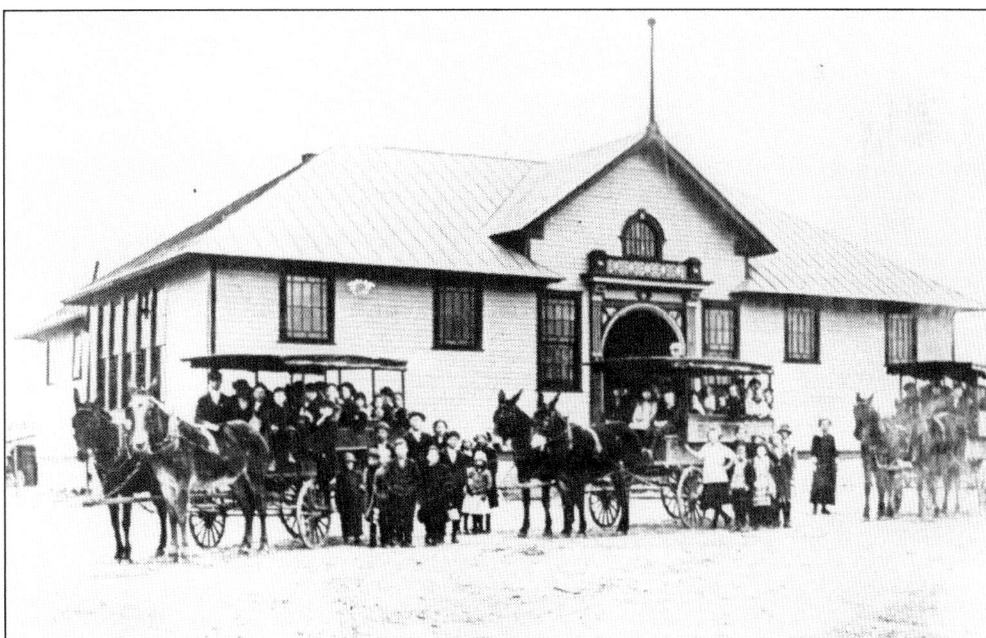

Leggett School, *c.* 1915, is shown here with the horse-drawn wagons that were used to transport the students. (BBH)

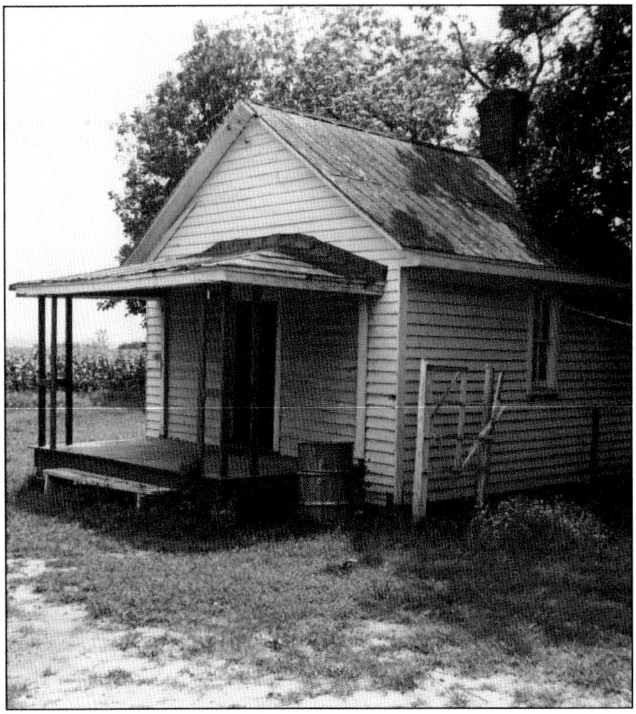

Governor Elias Carr of Edgecombe County and Governor C.B. Aycock of Wayne County both supported the establishment of public schools. This small, one-room school in Speed is an example of the many community schools that were developed through the efforts of Governors Carr and Aycock. This area was named Speed in 1903 for Dr. E.T. Speed. (ECML)

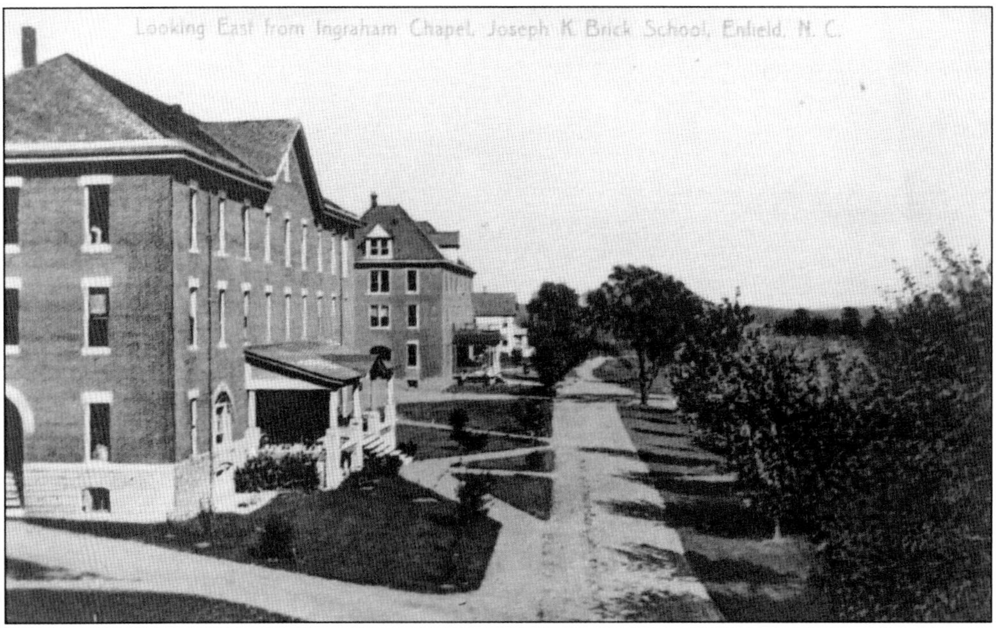

The Joseph K. Brick Agricultural, Industrial, and Normal School was founded in Brick, near Whitakers, in the 1890s and built on a farm owned by General L.G. Estes. In 1902 Mrs. Julia Brewster Brick of Brooklyn, New York, left a bequest of $500,000 to the American Missionary Association for the operation of the school. The school was a private academy for people of color and it recruited students from around the world. It became a junior college in the 1920s but closed in the 1930s because of a lack of funds. The headmaster for many years was Mr. Thomas Sewell Inborden. (ECML)

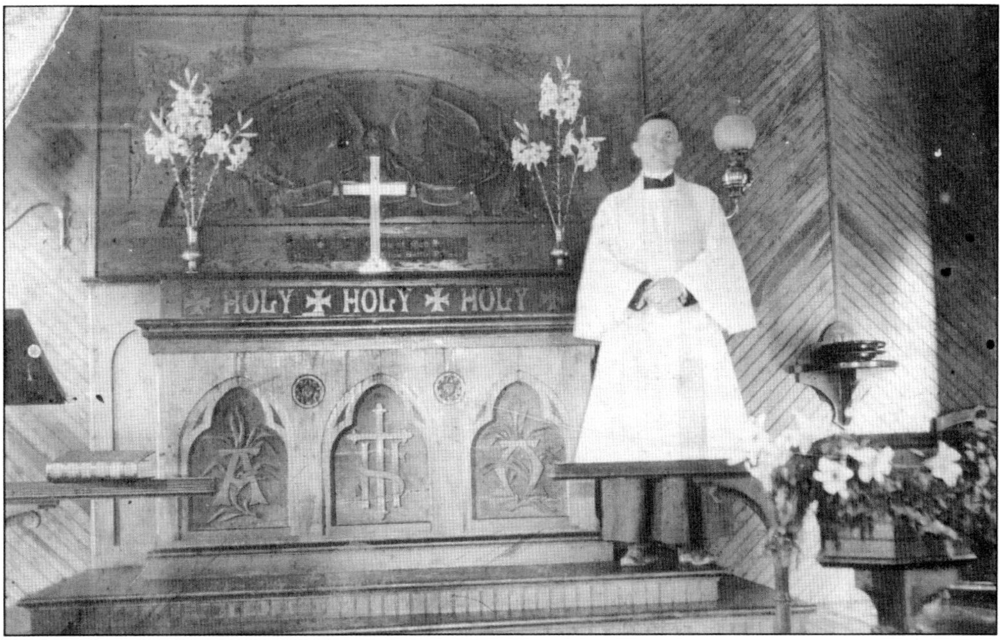

The Grace Episcopal Church, located at the northeast corner of the junction of NC 97 and Rte. 258, is another of Calvary Church's mission churches. Built in 1893, Grace is noted for the interior woodwork that was carved by Miss Kate Cheshire, who ran the parochial school here. The walls are clad in German siding, and Grace still has its original stained-glass windows. In this photograph, the Reverend Bertram Brown is standing by the carved altar. (ECML)

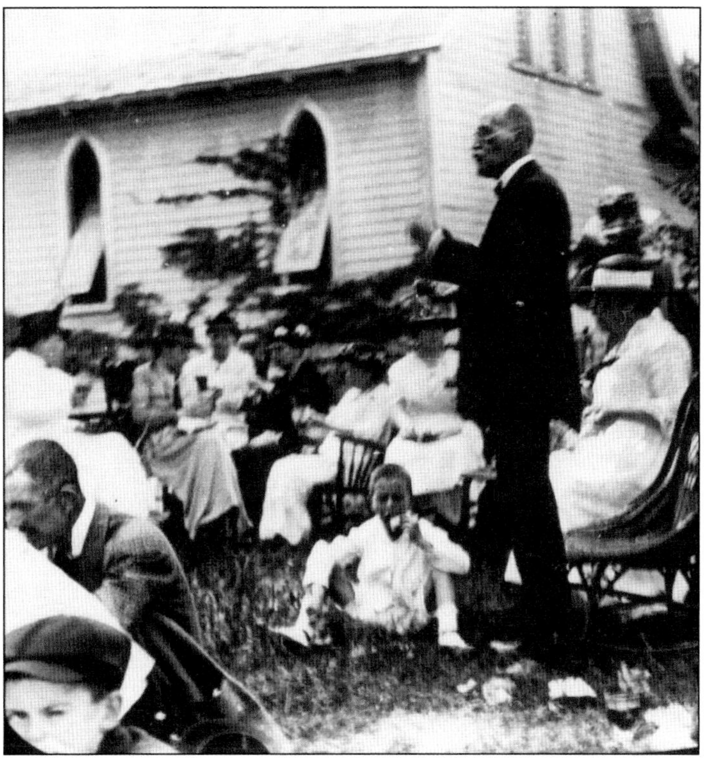

Members of the Grace Episcopal Church complete a homecoming service with dinner on the grounds about 1890. (ECML)

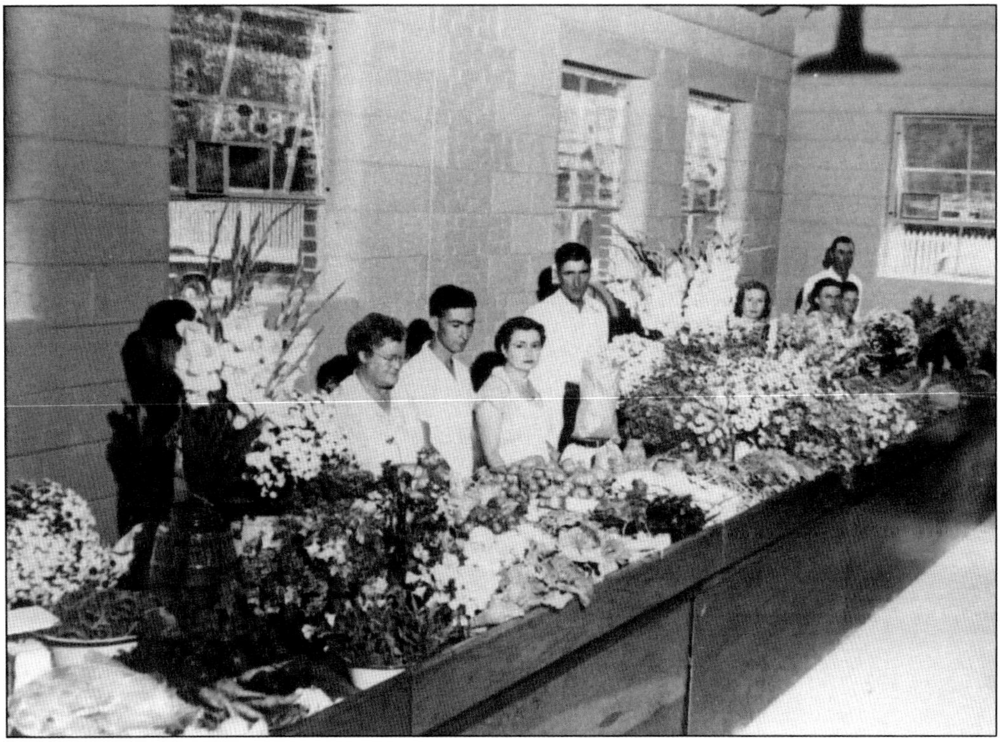

During the Depression, Edgecombe County received funds to establish a curb market near the train depot on Main Street in Rocky Mount to serve Edgecombe and Nash County farmers. The wives often brought canned goods, flowers, and fresh vegetables to sell. (ECML)

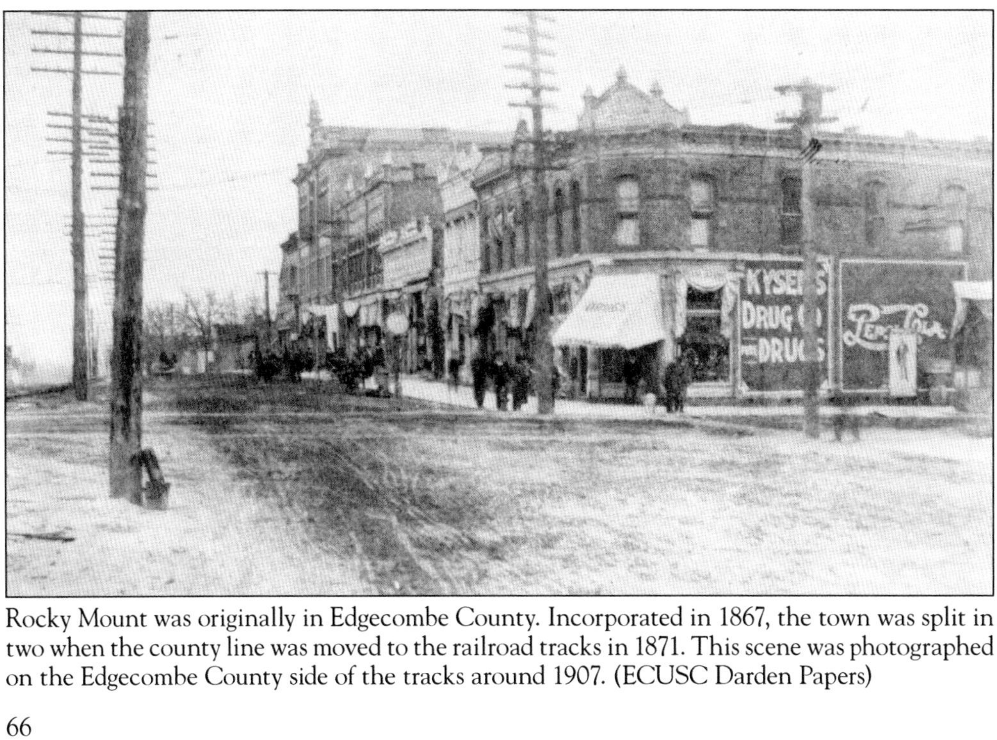

Rocky Mount was originally in Edgecombe County. Incorporated in 1867, the town was split in two when the county line was moved to the railroad tracks in 1871. This scene was photographed on the Edgecombe County side of the tracks around 1907. (ECUSC Darden Papers)

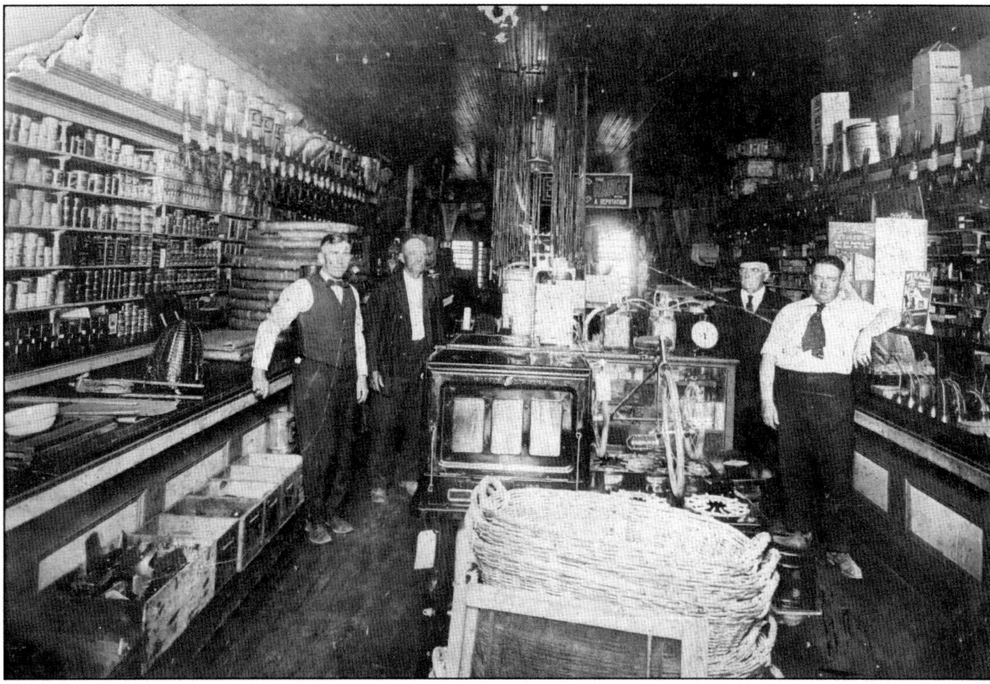

This hardware store was in Whitakers in the northern part of the county. (PC Jones)

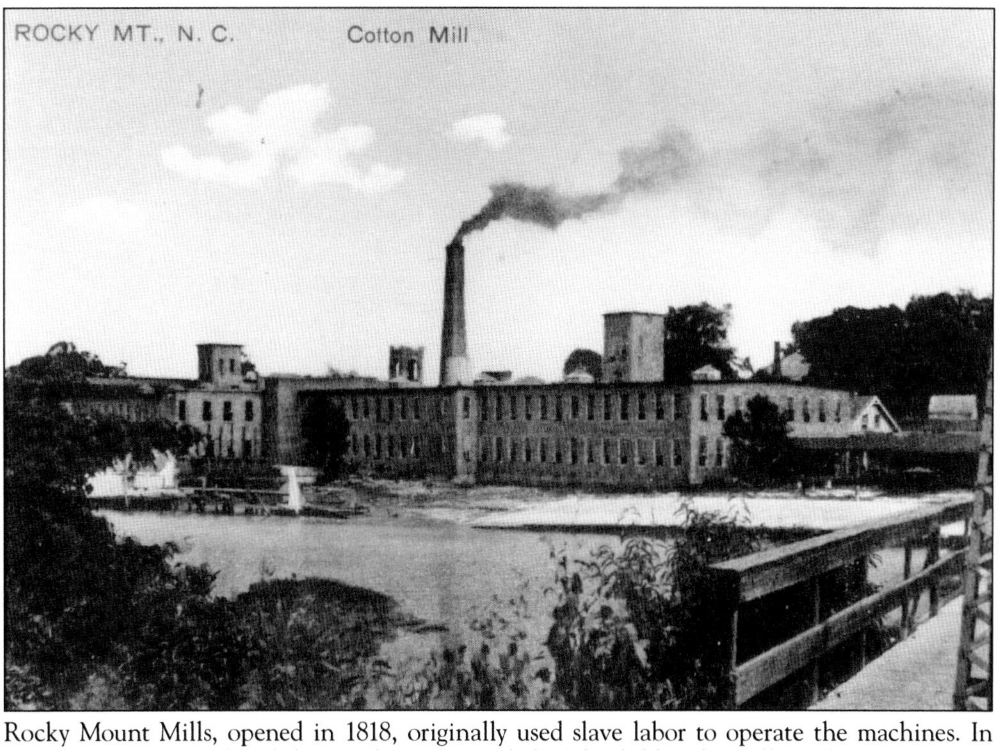

Rocky Mount Mills, opened in 1818, originally used slave labor to operate the machines. In the 1850s women replaced slaves, who were needed in the fields. The mill was burned in a raid in July 1863 but was rebuilt. Rocky Mount Mills closed in June 1996 after over 170 years of spinning cotton. (ECUSC)

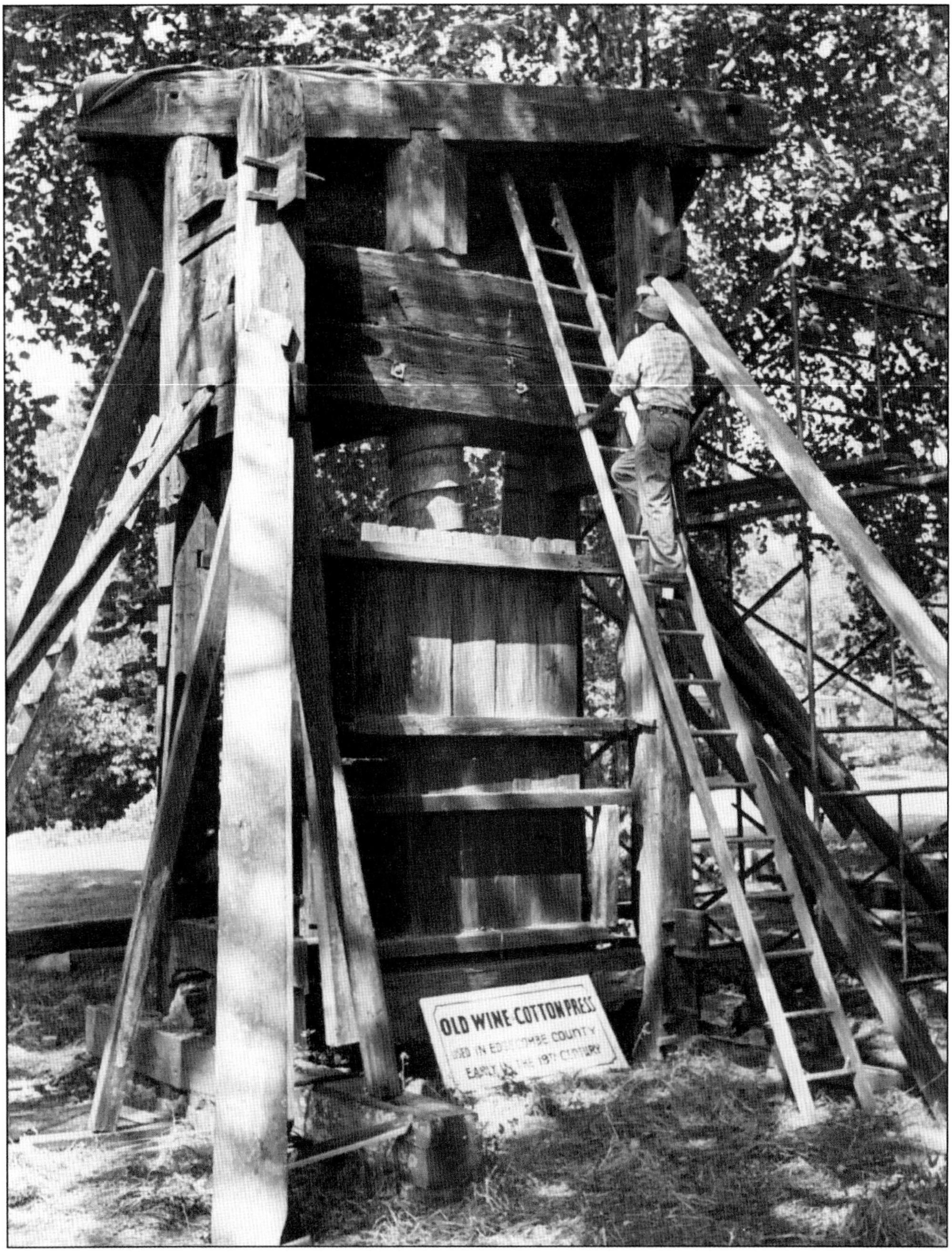

Cotton presses were prevalent in Edgecombe County beginning in 1800. To preserve part of the county's agricultural heritage, this cotton press, built around 1840, was moved from the Norfleet farm to the Town Common in 1960. The press used mule power to turn a large screw carved from a maple tree, to press cotton into 300 or 400-pound bales. When the cotton season was over, the press was also used to press fruit pulp to make cider, wine, and brandy. Edgecombe County was noted for its brandy exports back in the 1770s. (BBH)

Three

Working the Land

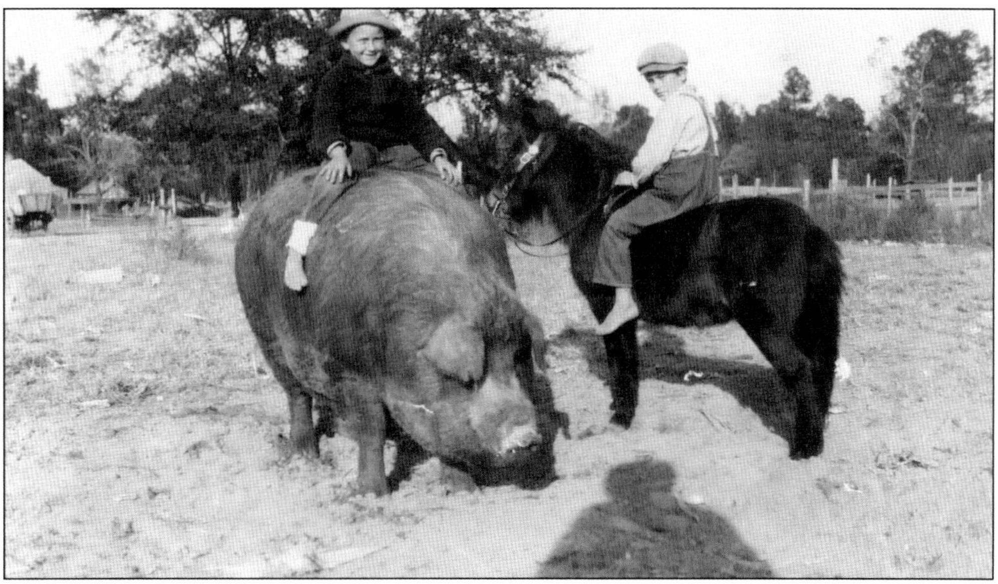

Most Edgecombe County farmers raised animals and grew vegetables for their families as well as raising crops for sale. Hogs and chickens could be found on most farms. Here young Sam Easton sits atop his 1,134-pound pet Duroc hog in 1928 while his brother Austin rides a pony. The hogs were usually slaughtered or sold before reaching this size. (PC Mayo family)

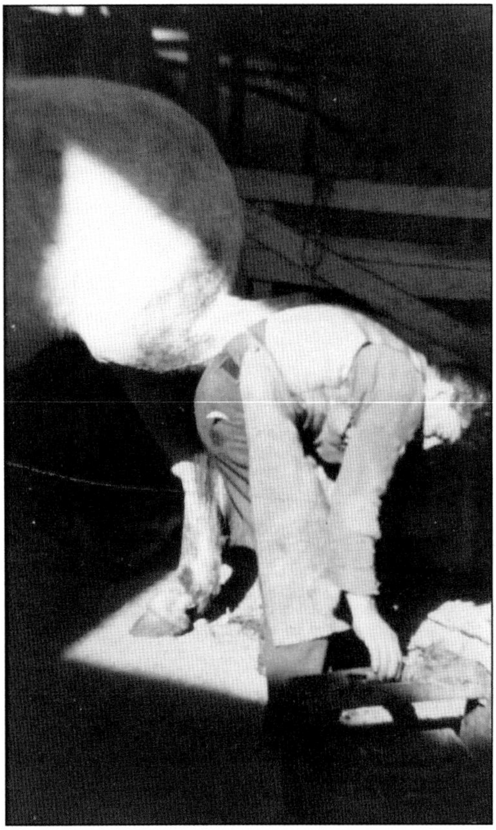

Mr. Frank Grayiel was the farrier at Winslow Stables and looked after many horses in the community. (PC Winslow)

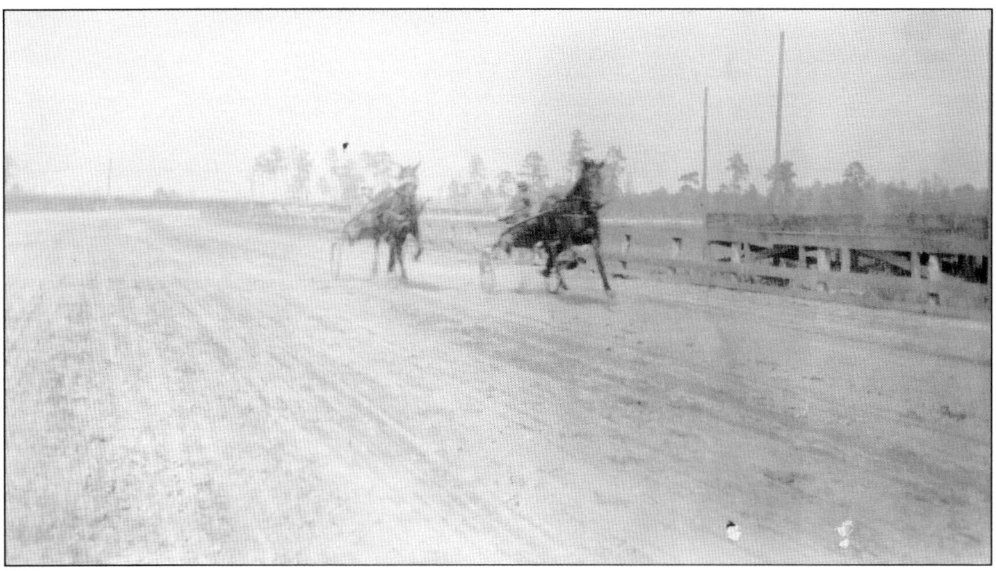

Horse racing has been a popular sport in Edgecombe County since the early nineteenth century. At least one farm specialized in raising horses rather than crops: Ben Mayo raised racehorses as well as thoroughbreds for riding at the Piney Grove Stock Farm in eastern Edgecombe County during the 1920s. This photograph shows the horse Anna Sue running a mile in 2.46 minutes in a 1926 harness race in Rocky Mount. (PC Mayo)

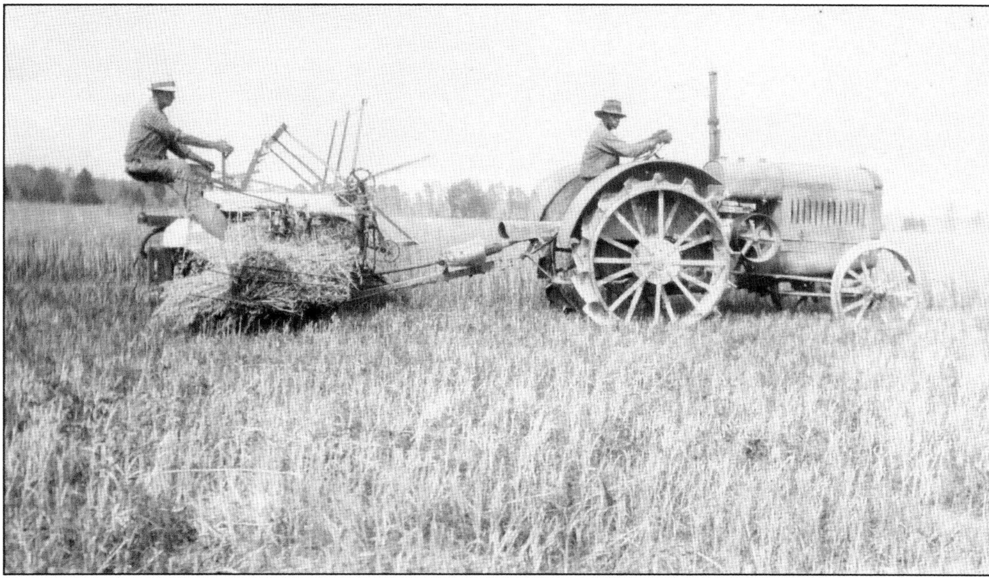

The Piney Grove Stock Farm raised grain to feed the horses there. C.C. Spurgin is on the binder and Isaac Freeman is driving the tractor in this 1928 photograph. (PC Mayo)

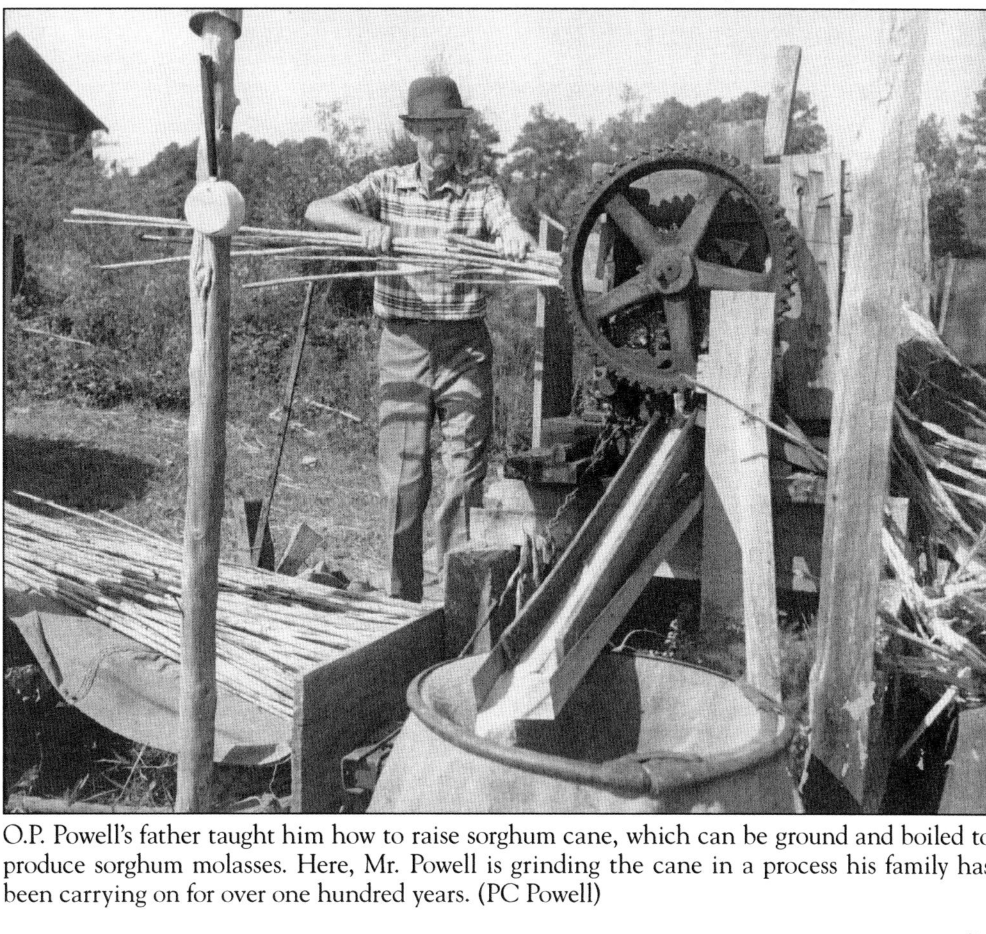

O.P. Powell's father taught him how to raise sorghum cane, which can be ground and boiled to produce sorghum molasses. Here, Mr. Powell is grinding the cane in a process his family has been carrying on for over one hundred years. (PC Powell)

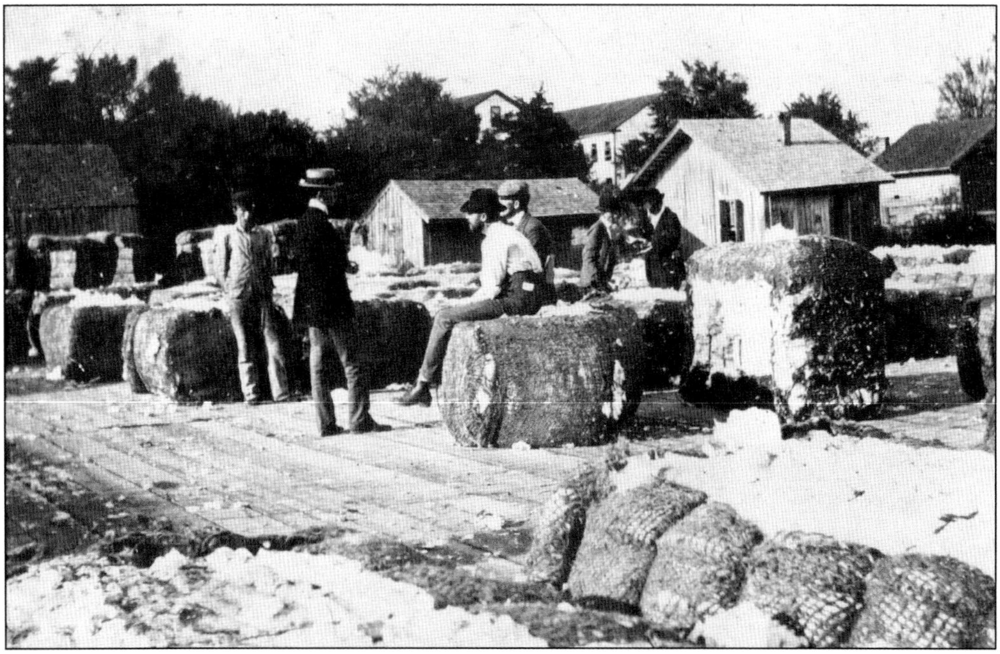

In 1840 Edgecombe County produced 2,445,000 pounds (approximately 6,000 400-pound bales) of seed cotton. In 1858 total cotton production for the county was recorded at 17,608 bales. Although corn, wheat, and sweet potatoes were produced, cotton was clearly the king crop in Edgecombe County prior to 1860. It was raised in great volume even after the War, with production in the 1880s averaging over 25,000 bales a year. Bales were formed at the numerous cotton presses throughout the county and then delivered to either the train depot or the river docks to be shipped to market. (ECML)

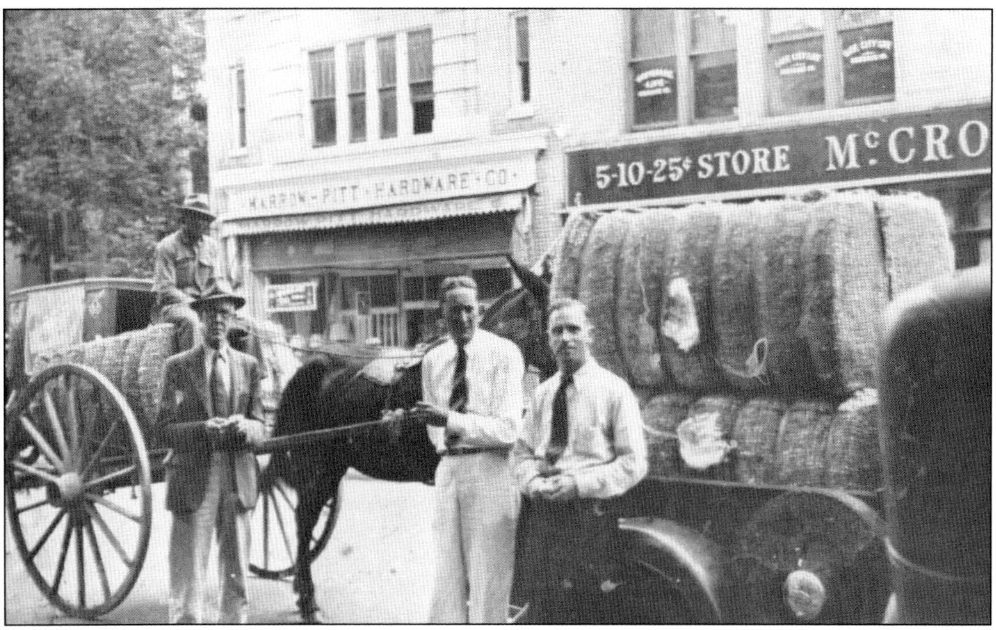

Cotton buyer Wat Smoot Sr. and his buyers stand in front of bales of cotton at the Cotton Market, located on the 300 block of Main Street in Tarboro. (BBH)

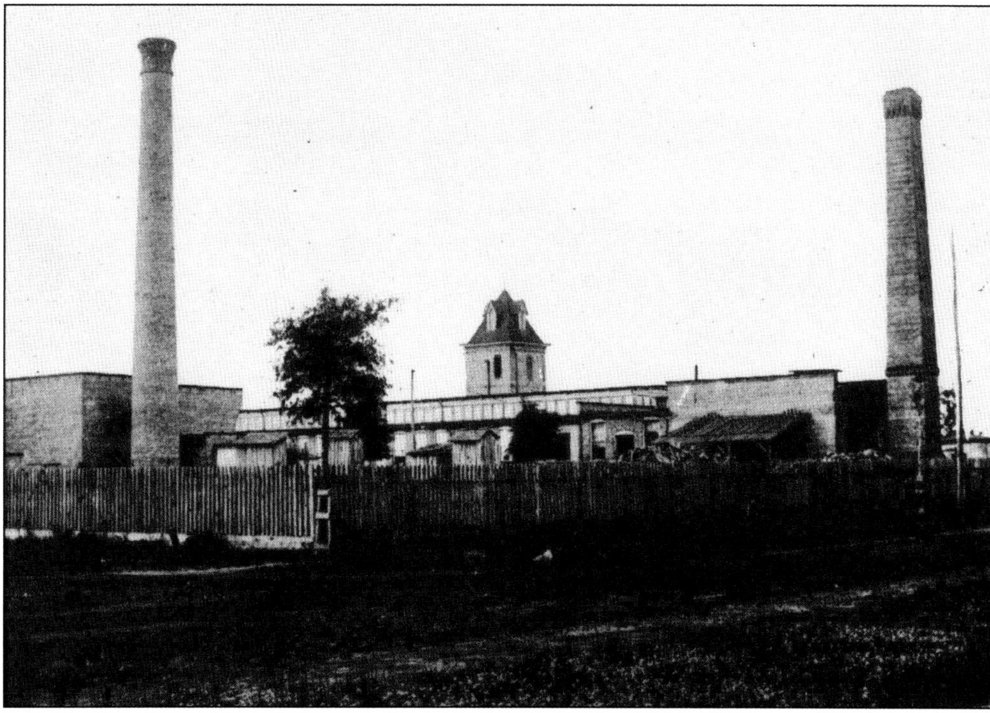

Over forty cotton gins were operated in the county at the turn of the century, leading to the development of several textile mills and five cotton oil seed companies. (BBH)

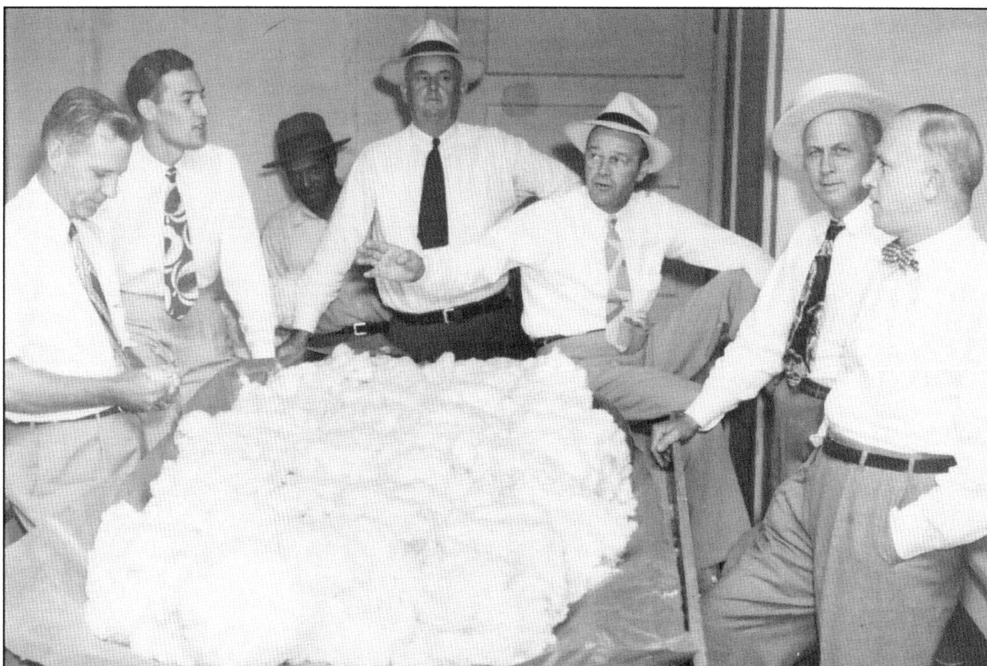

Cotton buyers discuss the quality and price of a 1940s cotton crop. They are, from left to right, as follows: unknown, Wat Smoot Jr., Mr. Davis, John Youngblood (sitting on the table), Sam Dean, and Wat Smoot Sr. (ECML)

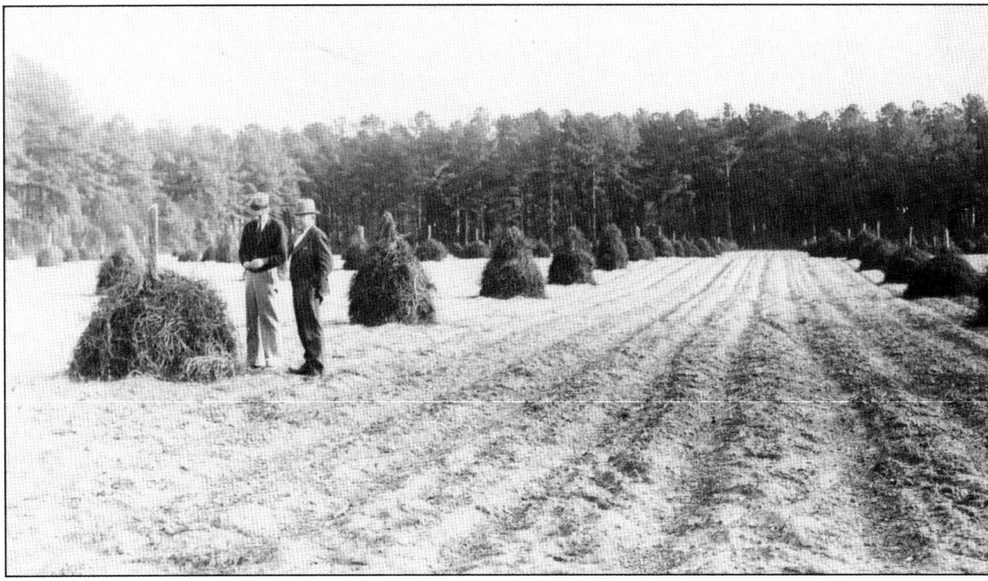

Peanuts were also important to the economy of Edgecombe County. Once the peanuts were dug and dried, the remaining straw was put in stacks to dry further for use as fodder for livestock. (ECML)

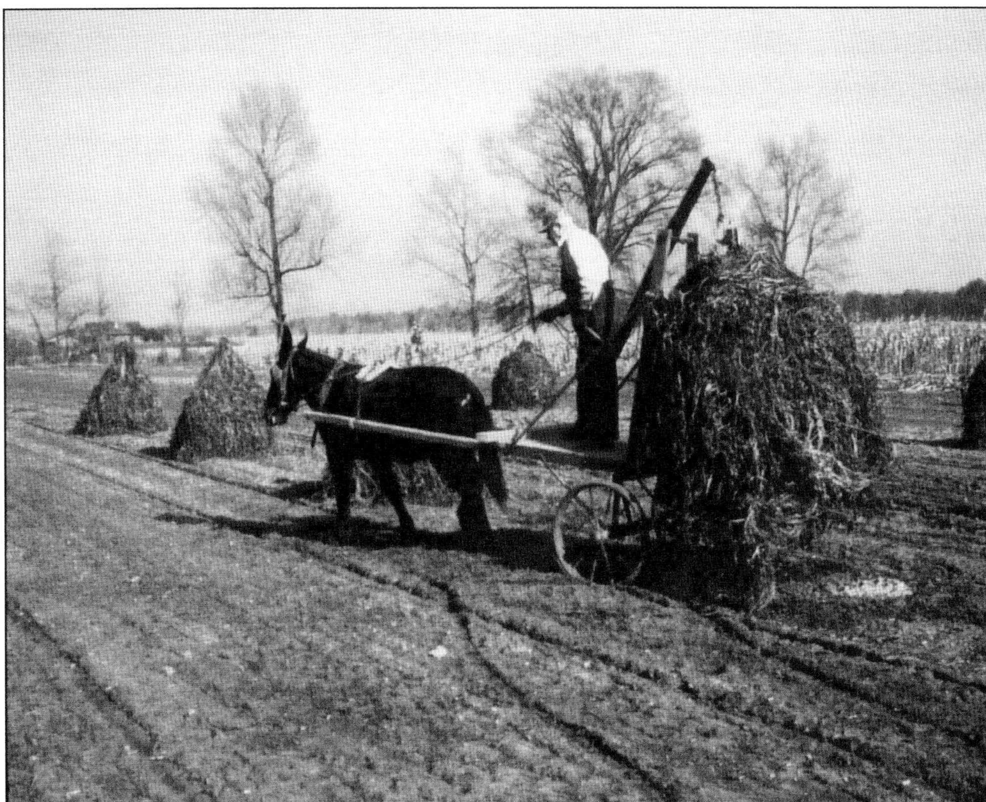

Stacks were sometimes carried to a barn or another field to feed the animals during the winter months. (PC Thigpen)

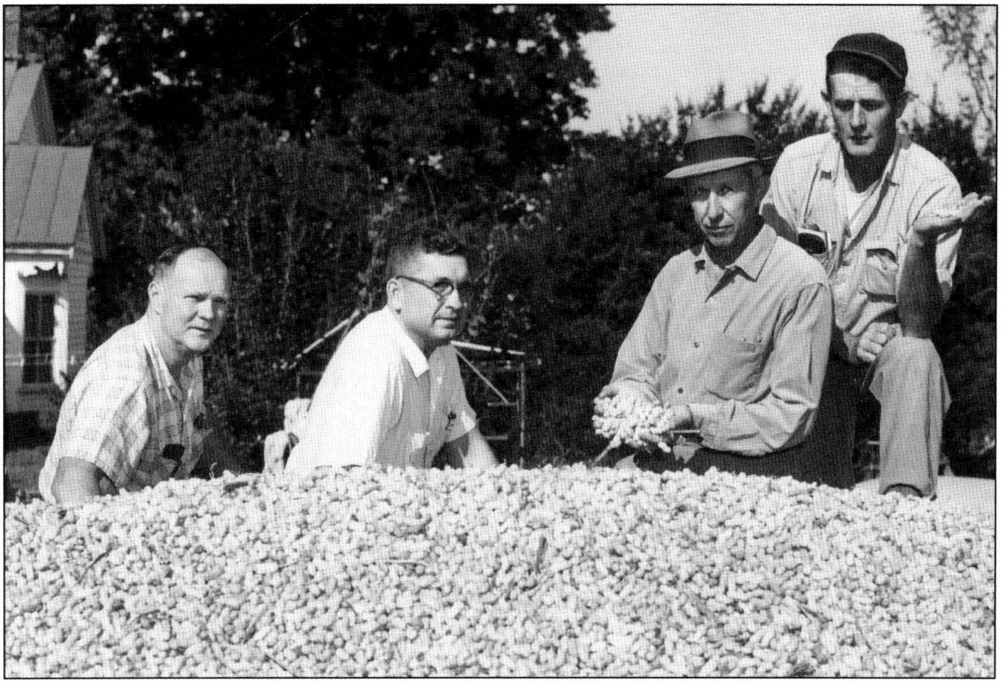

Berry Anderson and Robert Wolfe examine the peanut crop with the county agent. (BBH)

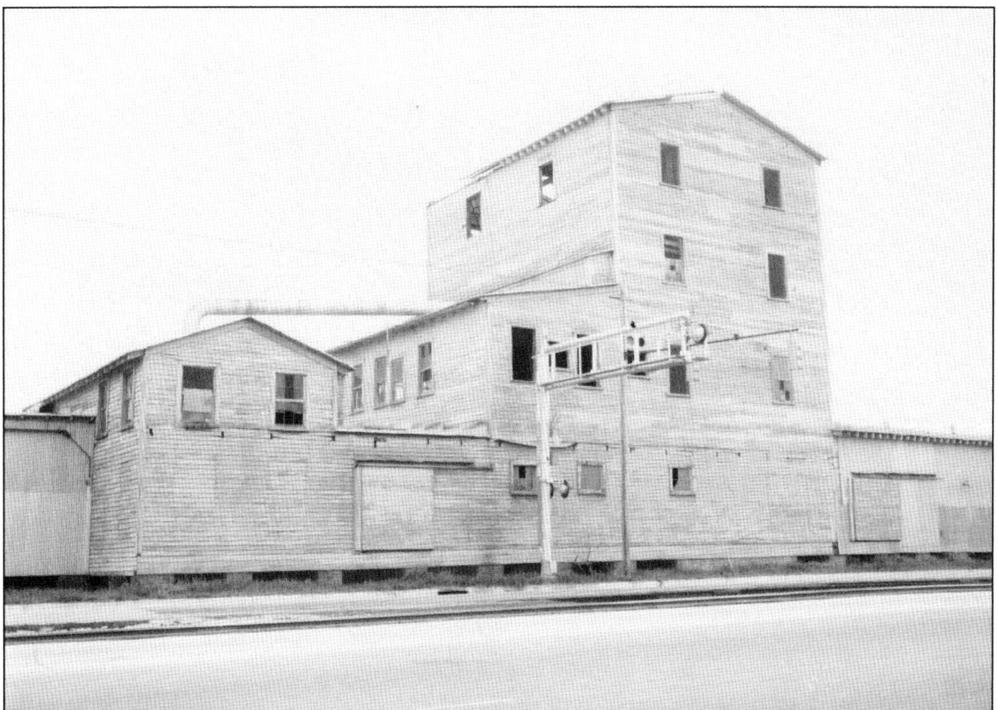

A peanut mill opened on Albemarle Avenue in 1891. In 1893 it became the Colombian Peanut Company, which also operated plants in Enfield, Scotland Neck, and Williamston. Other mills were located in Leggett and Battleboro. (ECML)

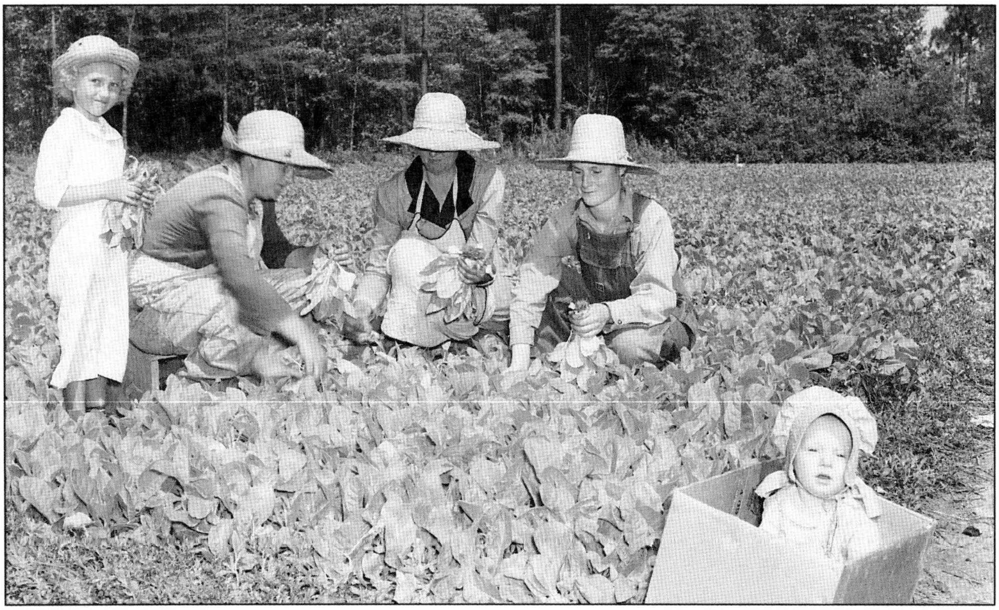

While the profits from tobacco were higher per acre grown than those from cotton, the labor was much more involved, and it kept entire families busy from April until late September. The seed beds were planted in early spring. By late April or May, the bed plants would be pulled and transplanted into a field to grow to maturity. Men usually plowed the fields to prepare them while the women in the family pulled the plants, as shown in this 1930s photograph of a seed bed near the Wilson County line. Daycare for toddlers consisted of a cardboard box or a wooden crate to keep the children out of trouble and away from snakes and other animals. (NA)

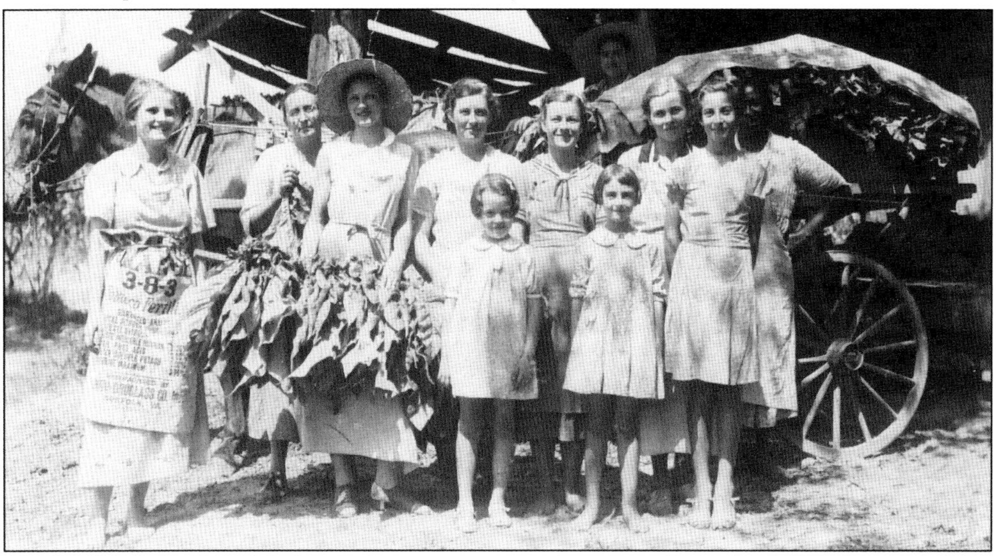

In 1934 the Smith-Douglas Fertilizer Company photographed the Webb family women in front of a tobacco barn near the Handy Corner Crossing in the Autry/Otter Creek Township. The women are, from left to right, as follows: (front row) Ora Webb, Elsie Lee Webb, Marie Parrish, Vera Webb, and Maudie Webb; (back row) Ellie Forbes Webb, Mary Belle Webb Whitley, Geneva Webb, Kitty Cummings Webb, and Lora Farmer. On a cart in the background is Bill Webb. (PC V. Stallings)

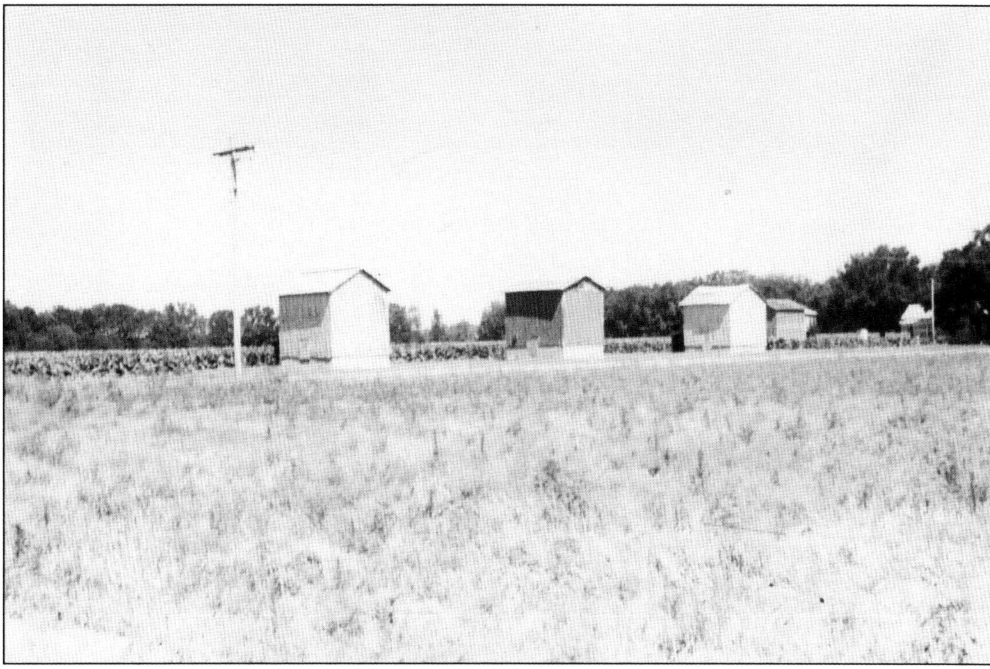

Tobacco barns like these, located near Crisp, could be found all over Edgecombe County, as nearby Farmville, Greenville, and Rocky Mount became major tobacco markets. (PC Crisp)

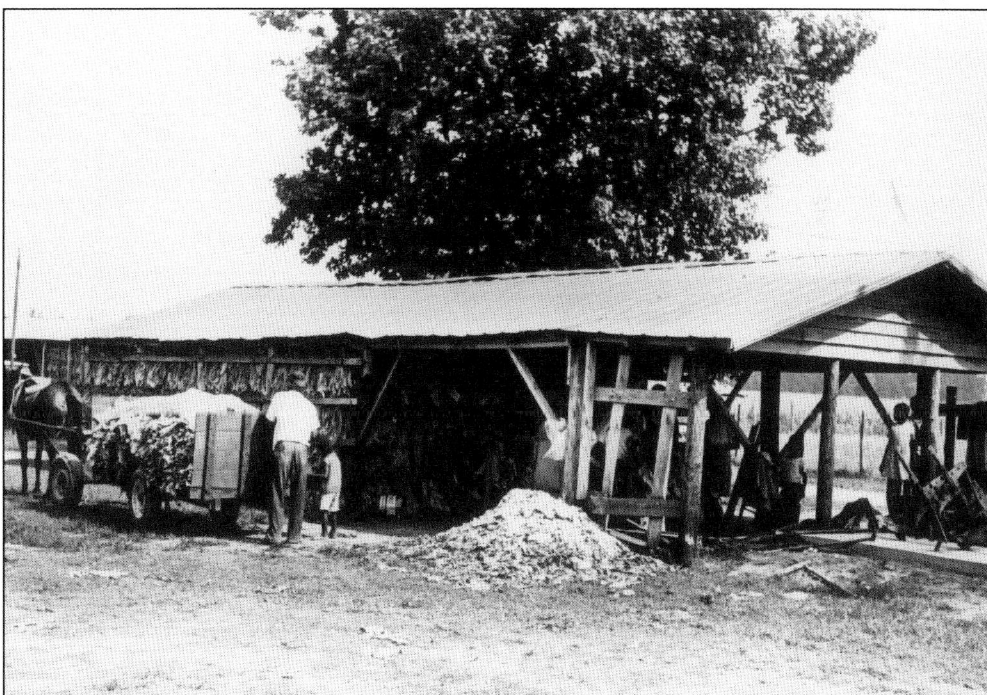

From July to early September tobacco would be barned by handlers and loopers who tied the leaves to a stick and hung the sticks in the barns to be cured by high heat. In this photograph, Enoch Armfield is removing a load of tobacco from a barn on the Thigpen farm. (PC Thigpen)

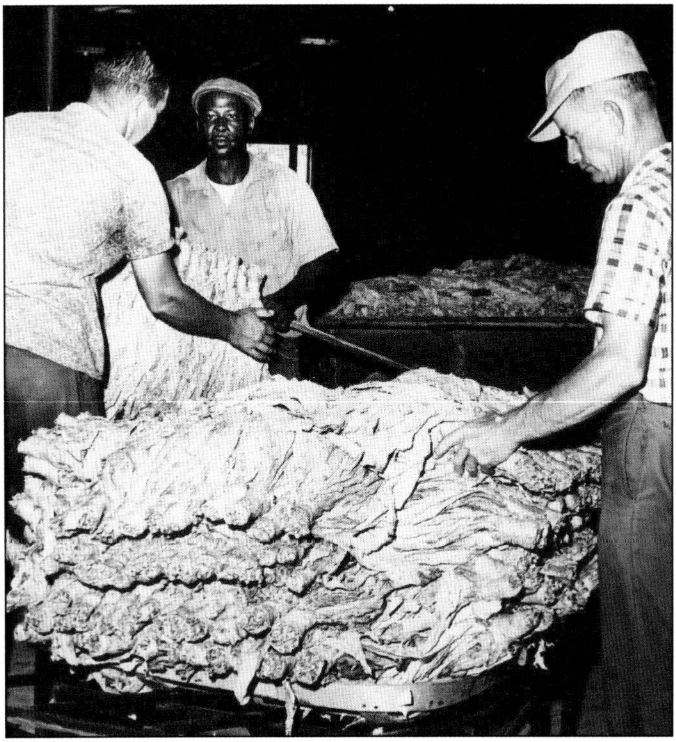

Once the tobacco was cured it was removed from the barn and tied into hands which were then graded on a grading table and bundled to take to market. (BBH)

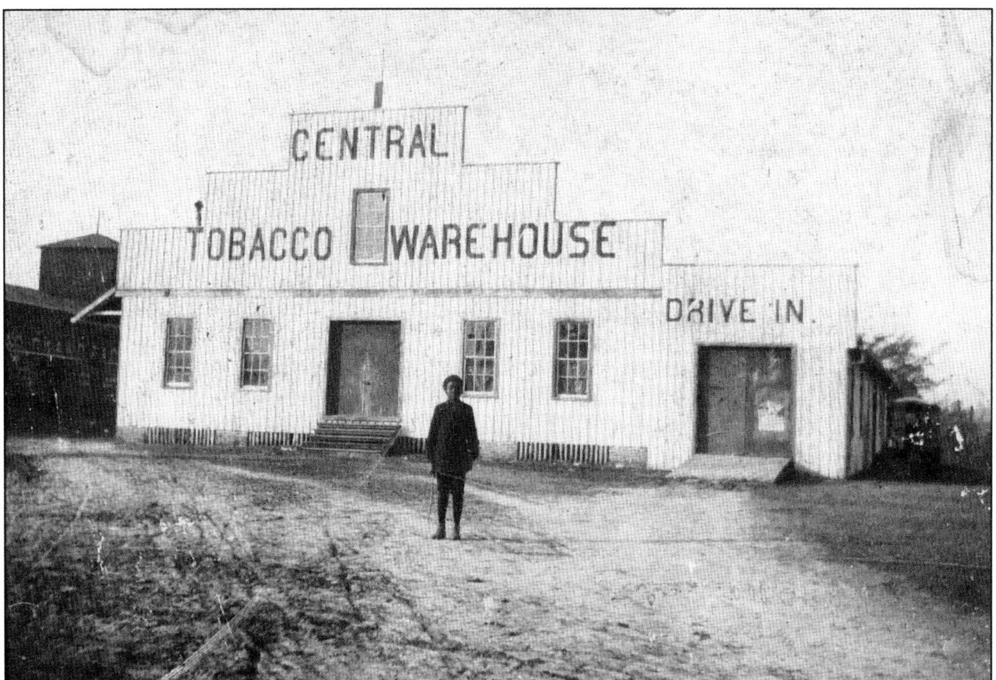

Although tobacco was a cash crop in the eighteenth century, it was replaced by cotton in the early nineteenth century and did not come back into Edgecombe County until the 1890s. Tarboro had its first auction in 1891 in the warehouse of the Central Tobacco Company. (ECML)

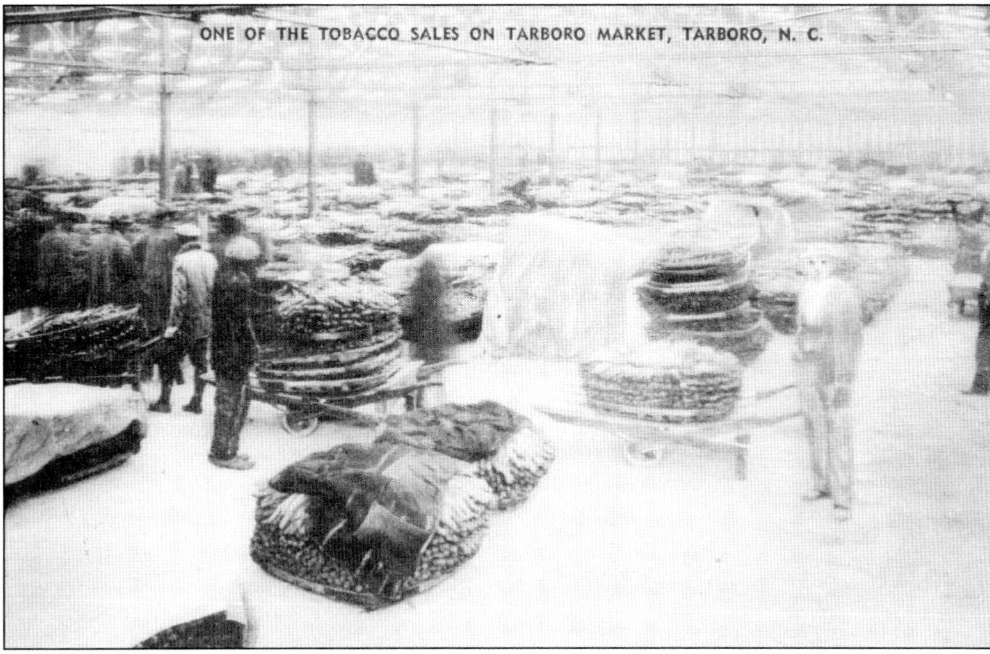

By 1910 Tarboro had four tobacco warehouses where farmers could bring their crop to be auctioned off. (PC Murphy)

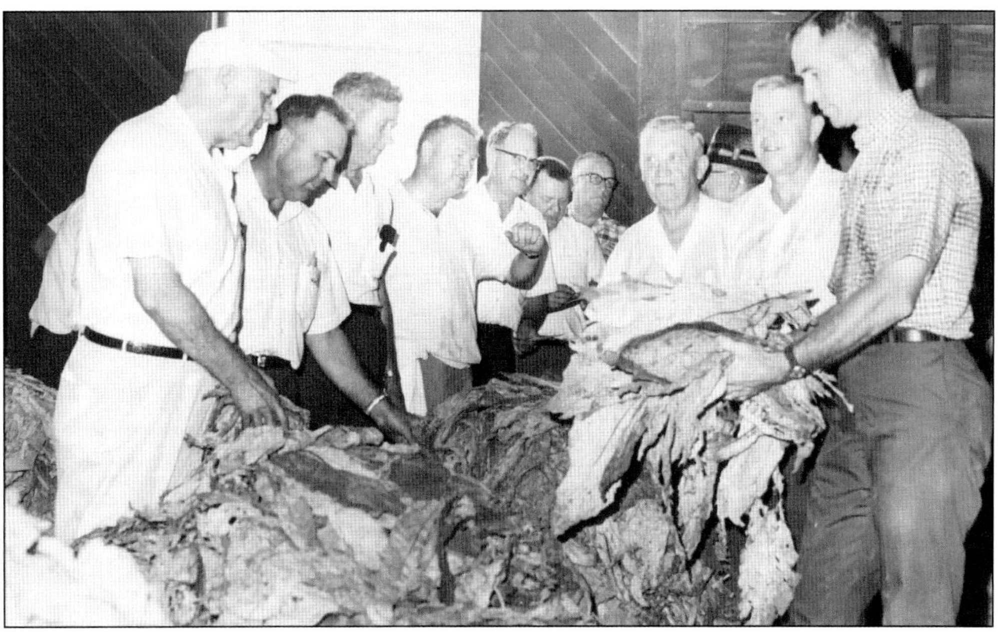

Don Price, Champ Batchelor (the auctioneer), W.G. Clark, and Don Gilliam Jr. are shown here at the opening of the tobacco market. (BBH)

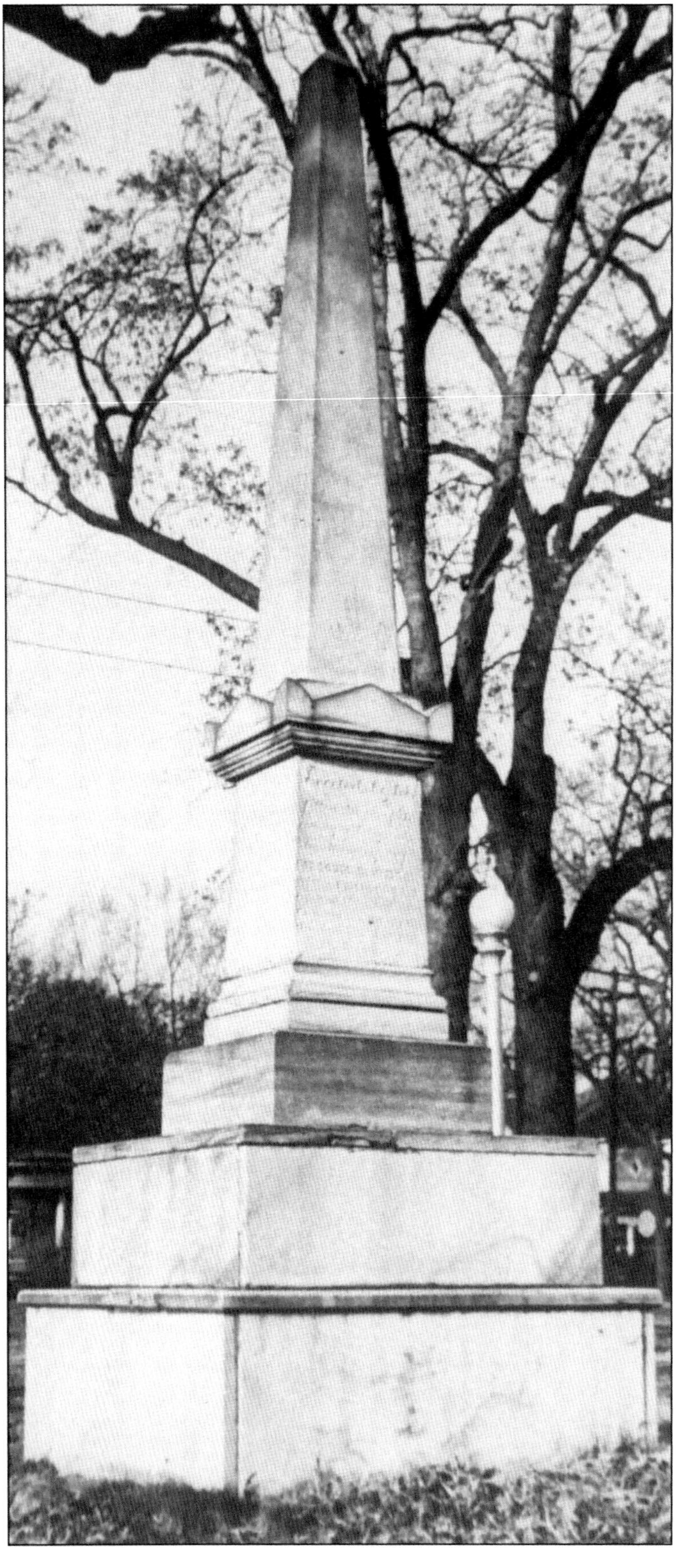

Louis Dicken Wilson was born in Edgecombe County in 1789. He served in the North Carolina General Assembly and the state senate during various terms between 1814 and 1846. He was also the Tarboro Tax Collector and a delegate to the 1835 North Carolina Constitutional Convention. One of the residents of "The Grove," Wilson was an advocate of public schools and libraries. In 1846, he resigned his seat in the state government and volunteered to serve in the Mexican War. Once commander of the 12th North Carolina Regiment, he rose to the rank of colonel. He died of yellow fever, received a Masonic service in Calvary Church, and was buried in the Old Town Cemetery. To honor Wilson, the residents of Edgecombe County placed this monument on Courthouse Square in 1850. They also changed the name of St. Joshua Street to Wilson Street. A new county, formed by the State of North Carolina from parts of Nash, Edgecombe, and Johnston Counties, was named Wilson County. In 1904 Wilson's monument was moved to the Town Common to allow for courthouse expansion. At that time, because his grave in the family cemetery was not being cared for, Wilson was once again buried, this time under his monument on the Town Common. (BBH)

Four

Soldiers and Statesmen

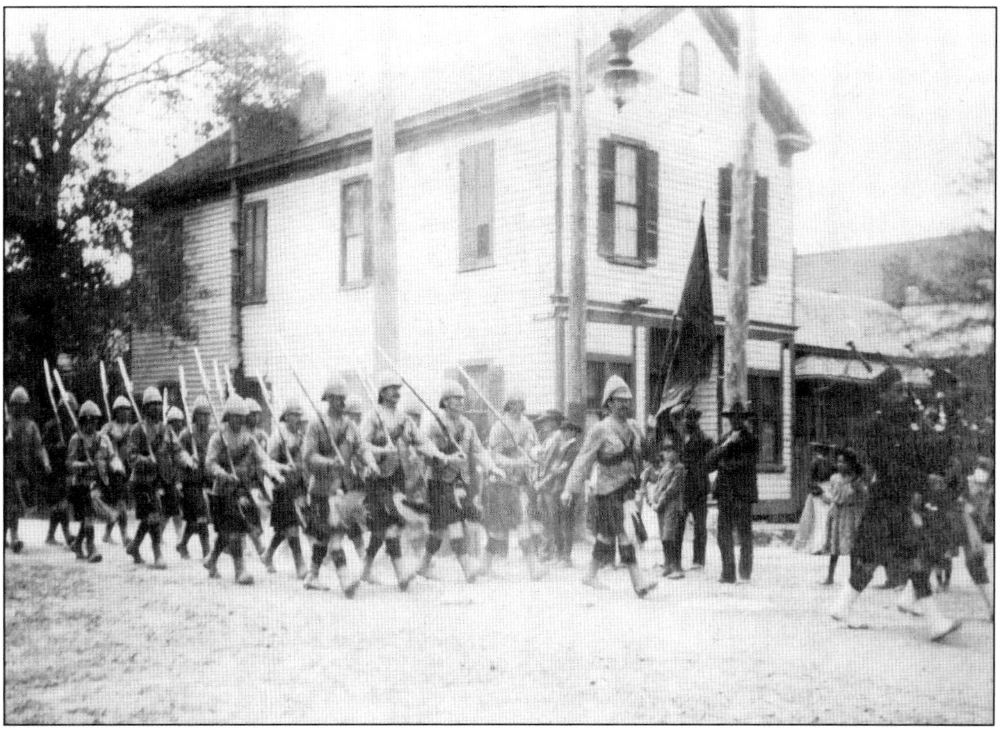

The Edgecombe Guards marched down Main Street in 1899 as part of a celebration for the Spanish-American War. The guards have been in existence since 1754 as part of the local militia. They served in all major national wars from the American Revolution through the Spanish-American War. (PC Simmons)

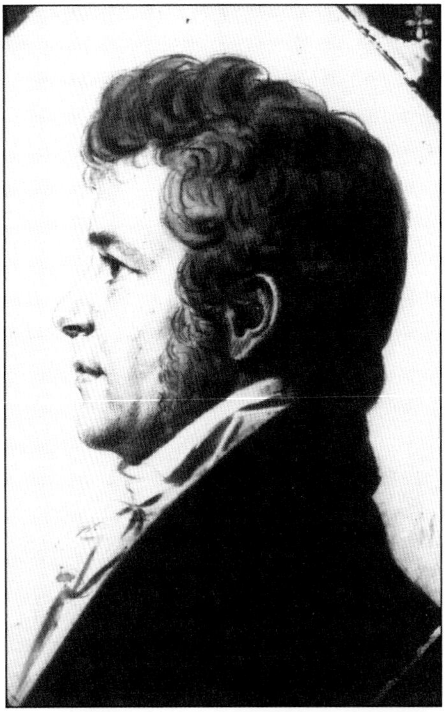

Thomas Blount was a landowner, merchant, congressmen, and Revolutionary War officer. His brother, John Gray, ran the shipping branch of the family business and helped establish the town of Washington, N.C. The Blount brothers were among the largest landowners in the new United States. They owned land from the Atlantic to the Mississippi and operated a shipping business as well as wharves, warehouses, sawmills, gristmills, tanneries, and cotton gins. They owned numerous slaves. Thomas managed the Tarboro branch of the business, running the shipping and mercantile operations. He served in the Revolutionary War, and was captured and taken to England as a prisoner of war. After the war he served as a trustee of the University of North Carolina, a commissioner of Raleigh, and a member of Congress from eastern North Carolina. Blount died in 1812 in Washington, D.C., and is buried in the Congressional Cemetery there. (NCDAH)

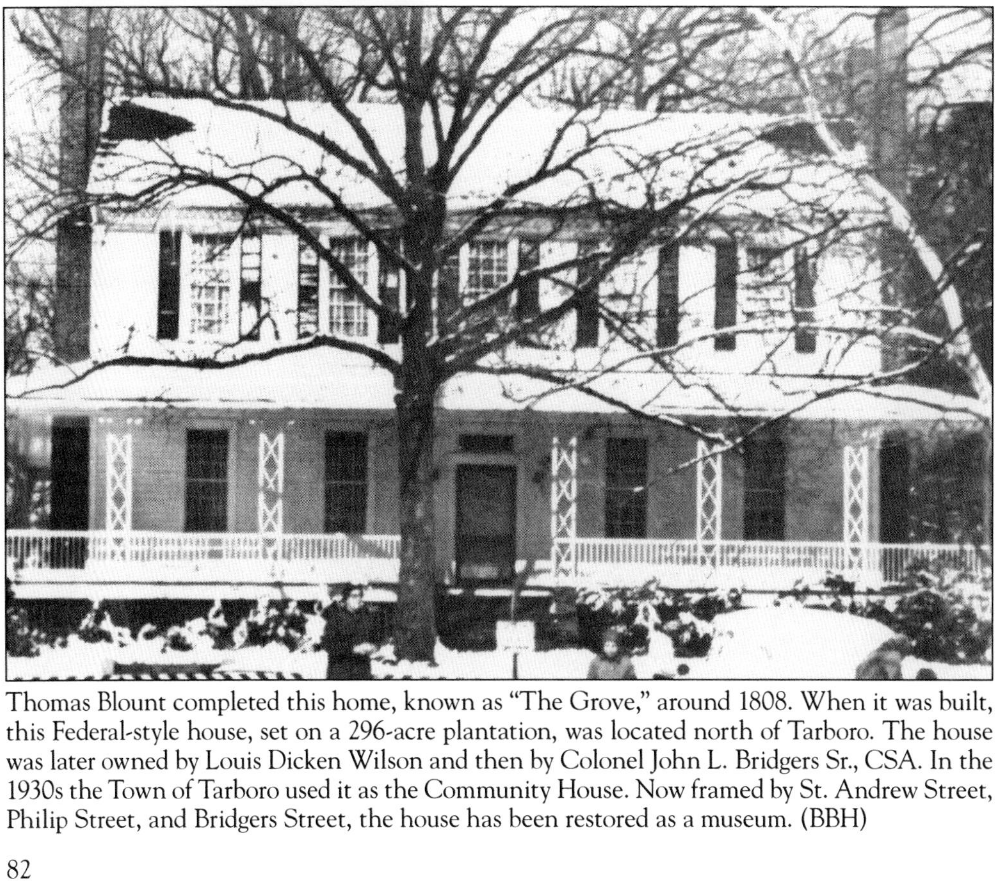

Thomas Blount completed this home, known as "The Grove," around 1808. When it was built, this Federal-style house, set on a 296-acre plantation, was located north of Tarboro. The house was later owned by Louis Dicken Wilson and then by Colonel John L. Bridgers Sr., CSA. In the 1930s the Town of Tarboro used it as the Community House. Now framed by St. Andrew Street, Philip Street, and Bridgers Street, the house has been restored as a museum. (BBH)

Mary "Jackie" Sumner was the second wife of Thomas Blount. They married in 1796 and built "The Grove." She lived ten years after the death of her husband and left her considerable fortune to various friends throughout the state. She also left enough money to establish Christ Episcopal Church in Raleigh and endowed a fund in Tarboro for the poor and for the relief of widows and orphans. She is buried in Calvary Churchyard. Legend has it that her original tombstone was destroyed by lightening and replaced by a gift from Christ Church. (BBH/MOR)

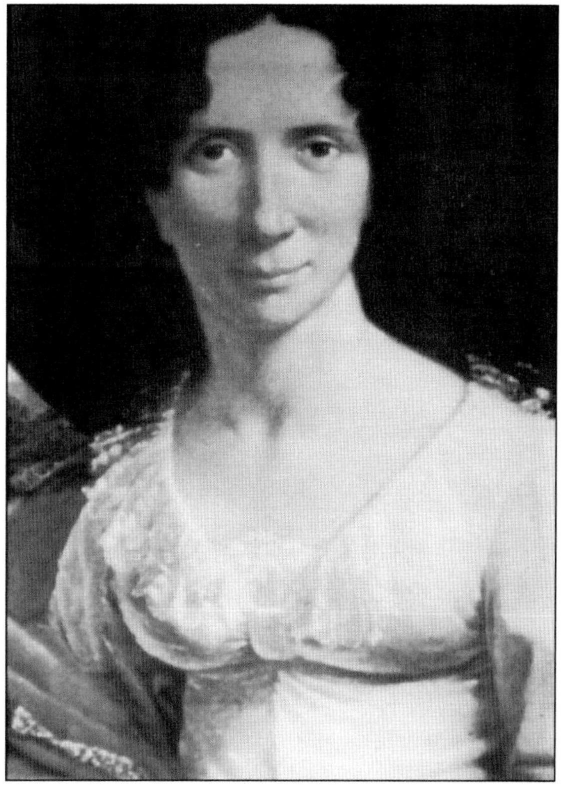

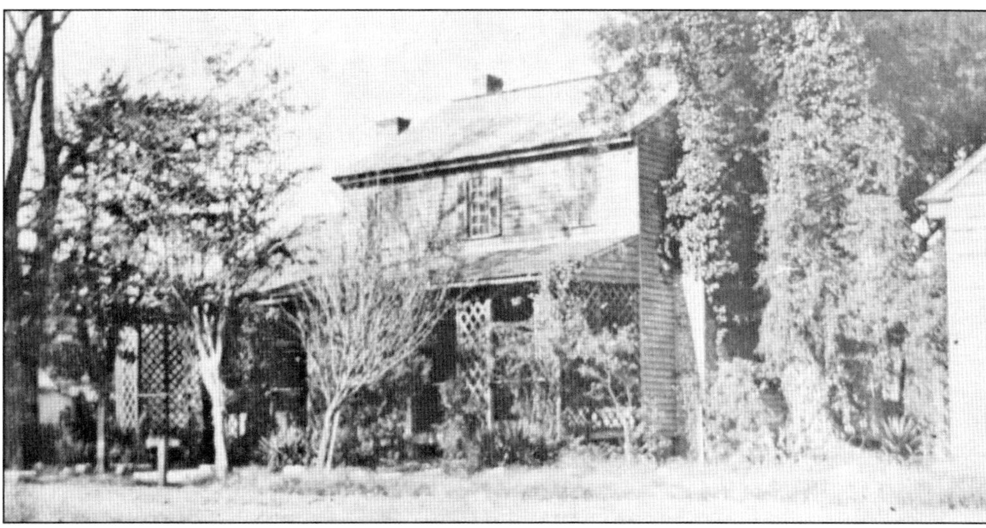

Theophilus Parker purchased a lot in 1808 and finished this vernacular, two-story house in 1810. Parker was the owner of the privateer *Snapdragon*, which saw duty in the War of 1812. It is believed that Thomas Blount helped Parker design the exposed hall stairway—one of the first of its type in town—in his home. In 1859 Dr. Joseph Blount Cheshire, the rector of Calvary Church, and his wife, Elizabeth Toole Parker (the daughter of Theophilus Parker), moved into the house with their daughter Kate, a gifted artist whose carvings adorn the interior of this and other buildings. Their son, Joseph B. Cheshire, became the fifth Episcopal bishop of North Carolina. (BBH)

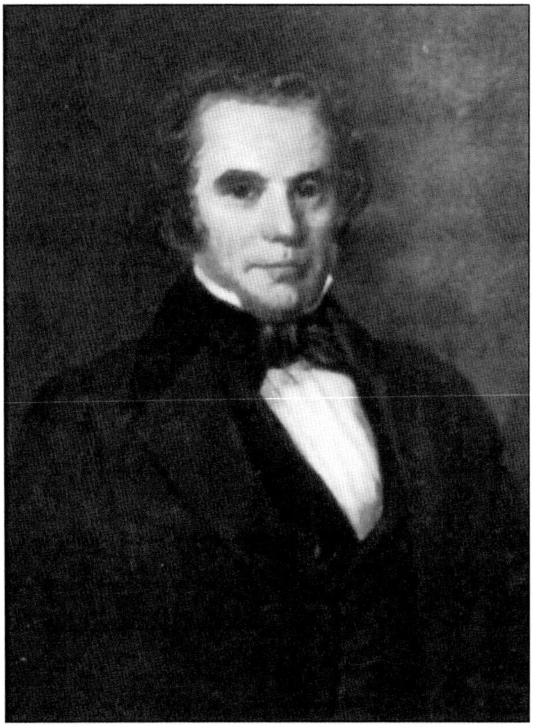

Henry Toole Clark became governor of North Carolina in 1861 after the death of John Ellis. As speaker of the senate, Clark inherited the position, but he did not run in the election of 1862, so his term was brief. He was born in 1808 on the family farm of his father, James West Clark, near Tarboro. His mother was Arabella Toole, the daughter of Henry Irwin Toole, who had served in the American Revolution. Clark graduated from the University of North Carolina in 1826 and practiced law while managing farms in North Carolina and Tennessee. He was elected to the North Carolina Senate in 1850 and continued to serve as a senator for the next decade. In 1850 he married Mary Weeks, the daughter of Theophilus Parker. When he retired from the governorship, he returned home and spent the rest of his life studying history and serving the county. He died in 1874. (PC Clark)

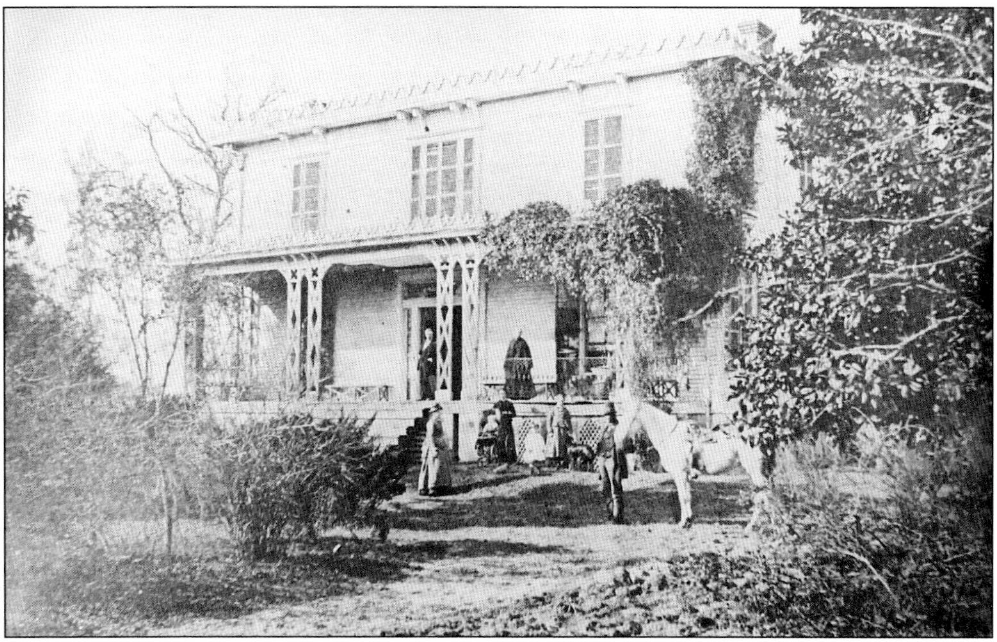

This photograph shows Governor Clark and his family relaxing at "Hilma" when the house was still in its original state. According to local legend, the Yankees raided this house on the way into Tarboro during the July 1863 raid and would have kidnapped the former governor had he been there. When the Tar River Bridge was ignited during the raid, Governor Clark was one of the first to raise a bucket brigade to put out the fire and save the bridge. He and his wife are buried in Calvary Churchyard. (BBH)

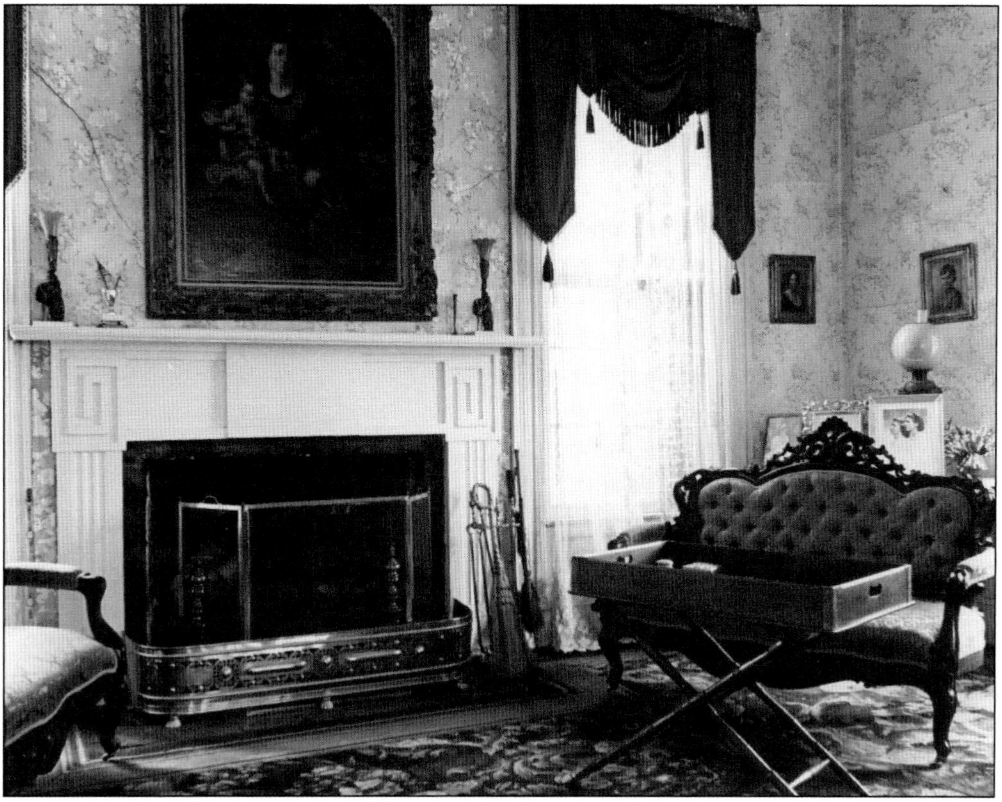

Jonas Carr, the father of Governor Elias Carr, built Bracebridge Hall in 1826. The older section of the house is a one-and-one-half-story frame structure. This room, the south parlor, maintains decor provided by Governor Carr and his wife at the turn of the century. (BBH)

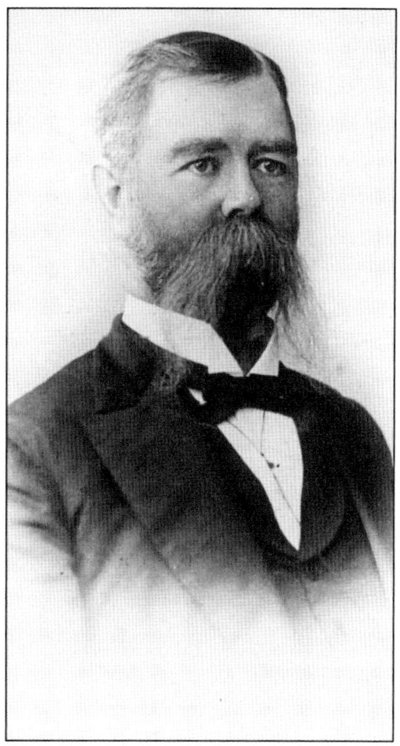

The son of Jonas Johnston Carr and Elizabeth Jane Hilliard, Elias Carr was one of three children born in the family home, Bracebridge Hall, near Old Sparta. Carr went to the University of North Carolina at Chapel Hill, then to the University of Virginia. In 1859 he married Eleanor Kearney and returned to his home and began to expand the plantation. He served briefly in the CSA, and after the War became an agricultural leader in both the county and the state, developing diversified farming techniques. He was the first president of North Carolina's Farmer's Association. In 1892 he was nominated as governor and elected. During his term as governor, he supported rural schools and compulsory education, and made efforts to improve road conditions. He is buried in the family cemetery on Colonial Road near his home, Bracebridge Hall. (NCDAH)

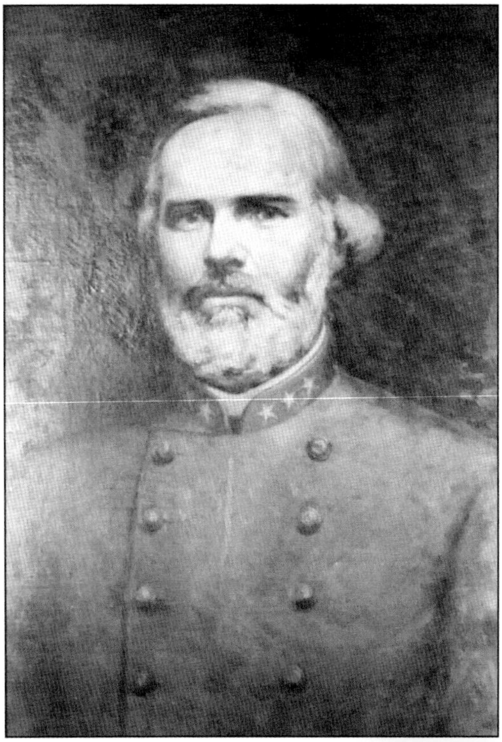

Edgecombe County wasted no time in organizing troops after North Carolina seceded from the Union, and soon had six companies, including the Edgecombe Guards, the Rocky Mount Light Infantry, the Edgecombe Rifles, the Confederate Guards, the Spartan Band, and the State Troops. The Edgecombe Guards, with more than 130 men including Second Lieutenant William G. Lewis, were led by Captain John L. Bridgers. Their first fight was at Bethel Church, Virginia, in June 1861. Bridgers was promoted to the rank of colonel and commanded Fort Macon. He lived in the former Blount house, "The Grove," from 1850 until 1881. (BBH)

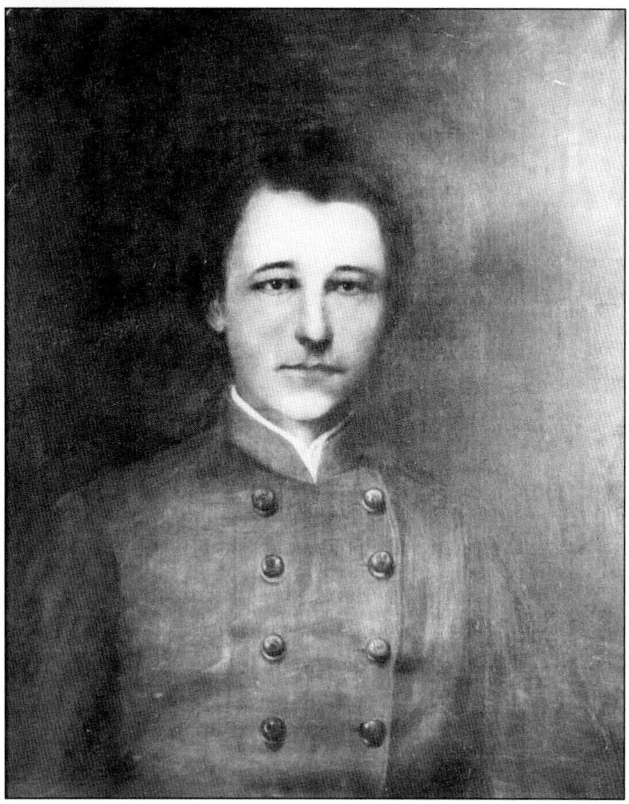

Born in Richmond, Virginia, in 1842, Henry Lawson Wyatt later moved to the Penny Hill community in Pitt County. Wyatt came to Tarboro in the late 1850s to apprentice as a carpenter to Francis Bond. He volunteered to serve in the Edgecombe Guards and was mustered into service in May 1861. When he was killed at the Battle of Bethel Church, Virginia, he became the first North Carolina soldier to die in the War Between the States. A statue of Wyatt stands on the capitol grounds in Raleigh. He is buried in the Hollywood Cemetery in Richmond, Virginia. (ECML/NCDAH)

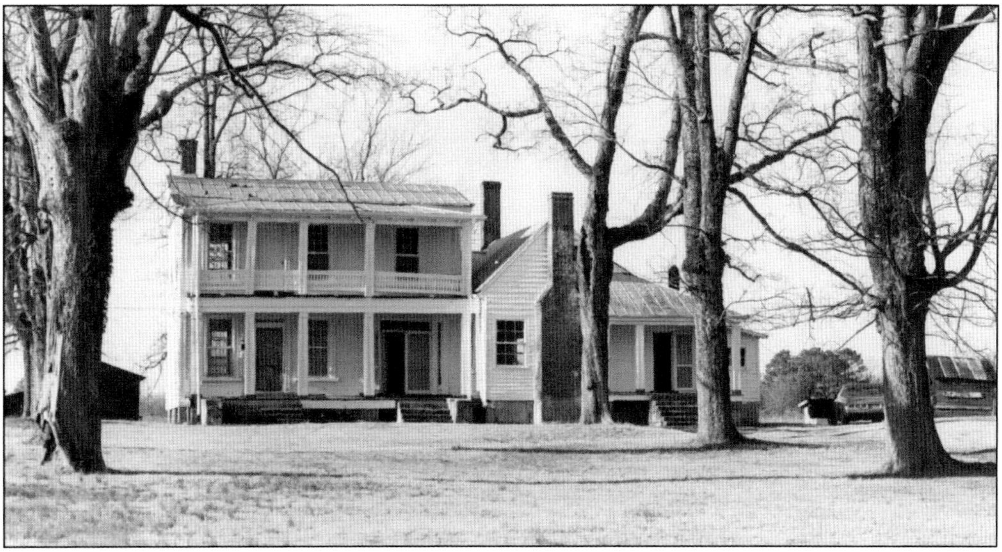

Located southeast of Tarboro, "Danielhurst" served as both a manse and a church. The oldest section was originally a one-story frame house. It was built in the early nineteenth century by John H. Daniel, a Primitive Baptist minister for at least three local churches. The two-story, Greek Revival-style block was constructed in the 1850s to serve as a church. A private school operating in the 1860s was located nearby. In the woods behind the house is the site of the Civil War skirmish known as the Battle of Daniel's Schoolhouse. After the Yankees raided Rocky Mount and Tarboro in July 1863, Confederate forces from nearby Fort Branch ambushed the Union troops, killing two of the Twelfth New York Cavalry and taking numerous prisoners. The house passed to Daniel's daughter, Ann Rouse, and her daughter Effie, who married David Gillespie. The Gillespies taught at Tarboro Female Academy. (ECML)

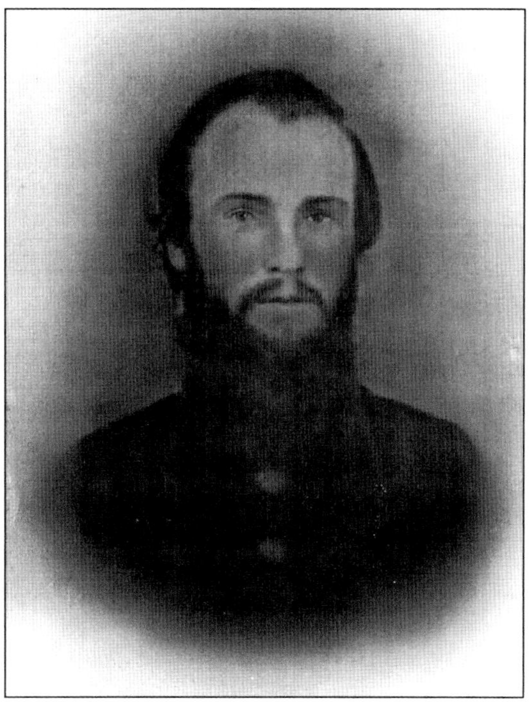

Lorenzo Dow Eagles of the Crisp community joined the Spartan Band, one of the six companies raised in Edgecombe County during the early months of the War. Eagles was killed at Spotsylvania Courthouse. Many other Edgecombe County men died in Virginia between 1861 and 1865. Fred Walker, W.F. Womble, J.H. Jackson, and H. Meares were all killed near Richmond. William Everett, John Bryan, William Dew, and John W. Robertson died at Mechanicsville. Sergeant Sam T. Williford and Privates James Walston, Hardy Webb, and James O'Neal were all killed at Malvern Hill. Ivey Foreman, a naval officer, died in the Richmond Hospital. Because the Wayside Hospital was located in Tarboro, numerous soldiers were buried here. Many were later removed and returned to their home areas. (PC Gulley)

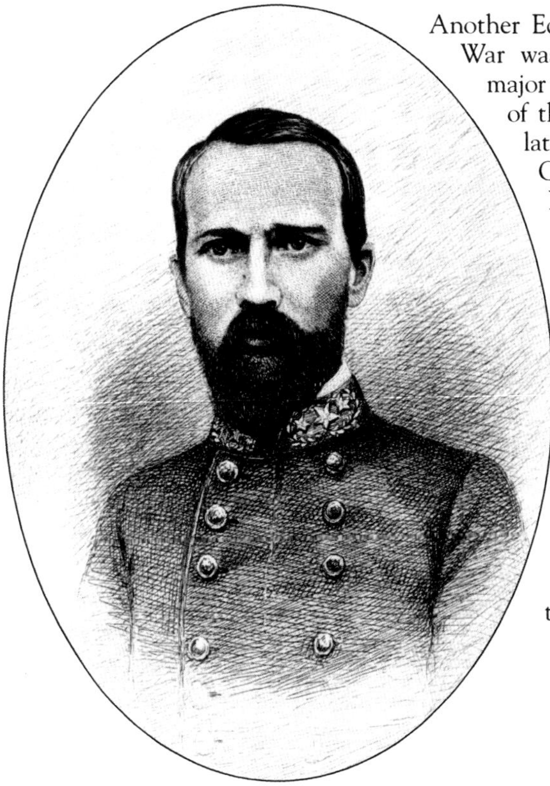

Another Edgecombe County resident to die in the War was William Dorsey Pender, the youngest major general in the Confederacy. A member of the Third North Carolina Volunteers and later of the Thirteenth Regiment of North Carolina Troops, part of Lee's Army of Northern Virginia, Pender fought at Seven Pines and was promoted to the rank of brigadier general. He served under D.H. Hill in Seven Days Battles, and was wounded at Second Manassas, and again at Fredericksburg. He carried on the attack at Chancellorsville after the death of Stonewall Jackson and was wounded three times. He was promoted to the rank of major general in May 1863, then went to Gettysburg, PA, where he was again wounded. He died on July 18, 1863. His grave in Calvary Churchyard is surrounded by cannon balls put there by the Edgecombe Guards. (ECML/NCDAH)

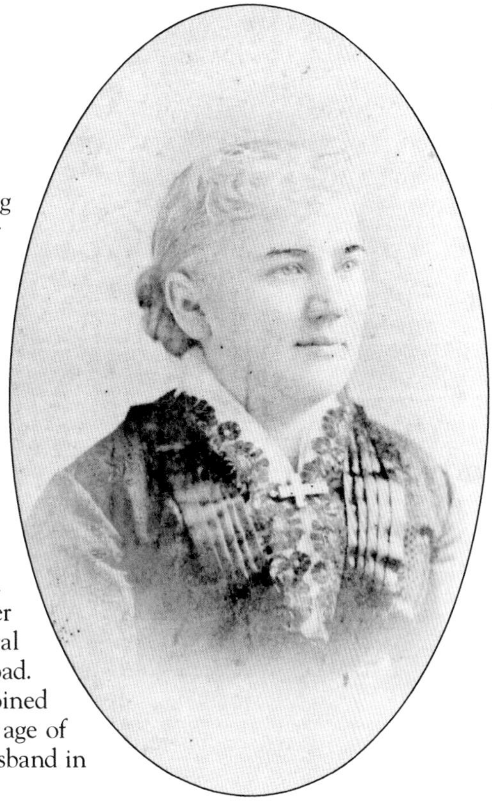

Mary Shepperd was born in 1840 in Good Spring near Salisbury, North Carolina. When her brother, Samuel Turner Shepperd, a West Point cadet, brought home a classmate, William Dorsey Pender, for a visit, Mary and Pender fell in love. The couple married four years later, in March 1859, when Mary was nineteen. When "Fanny," as Pender called her, received the news of her husband's death, she "closeted herself in her room for three days during which her hair reputedly turned white." Her third son, Stephen, was born four months later. Fanny raised their three boys, never remarrying. She taught at the Tarboro Female Academy, and in 1885 she became postmistress of Tarboro. Her oldest son, Samuel Turner, became the general agent for the Carolina and Northwestern Railroad. Dorsey Jr. became a lawyer, and Stephen joined the cotton business. Fanny died in 1922 at the age of eighty-two and is buried next to her beloved husband in Calvary Churchyard. (ECML)

Born in 1832 in Scotland Neck, Halifax County, William R. Cox studied law at Franklin College, TN. He practiced law in Nashville before relocating to Raleigh in the 1850s. He acquired a plantation in Edgecombe County before the War. Cox served in Lee's Army of Northern Virginia under Stonewall Jackson and was promoted to the rank of brigadier general. Wounded eleven times, he surrendered after leading the last charge at Appamatox. After the War he was appointed district court judge, and he served in that capacity for three terms. He also became active in public education and founded the *NC Journal of Education*. (ECML)

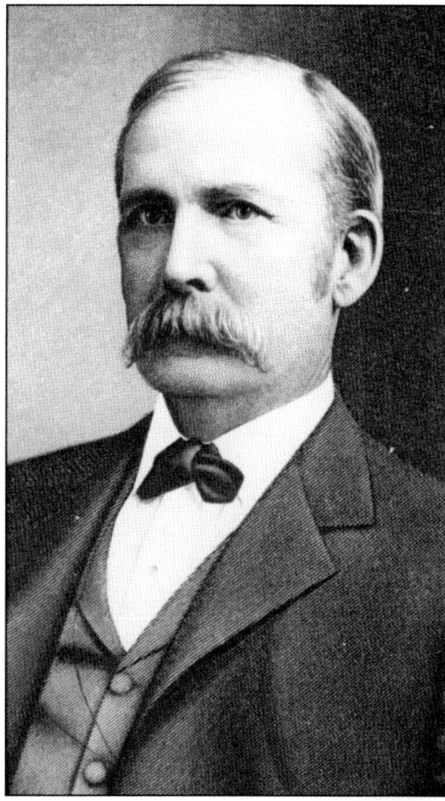

A North Carolina Historical Marker near the Kingsboro exit on old Highway 64 between Tarboro and Rocky Mount marks the site of the Cox farm home. Cox also had a home in Raleigh, where he lived for many years. He married three times. His first wife was Penelope Battle, the daughter of James Smith Battle. His second wife, Frances Lyman, had two children, a son and a daughter. His third wife was a widow, Mrs. Herbert A. Claiborne of Virginia. A grand master of the Masons, Cox is buried in Oakwood Cemetery in Raleigh. (BBH)

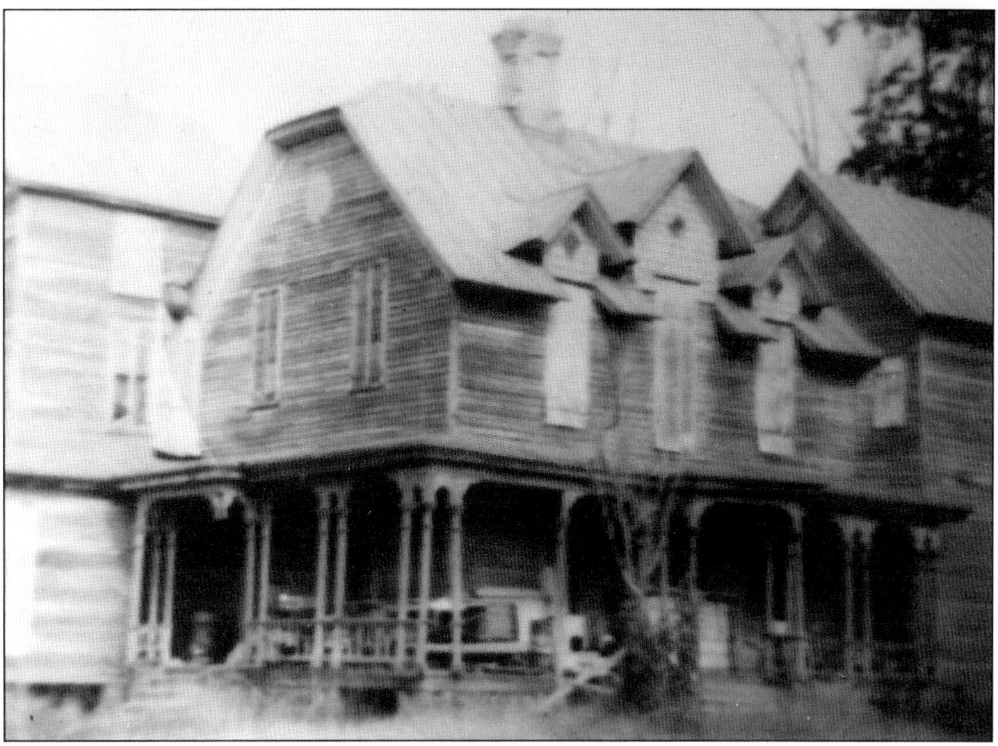

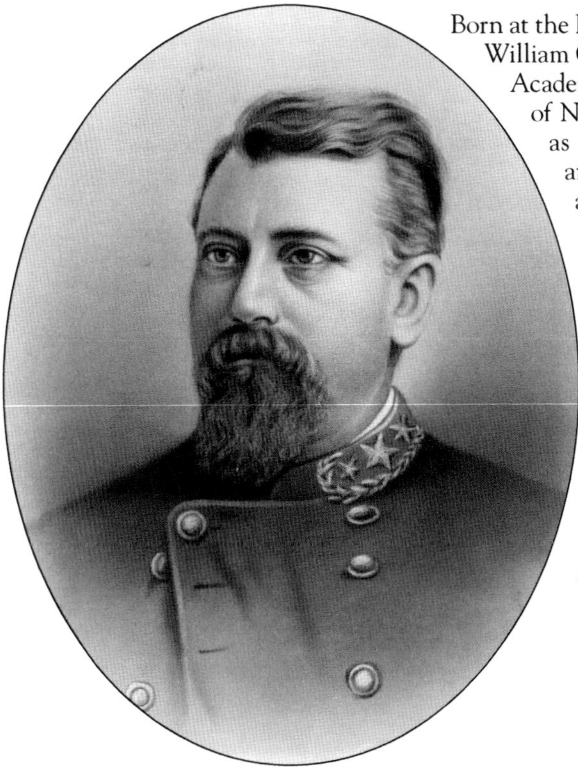

Born at the Falls of the Tar in Rocky Mount in 1835, William Gaston Lewis attended Raleigh Military Academy, then graduated from the University of North Carolina-Chapel Hill. He worked as a civil engineer, a job he returned to after service in the CSA. He first saw action at the Battle of Bethel Church, Virginia, as second lieutenant of the Edgecombe Guards. Afterwards he was assigned to Lee's Army of Northern Virginia. He returned to North Carolina in 1863 and participated in the Battle of Plymouth in April 1864. After the War he became the general superintendent of the railroad and worked as survey engineer for George Vanderbilt's estate, "Biltmore." Lewis married Martha Lucinda Pender. He is buried in Willowdale Cemetery in Goldsboro. (NCDAH)

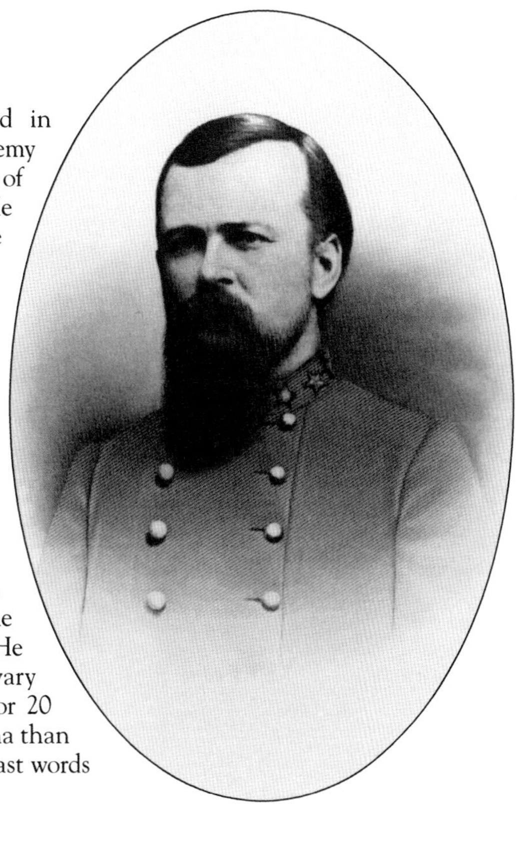

William L. Saunders was born and raised in Raleigh. He attended the Raleigh Academy before graduating from the University of North Carolina-Chapel Hill in 1854. He was wounded four times during his service in the CSA. In February 1864 Saunders married Florida Cotten, a relative of John Whitaker Cotten. She died within a year but Saunders remained friends with his in-laws. In 1870 Saunders testified before a special Congressional hearing on the activities of the Ku Klux Klan, at which his only response was "I Decline to Answer." Saunders served as secretary of state of North Carolina from 1879 to 1889 and during that time he collected, organized, and edited the multi-volume *North Carolina Colonial Records*. He also served on the board of trustees for the University of North Carolina-Chapel Hill. He is buried in the Cotten family plot in Calvary Churchyard. His tombstone declares that "for 20 years he exerted more power in North Carolina than any other man" and ends with his infamous last words to Congress, "I decline to answer." (ECML)

Henry L. Staton was the son of Dr. L.L. Staton, who had attended the Virginia Military Institute in 1870. This photograph of Henry was taken at VMI in 1892, a year before he graduated. He later obtained a law degree from the University of North Carolina-Chapel Hill and practiced law in New York. (BBH)

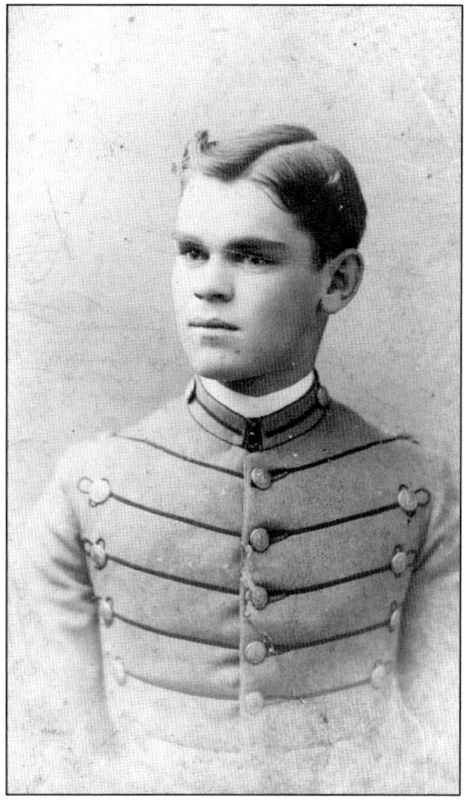

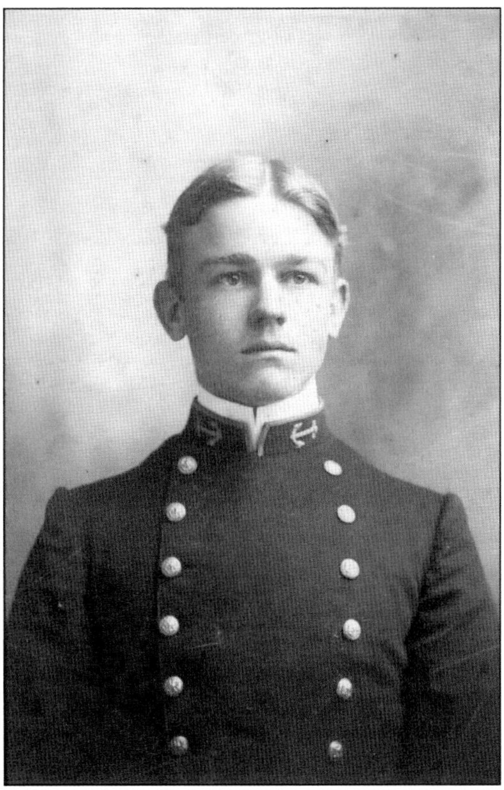

Aldolphus Staton, the son of Dr. L.L. Staton, attended the Virginia Military Institute for one year before graduating from the United States Naval Academy. He later earned a law degree from George Washington University. As chief of the Bureau of Navigation in Washington, D.C., he commanded numerous ships during the two world wars, and achieved the rank of rear admiral. He is buried in Arlington National Cemetery. (BBH)

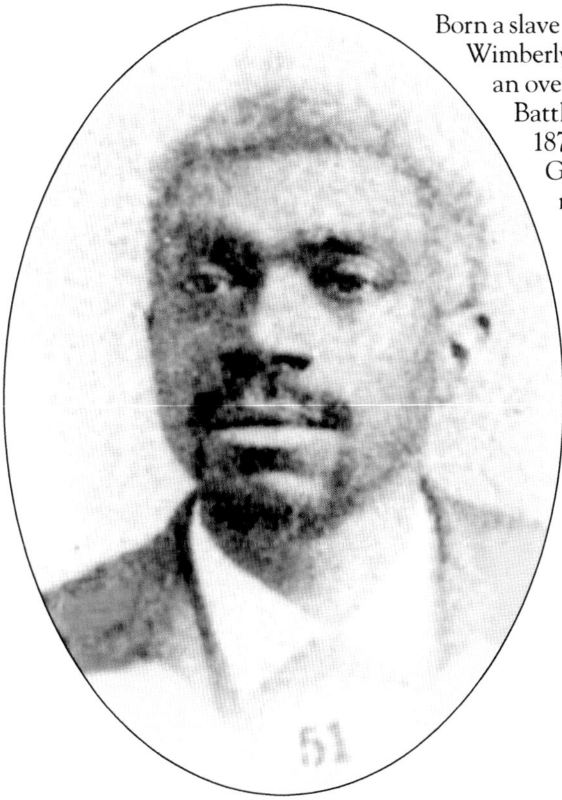

Born a slave to the James S. Battle family in 1848, Dred Wimberly agreed to stay after the War and become an overseer for his former owner, Kemp Plummer Battle. He later moved to Rocky Mount and in 1879 he was elected to the North Carolina General Assembly. In 1889 he became a member of the state senate. After serving in North Carolina, Wimberly went to Washington, D.C., as custodian in the House of Representatives. Wimberly married twice and fathered a total of eighteen children. His descendants still live in the family home on Raleigh Street in Rocky Mount, across from Pineview Cemetery, where the North Carolina Historical Marker now stands. Wimberly died in 1937 and is buried in Unity Cemetery in Rocky Mount. (NCDAH)

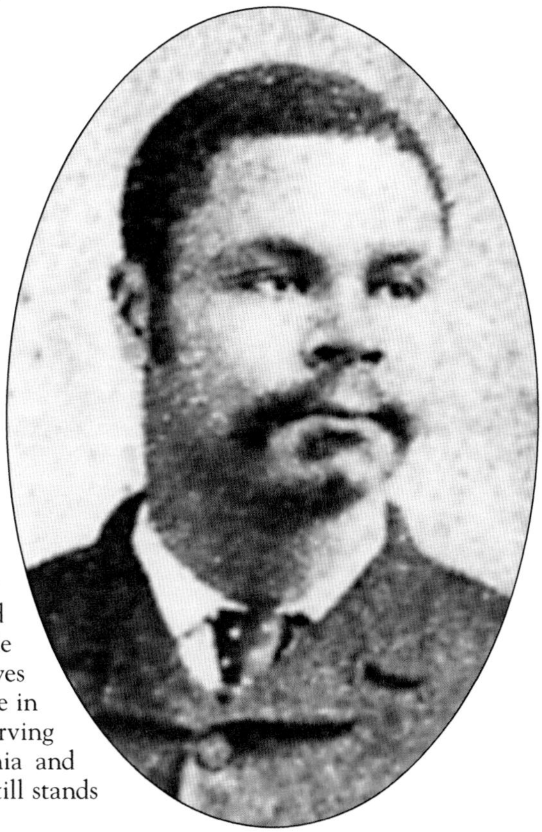

George Henry White was born in 1852 in Bladen County. After graduating from Howard University, he practiced law in New Bern. His first wife was Fannie B. Randolph, with whom he had one child. After Fannie's death, White married Cora Lina Cherry, the daughter of Henry Cherry of Tarboro. They had two children, Mary and George Jr. White served as solicitor and prosecutor of the second judicial district. He was elected to the House of Representatives in 1896 and was the last black man to serve in Congress until after World War II. After serving in Congress, White moved to Philadelphia and spent the rest of his life there. His house still stands on Granville Street. (NCDAH/UNC)

Born in Edgecombe County, Elijah Longstreet Daughtridge attended a private academy in Mebane and then worked on the family farm near Rocky Mount. In addition to farming, he was the owner and operator of the Daughtridge Supply Company and the president of the Planters Cotton Oil and Fertilizer Company. His work in politics began after he was elected an alderman in Rocky Mount in 1898. He served in the North Carolina General Assembly from 1901 to 1904 and on the state board of agriculture. In 1906 he became president of the North Carolina Fair Association. In 1912 he defeated an Edgecombe County rival, James Gaskill, for the lieutenant governor's seat and served in that role until 1917. He was vice president of the North Carolina Good Roads Association and later a director of the Southern Commercial Congress. Married to Mary W. Odom, Daughtridge had five children. He is buried in Pineview Cemetery in Rocky Mount. (NCDAH)

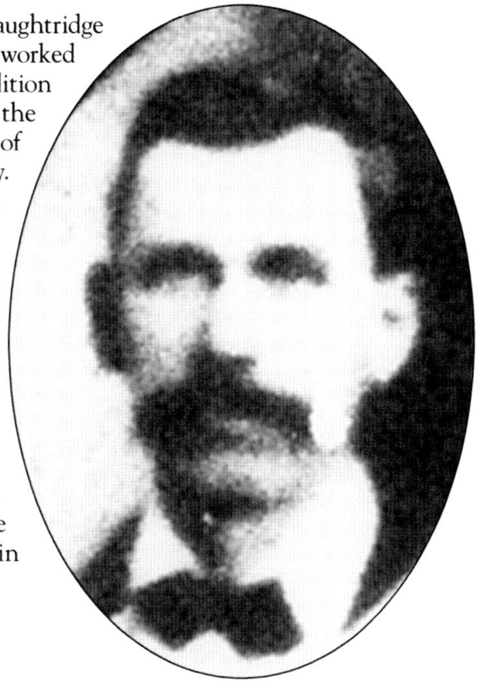

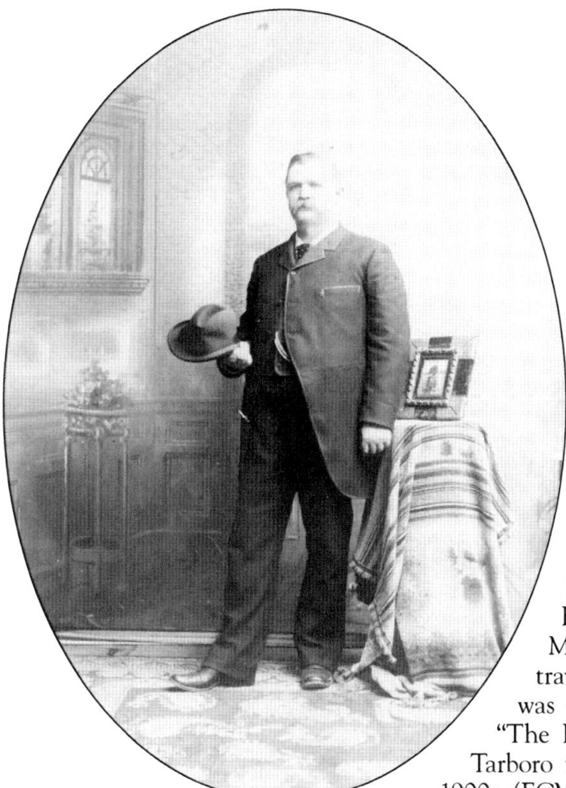

Local sources say that William E. Fountain came to Tarboro from Baltimore, Maryland, and founded Fountain Mills. He traveled by a private Pullman car, which was often seen on Albemarle Avenue near "The Barracks." Fountain served as mayor of Tarboro for eight terms in the 1890s and early 1900s. (ECML)

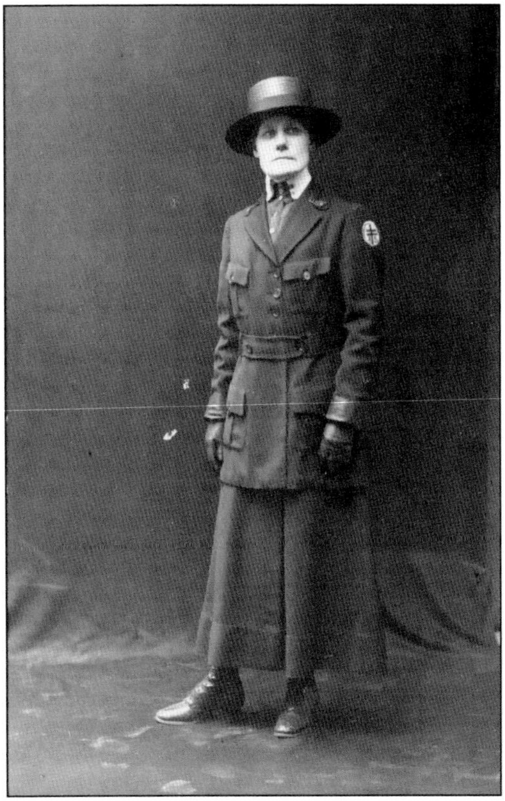

Originally from Virginia, Mattie Shackleford earned her medical training as a nurse at Norfolk Memorial Hospital. In World War I she trained Red Cross nurses. After the war she became the nursing supervisor at Pittman Sanatorium and taught home health nursing. A very community-spirited person, she became the first female commander of the local American Legion Post, and during the 1930s she supported the development of a new county home for the poor. She also cleaned up the Old Town Cemetery behind Howard Memorial Church and constructed a Memory Chapel for veterans of Edgecombe County. Long a leader of parades and special services on holidays and Veterans Day celebrations, Miss Mattie is remembered as the spokesperson for patriotism. She never married, but she considered Tarboro and her veterans her family. Her marker is in the Old Town Cemetery next to the Memory Chapel. (ECML)

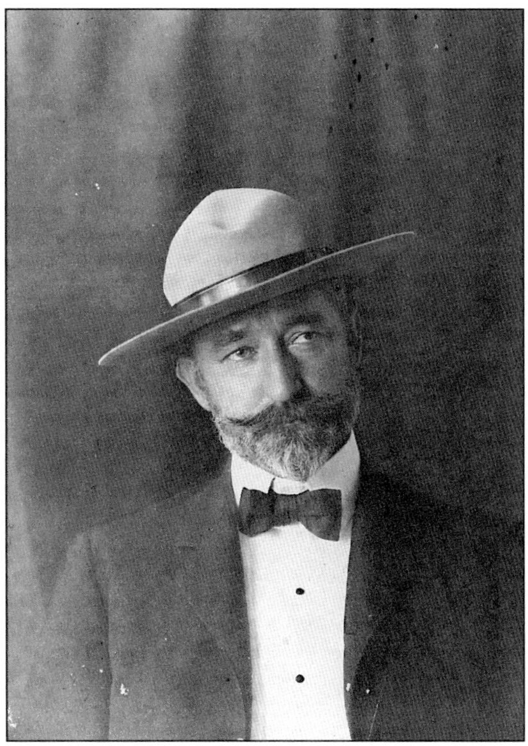

Samuel Westray Battle, the son of William S. and Elizabeth Dancy Battle, was a surgeon in the United States Navy and was in charge of the U.S. Naval Hospital in Pensacola, Florida. He was also surgeon general of the North Carolina National Guard. He retired from the military in 1884 and moved to Asheville, where he was director of the Clarence Barker Hospital. (BBH)

Brooks Peters, 2nd lieutenant, was at Eaton, Pennsylvania, just before going overseas in 1918 to serve in World War I. (BBH)

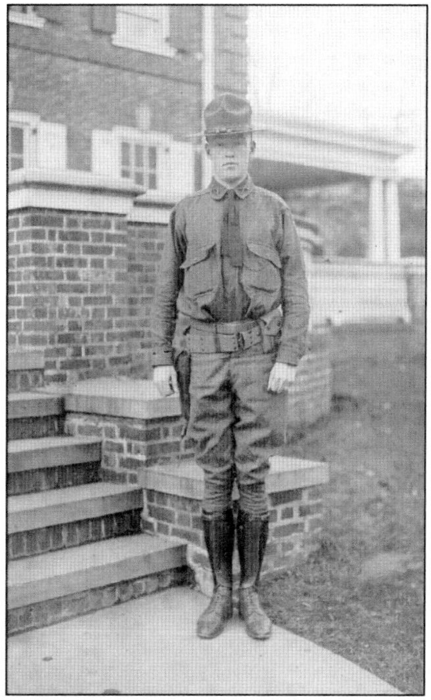

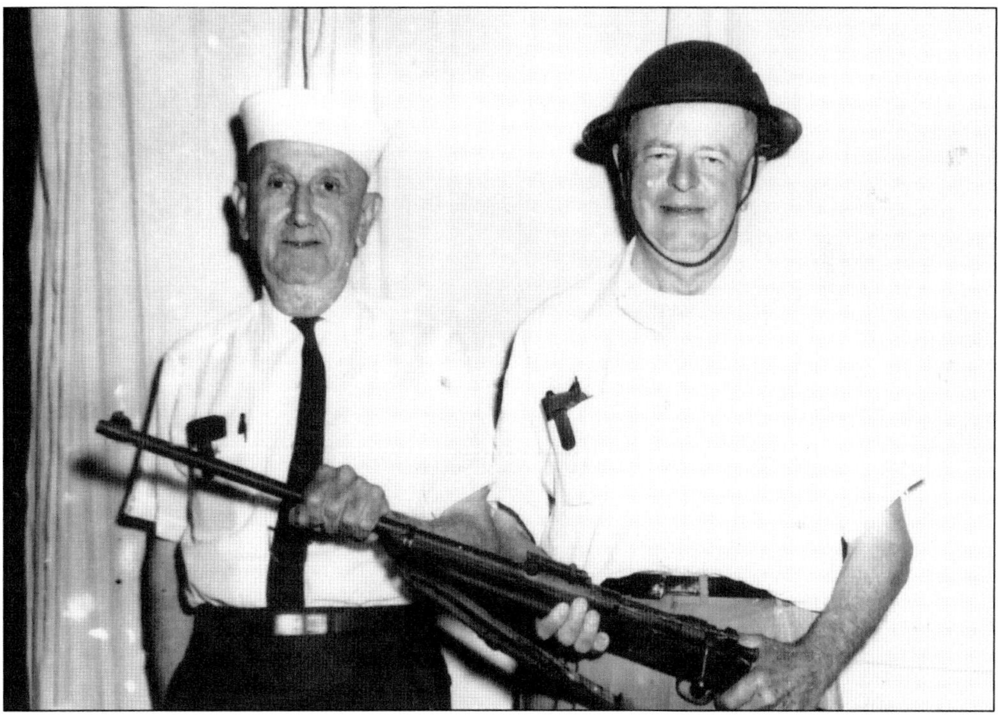

Maury Stancil and Nick Constantine were two of the World War I veterans from Edgecombe County. Among the two hundred North Carolinians who received the Distinguished Service Cross for great bravery in World War I were five men from Edgecombe County: Sam R. Brown of Macclesfield; Thomas Carlisle and Thomas R. Royster of Tarboro; and Garland Spain and Charles F. Stephenson of Rocky Mount. (BBH)

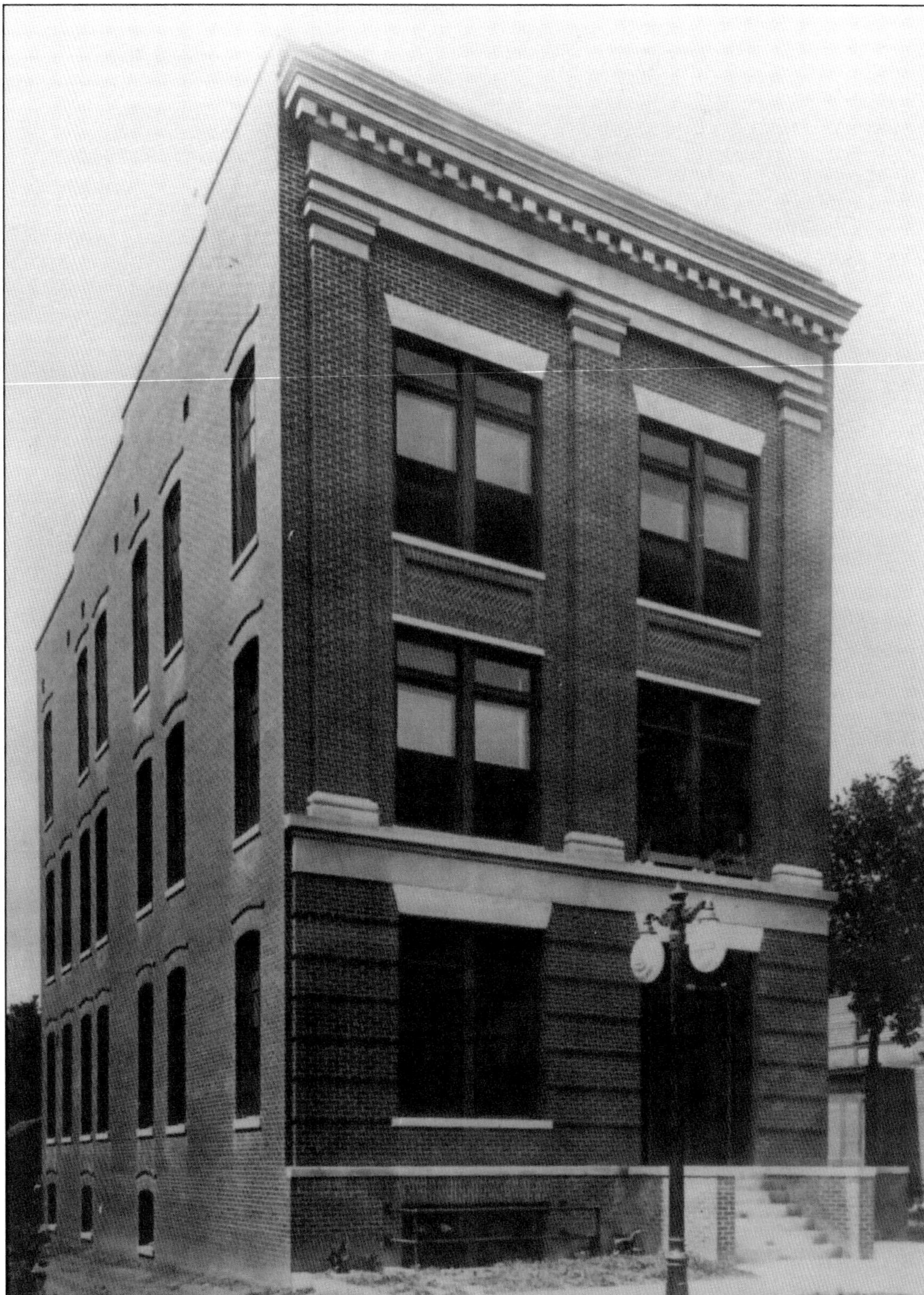

In 1895, three men formed a partnership to create the Carolina Telephone and Telegraph Company. Within two decades, the business had expanded so that the company needed an administrative building. In 1912 CTT opened this "skyscraper" on St. James Street in Tarboro. The company continued to grow and prosper for a century, and was recently acquired by Sprint. (CTT)

Five

EARNING A LIVING

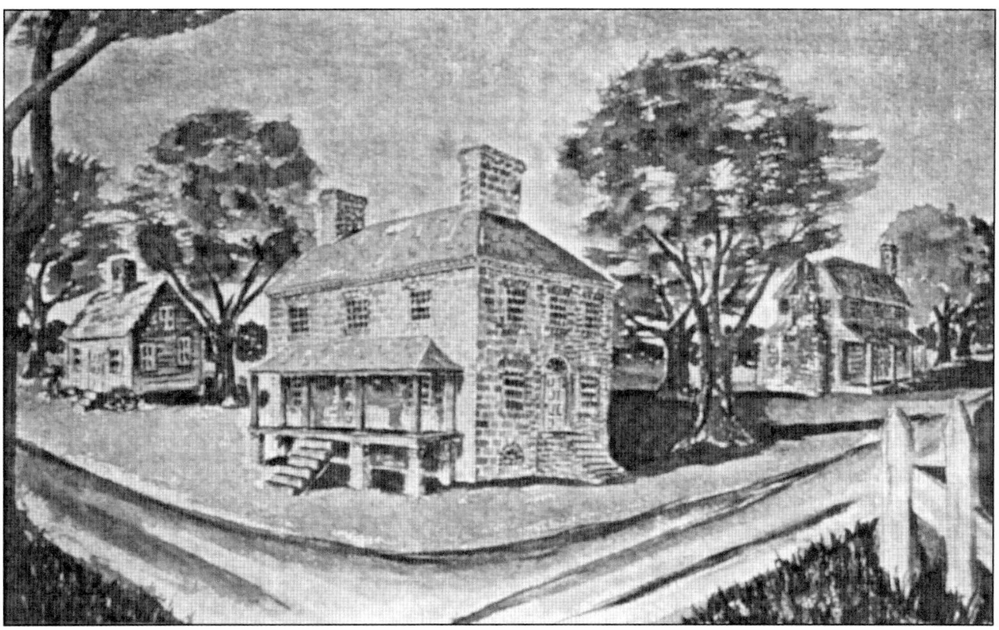

Banking has been a part of Tarboro and Edgecombe County since 1811, when a branch of the State Bank of North Carolina opened with Thomas Blount as president. Barrow's Vault may have been the first bank in the area, and was located in a brick building, as portrayed in the above painting. Other banks included the Edgecombe Bank and Trust, Co., the Bank of Tarboro (with cashier Peter Payne Lawrence), Edgecombe Homestead and Loan, Farmer's Banking and Trust, and Tarboro Savings and Loan Company. (BBH/Amanda Peterson)

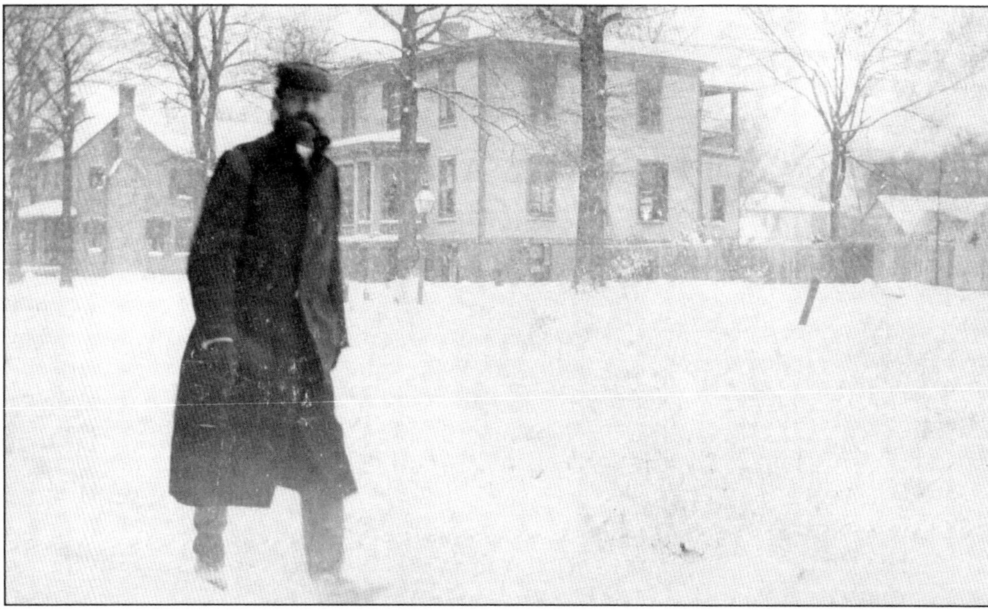

Buck Powell, seen here walking across the Town Common in the snow, was the first president of Carolina Telephone and Telegraph. (ECML)

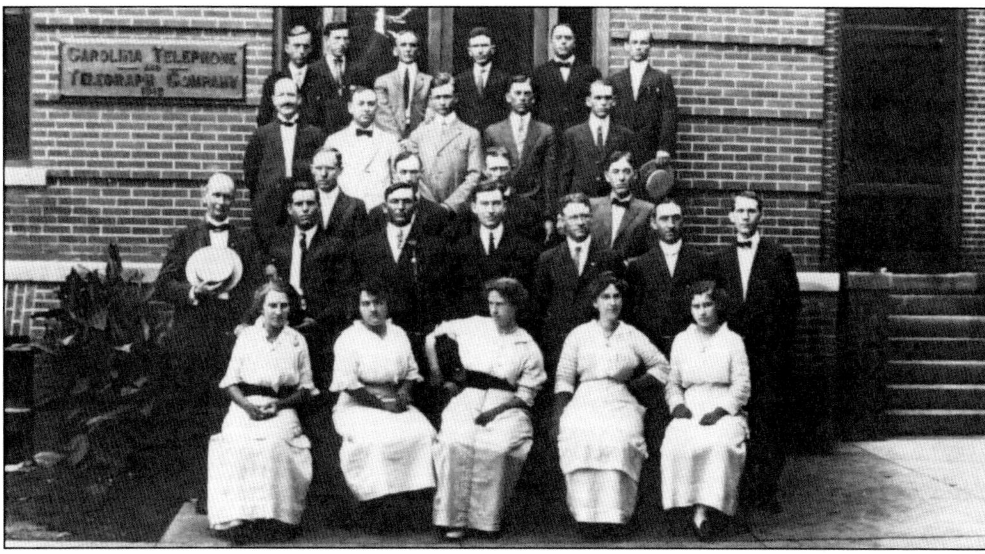

On June 25, 1915, all Carolina Telephone and Telegraph Company managers met at the administrative office on St. James Street. They are, from left to right, as follows: (front row) Mrs. Lloyd, Annie Bogey, Emily Austin, Lottie Cosby, and Miss Hyman; (second row) Almond Hart (auditor), Jim Scotton (general foreman), Ransome Strickland (supervisor), Mr. Henderson (from Southern Bell in Atlanta), Mr. McClure (general manager), Mattie Matthews (equipment installer), and J.B. Foster (traffic manager); (third row) J.W Dillahunt (Smithfield manager), Mr. Weaver (Scotland Neck manager), and E.J. Nobles (Dunn manager); (fourth row) Dave Ball (Washington manager), Mr. Whitmore (Wilson manager), H.H. Hardy (Tarboro), Bob Jones Lillington manager, and E. H. Dixon, Jr, (Benson manager); (back row) unamed (Red Springs manager), Joe Terrell (Tarboro office), J.R. Boyd (Fayetteville manager), and Tom Collins Sr. (Tarboro). (CTT)

John Porter demonstrates the latest switchboard equipment to area businessmen. (ECUSC Porter Papers)

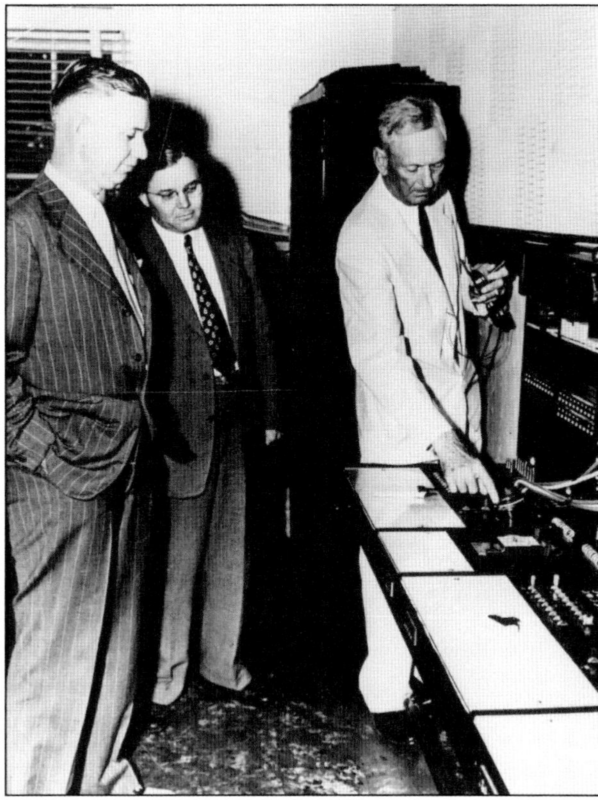

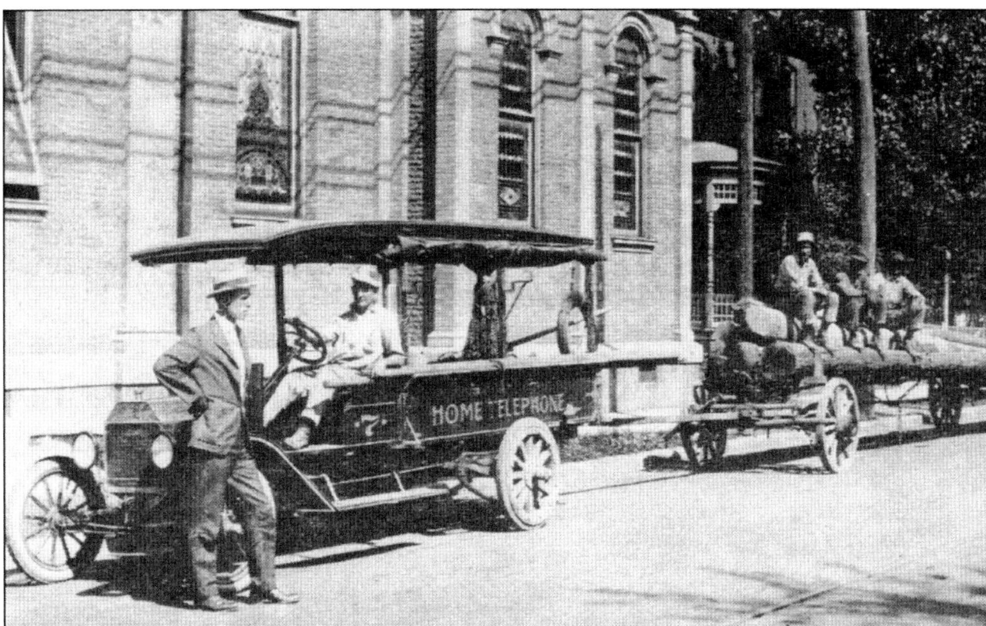

The telephone company was among the first businesses to use gasoline-powered trucks in place of horse power. (CTT)

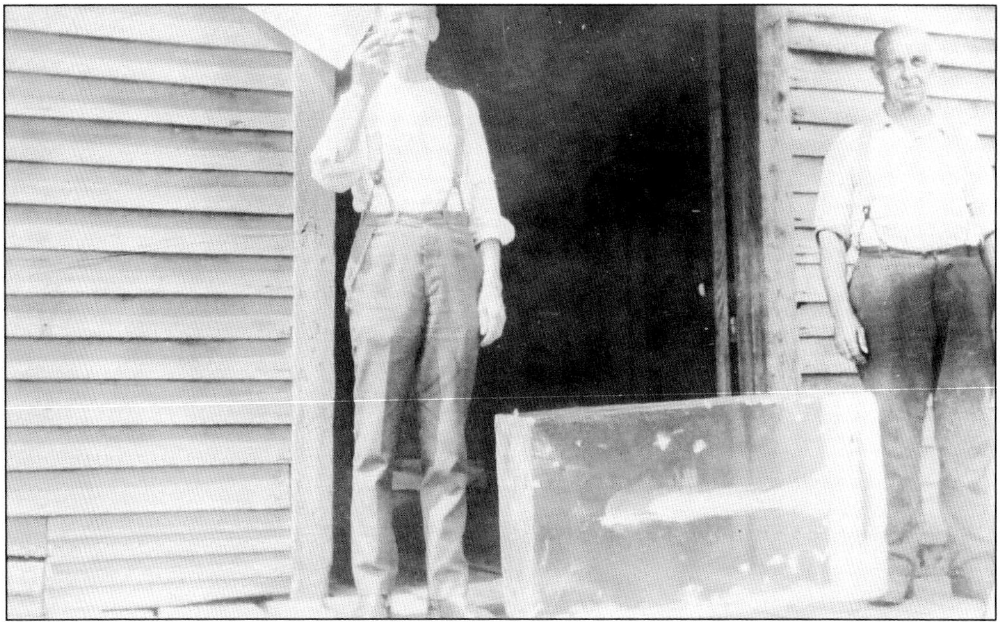

The Tarboro Ice Company provided ice and stored meat for area residents. (PC Spain)

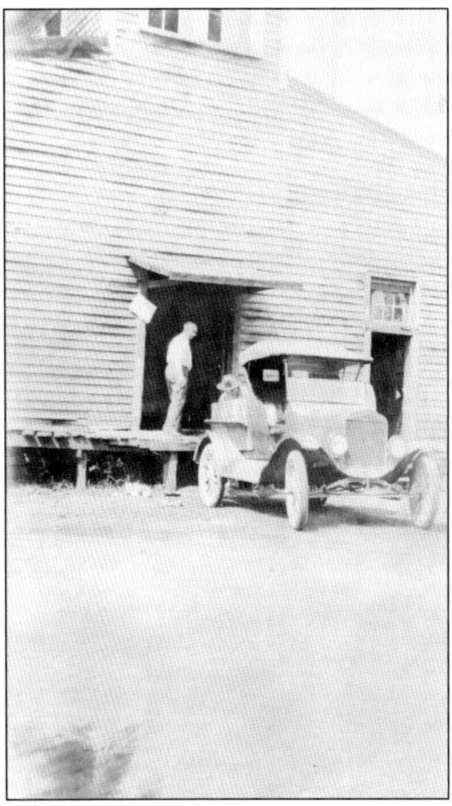

The Ice Company opened in around 1900 and in the 1930s was managed by L.P. Waldo. (PC Spain)

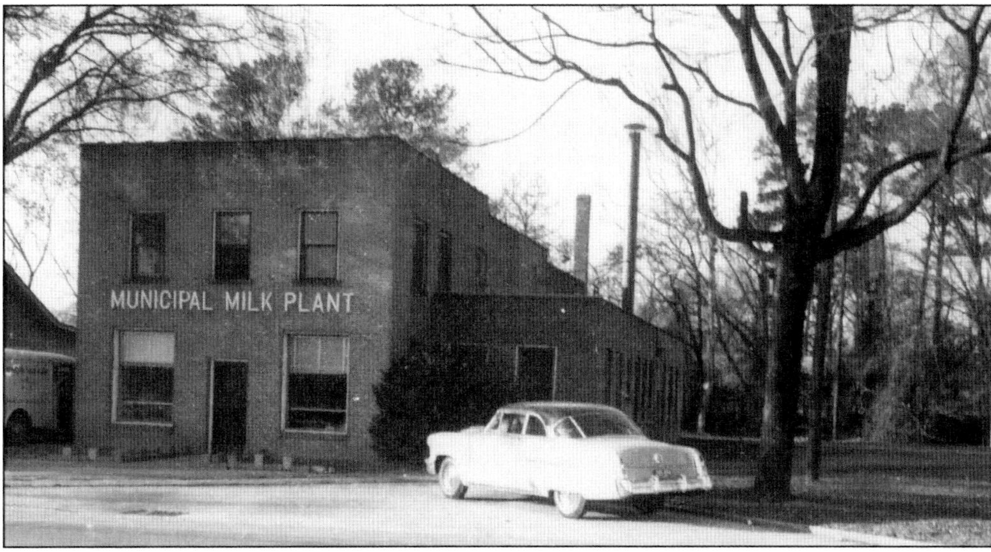

Founded in 1918, the Municipal Milk Plant of Tarboro was the only city-owned milk plant in the United States. Located at the corner of Wilson Street and Albemarle Avenue, it was built after an outbreak of colitis attributed to bad milk. A town ordinance requiring milk to be pasteurized resulted in the creation of the plant. By 1940 the plant not only pasteurized milk, but also processed chocolate milk, butter, and whipping cream. Milk was supplied by several dairy farms in the county including those belonging to George Holderness, Berry Lewis, and E.C. Winslow. (BBH)

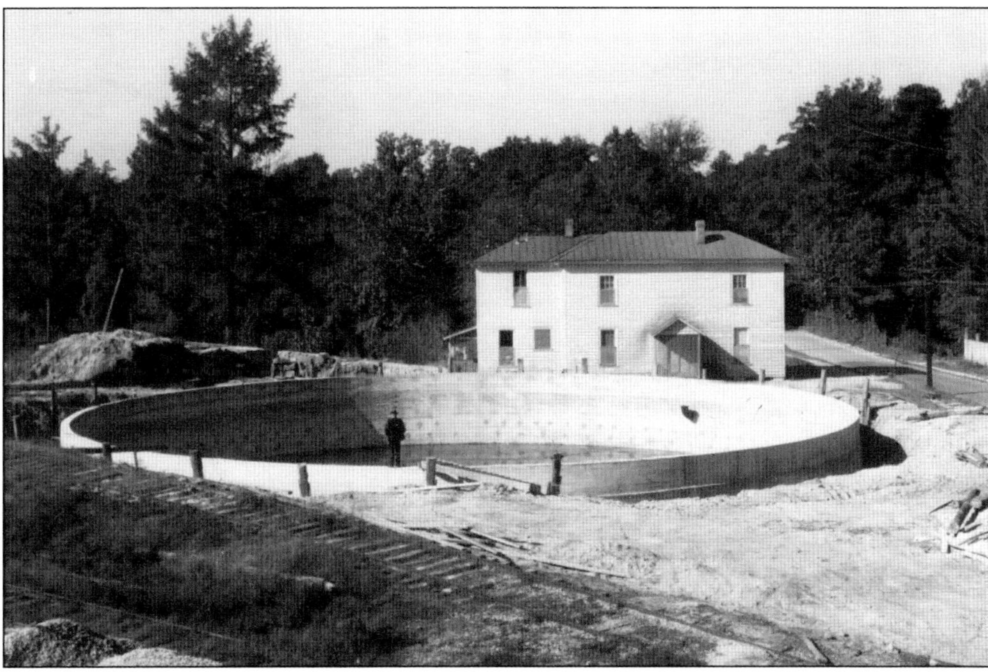

As a result of the Depression-era projects of the Work Project Administration, Tarboro acquired a new water treatment plant on the corner of Wilson Street and Albemarle Avenue. The building in the background of this photograph served as a boarding house for girls attending the Tarboro Female Academy during the 1880s. (NA in ECML)

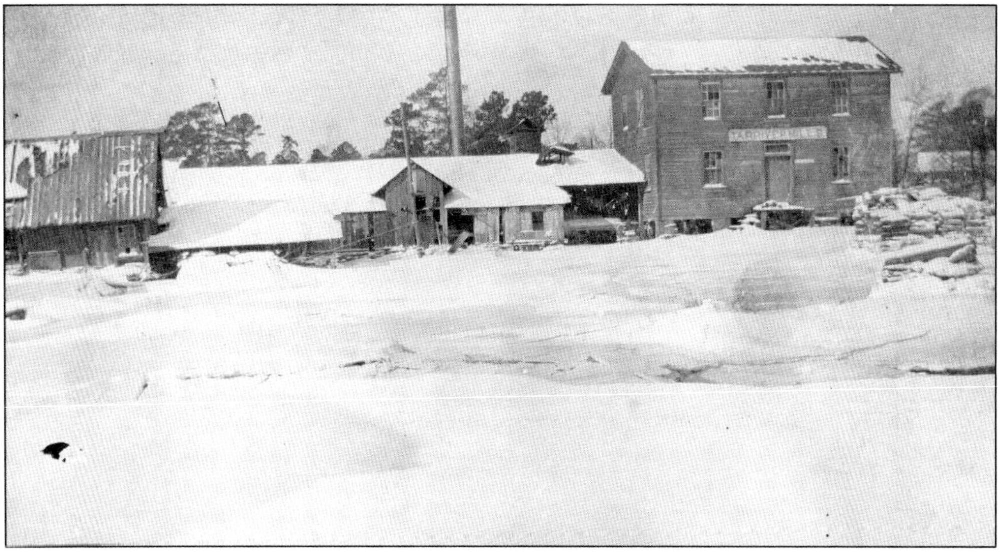

The Tarboro Lumber Company, located across the Tar River in the 1800s, supplied the area with wood for building. In 1935 the Tarboro Builders Supply Company opened with J.M. Britt as president. This company was soon purchased by C.H. Henderson and became the Henderson Lumber Company. A lumber company in Leggett specialized in basket bottoms and hampers. (ECML)

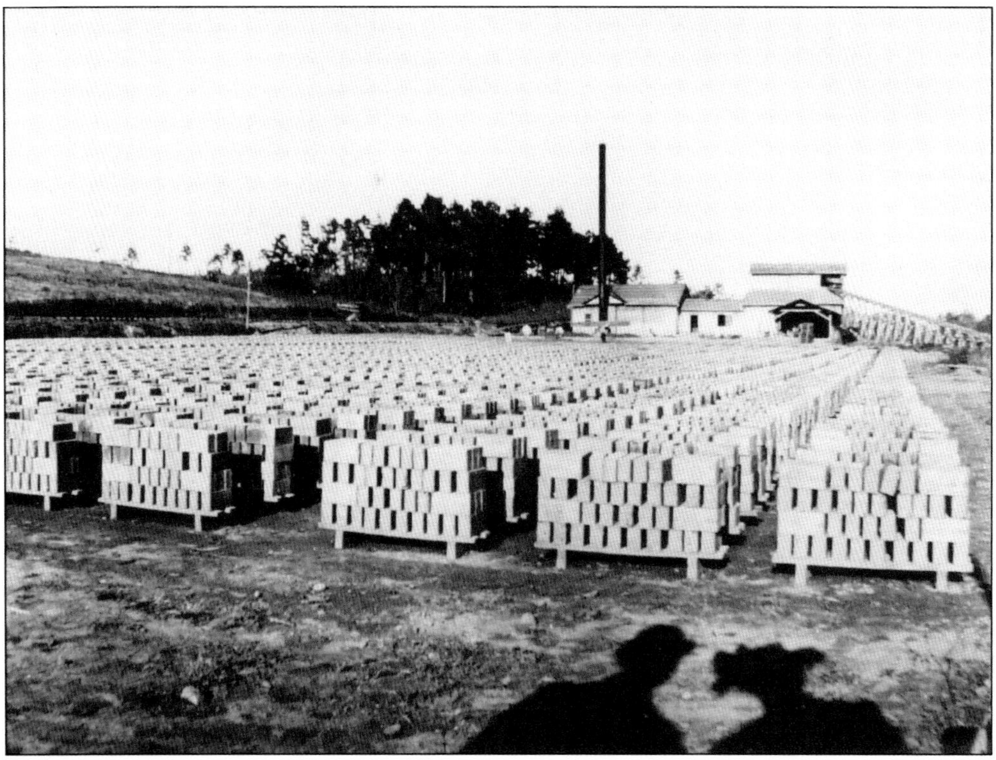

The first brickyard in Tarboro was established in the late 1850s when William Percival was contracted to build Calvary Church and "The Barracks." By the 1880s there were at least four brickyards in the county. (ECUSC Austin Family Papers)

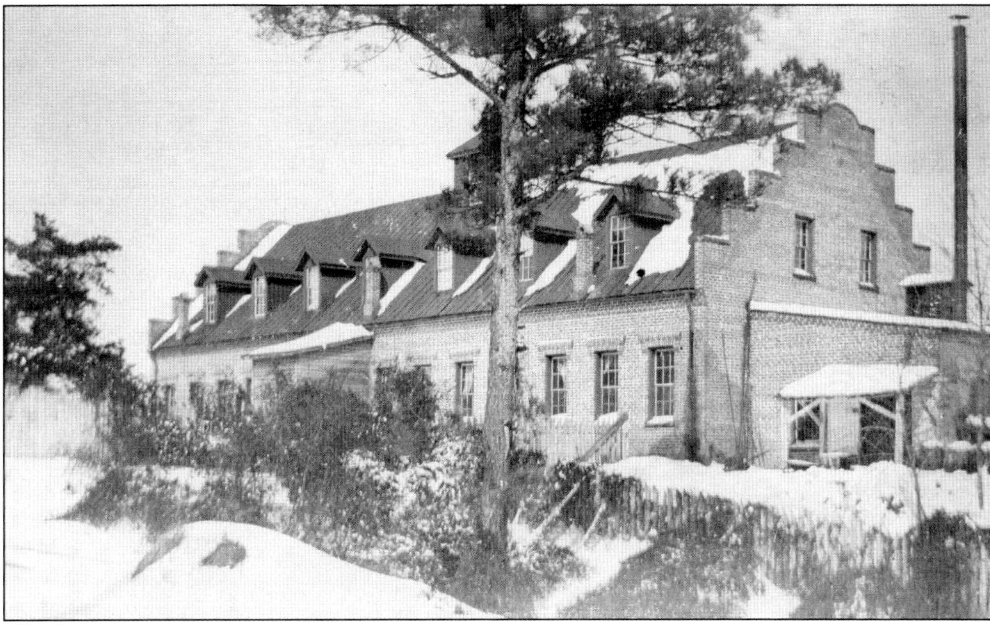

John F. Shackleford started the Riverview Mill in 1888 and employed over eighty-two citizens to produce socks and stockings for men, women, and children. Most of the employees were women, including a forewoman, Victoria Snell. The mill was located on Water Street near Albemarle Avenue. (ECML)

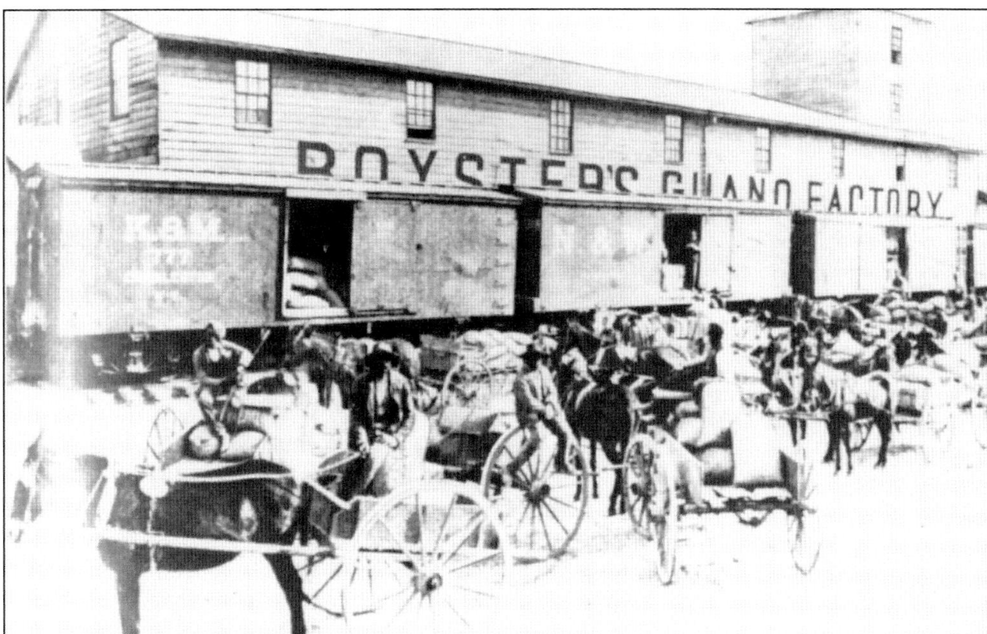

In 1885 Frank S. Royster established his first Guano fertilizer plant in Tarboro. By the 1930s, the company had fourteen plants in nine states. Although it moved its headquarters to Norfolk at the turn of the century, in 1990 the company came back to Tarboro where it originated and merged with another local agricultural firm, W.S. Clark, Co., which had been established in 1872. (BBH)

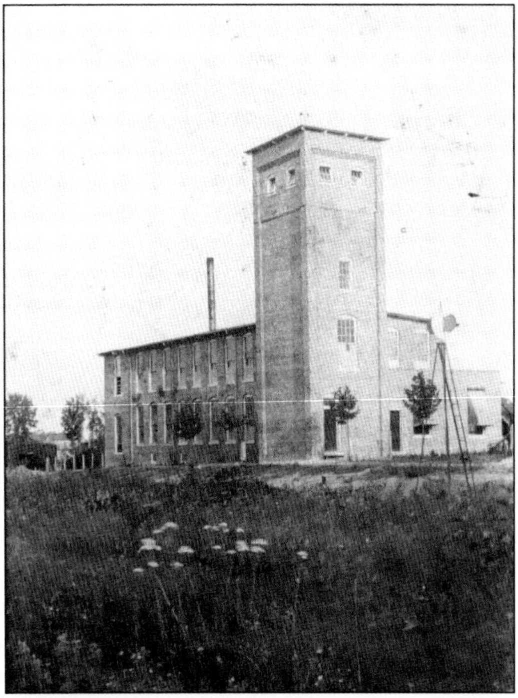

George Howard Jr., Job Cobb, and Henry T. Bryant founded Runnymede Mills in 1889. Called Runnymede because it was built near the Runnymede racetrack, the mill village included seventy-two homes for employees. During the wars, the mill produced hosiery for the Army, the Navy, and the Marine Corps. The mill produced hose for men and women and in the 1930s its average output was 1,700 dozen pairs of hose per day. (ECML)

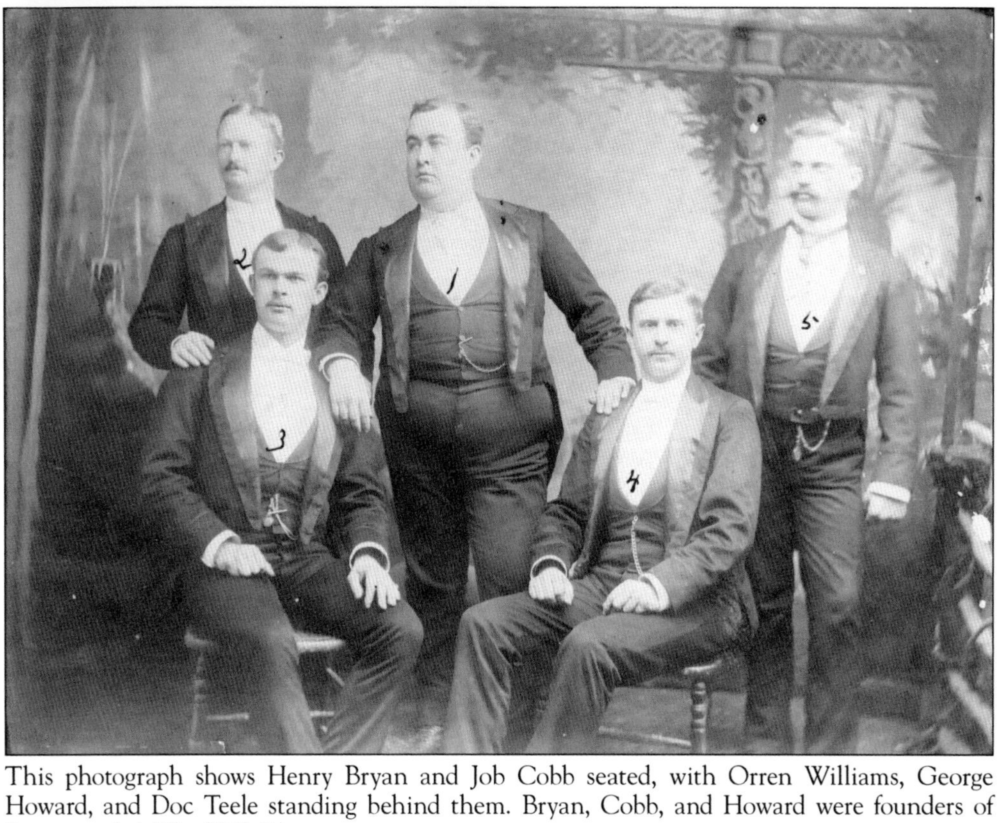

This photograph shows Henry Bryan and Job Cobb seated, with Orren Williams, George Howard, and Doc Teele standing behind them. Bryan, Cobb, and Howard were founders of Runnymede Mills. (ECML)

Many mill villages, such as the one at Runnymede, provided schools for the children of the workers, which the children attended until they were old enough to begin work in the mills. Sarah (Sallie) Howard Pitt, born in 1868, taught in the two-room school at Runnymede. After the village became a part of Tarboro, she taught in the Tarboro Public School. Ms. Pitt died in 1931. (ECML)

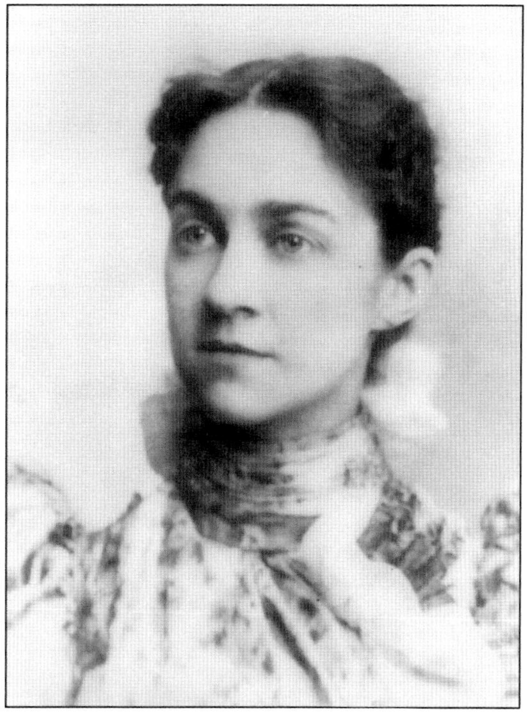

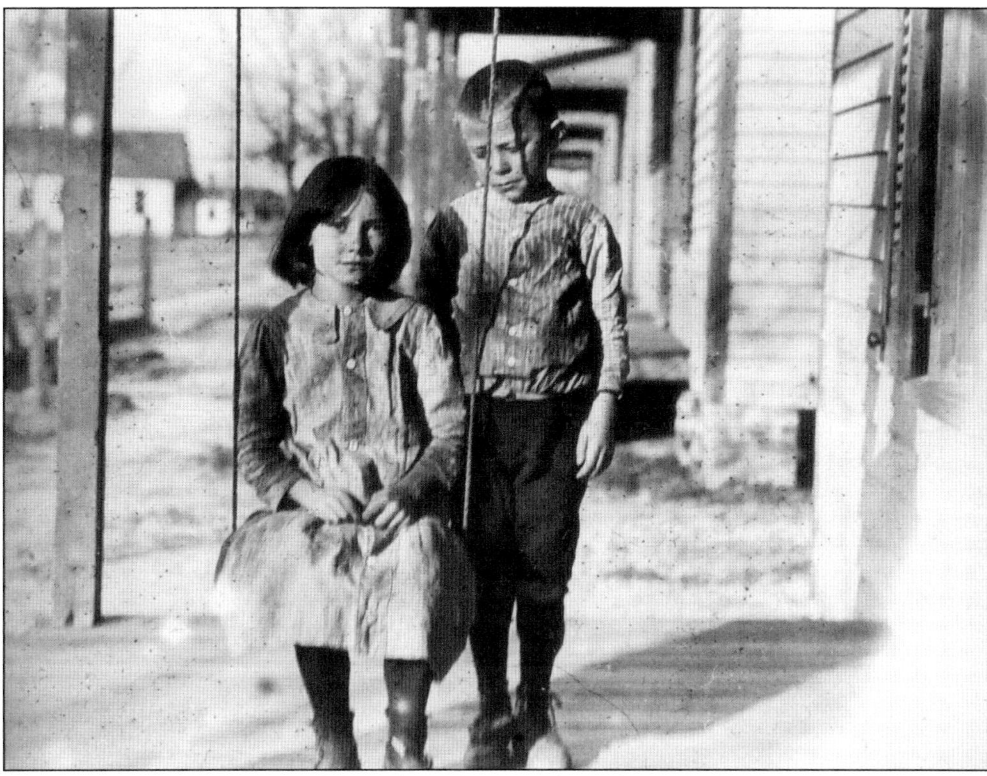

Most children in mill towns did not have long to play. The mills did provide schools for the younger children, but children as young as fourteen could go to work in the mills. (ECML)

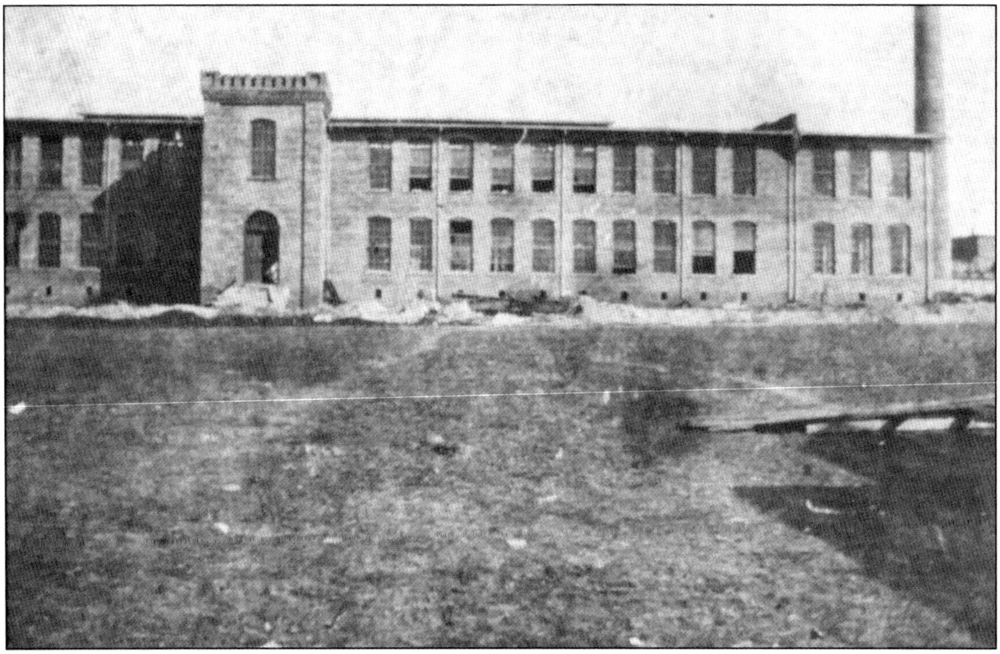

The first cotton mill in Tarboro, the Tarboro Cotton Factory was opened in 1887 by W.A. Hart, John H. Rodgers, and W.C. Hill. In 1916 it became the Hart Cotton Mills and later it became part of Burlington Industries. The plant employed over six hundred workers when it was at its peak of production. (ECML)

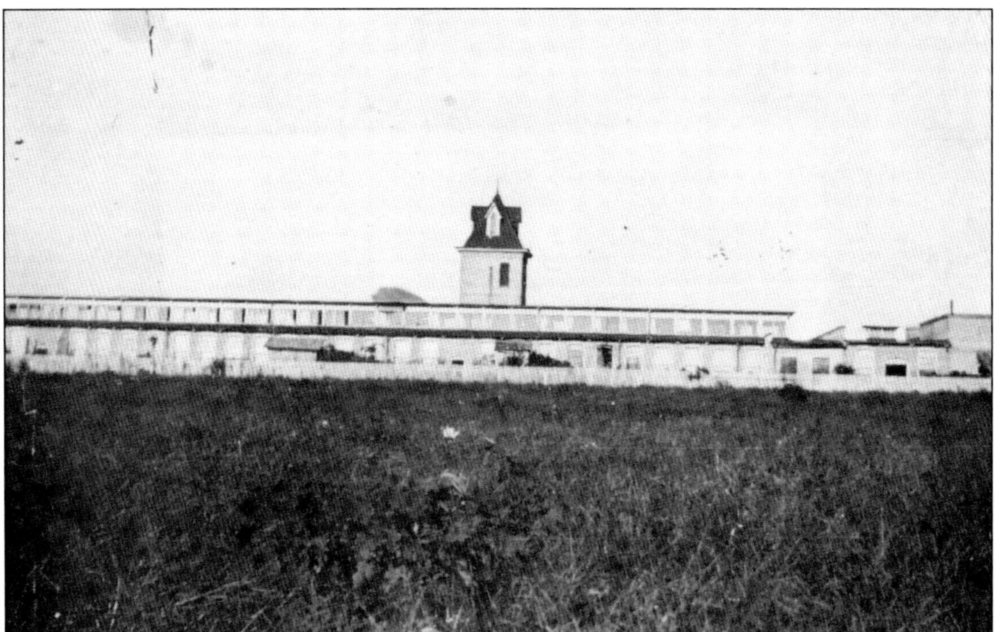

The Tarboro Knitting Company, formerly supervised by C.W. Jeffreys, was purchased by the Mayo brothers in 1931. The Mayo Knitting Mills originally employed thirty-five people and produced children's stockings. (ECML)

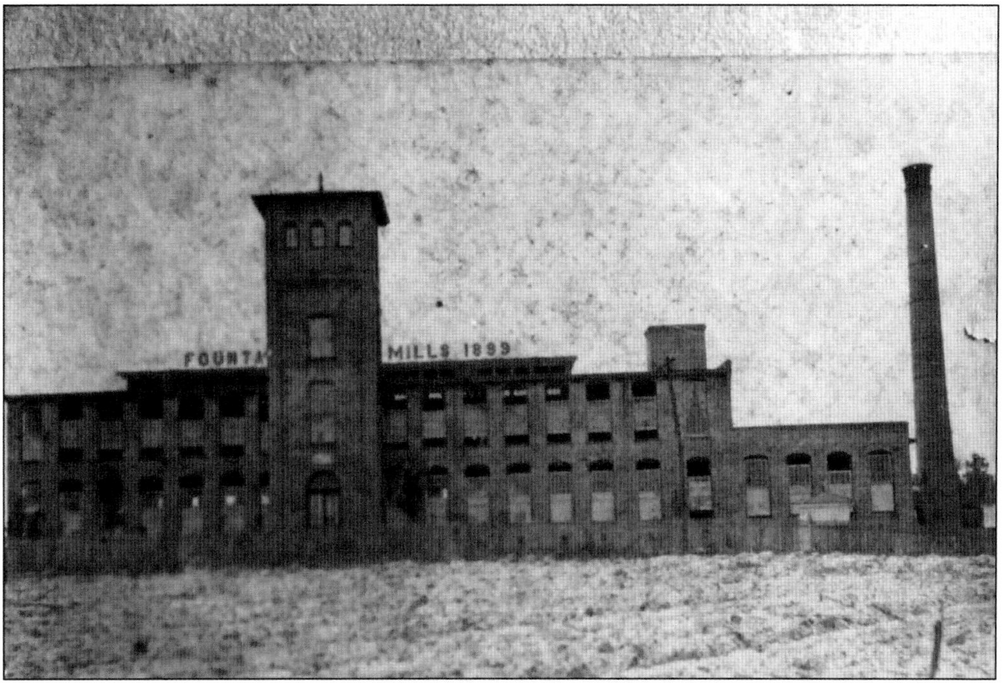

By the 1930s the Hart and Fountain Mills were combined with Captain Henry Smith as the general manager of both. William C. Hill was the president of Fountain Mills and John H. Rodgers was the president of Hart Mills. (ECML)

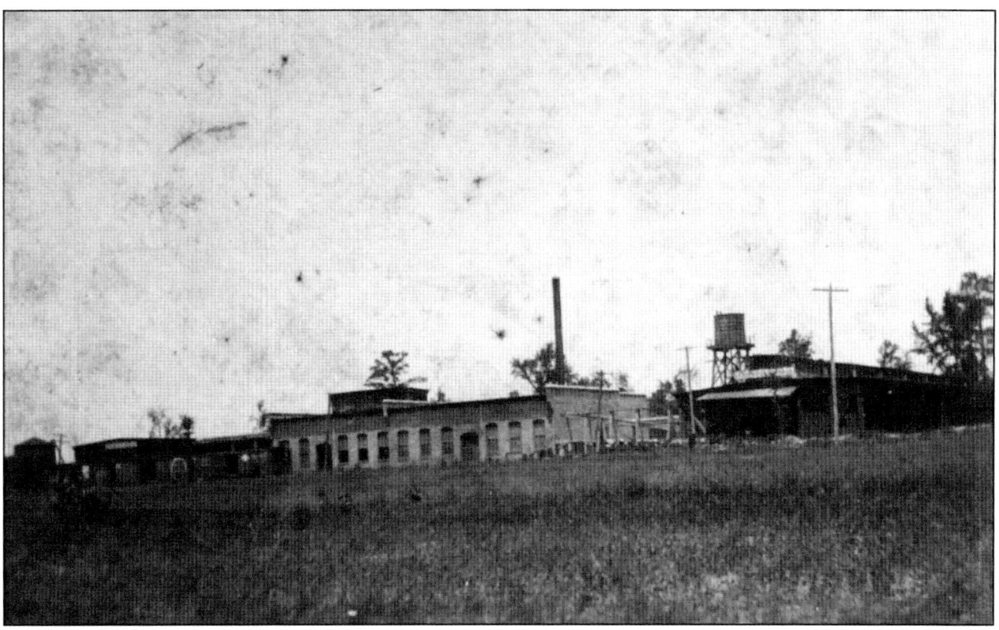

The Cotton Oil Company is shown here around 1885. Cotton oil was used to clean furniture, polish items, and preserve wood. (ECML)

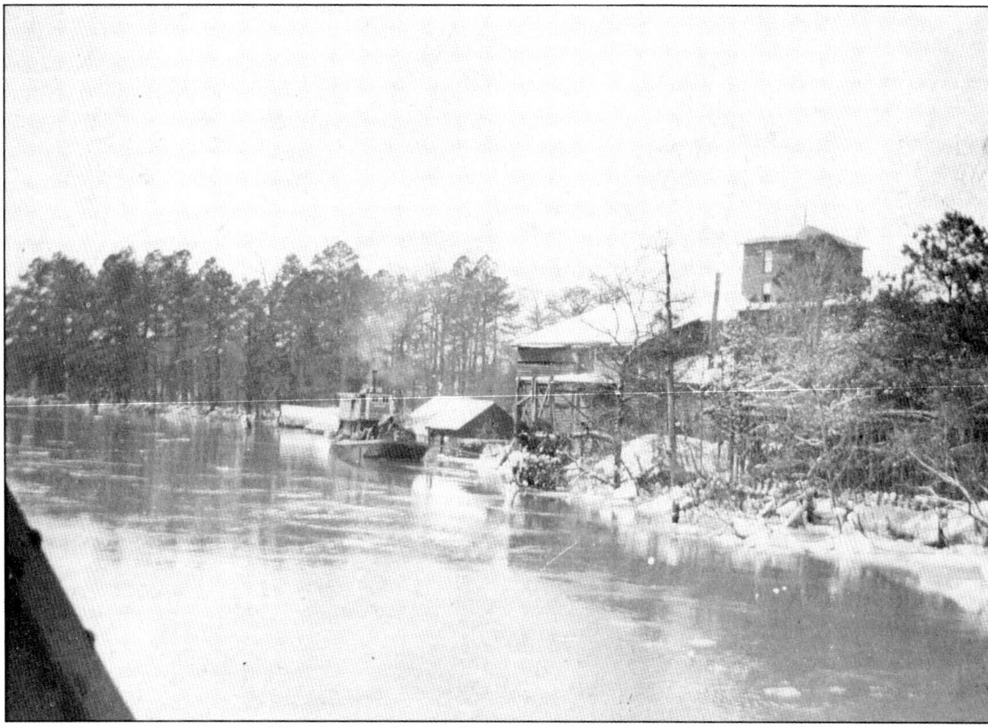

According to the 1891 publication, *Edgecombe County North Carolina: Her People and Resources. The Foremost Agricultural Section of the State*, Tarboro had much to offer. The author noted: "No town in the State has superior railroad and navigation facilities. Four lines of railroads and three steamboat lines give to Tarboro all the benefits and advantages of cheap freights and easy communication with all sections." The steamboats docked near the warehouse district where Hendricks Creek flowed into the Tar River. (ECML)

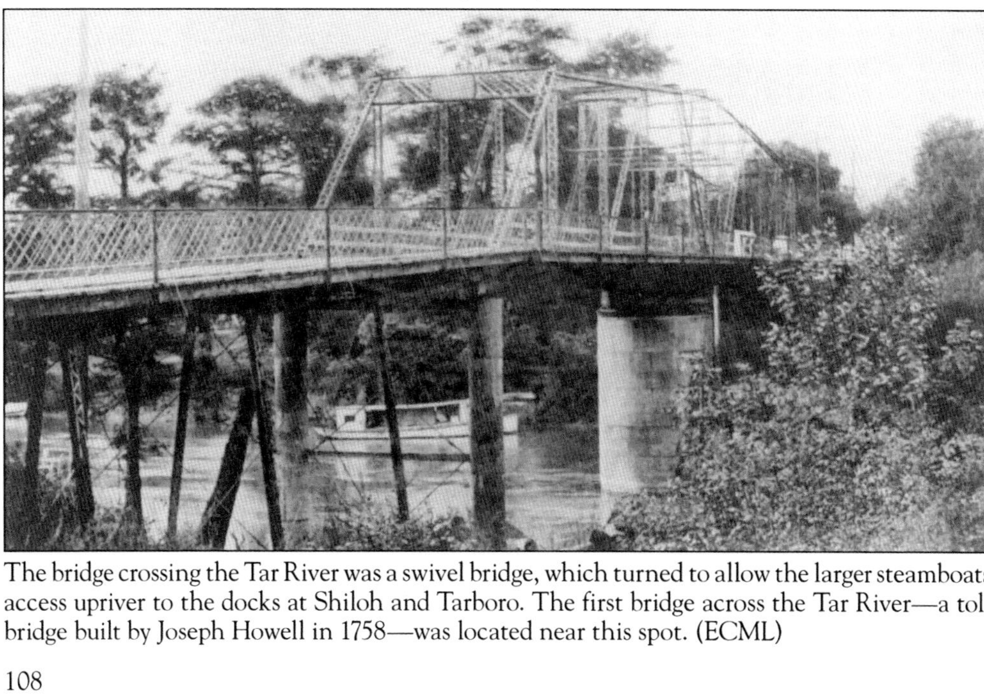

The bridge crossing the Tar River was a swivel bridge, which turned to allow the larger steamboats access upriver to the docks at Shiloh and Tarboro. The first bridge across the Tar River—a toll bridge built by Joseph Howell in 1758—was located near this spot. (ECML)

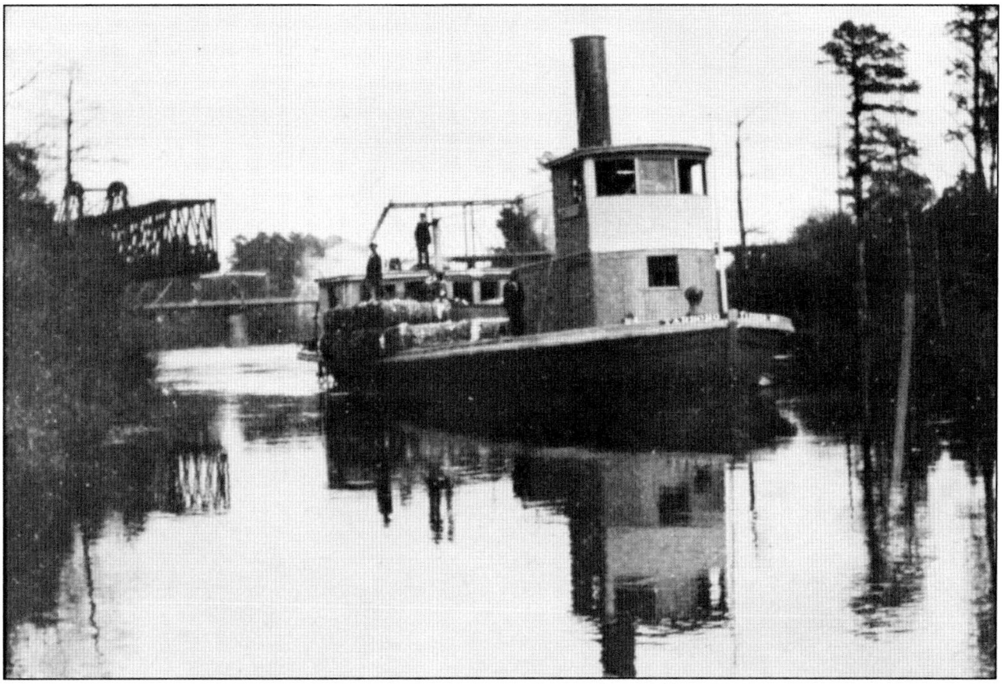

The Tar River winds through Edgecombe County from the fall line on the western edge of the county through the southeast and on through neighboring Pitt and Beaufort Counties before merging with the Pamlico River and flowing into the Pamlico Sound. Tarboro was the head of navigation on the river, which connected residents to the coastal ports. As early as the 1770s boats were sending goods up and down the river. Here the steamboat *Tarboro* crosses under the swivel bridge on its way to the loading wharf. (BBH)

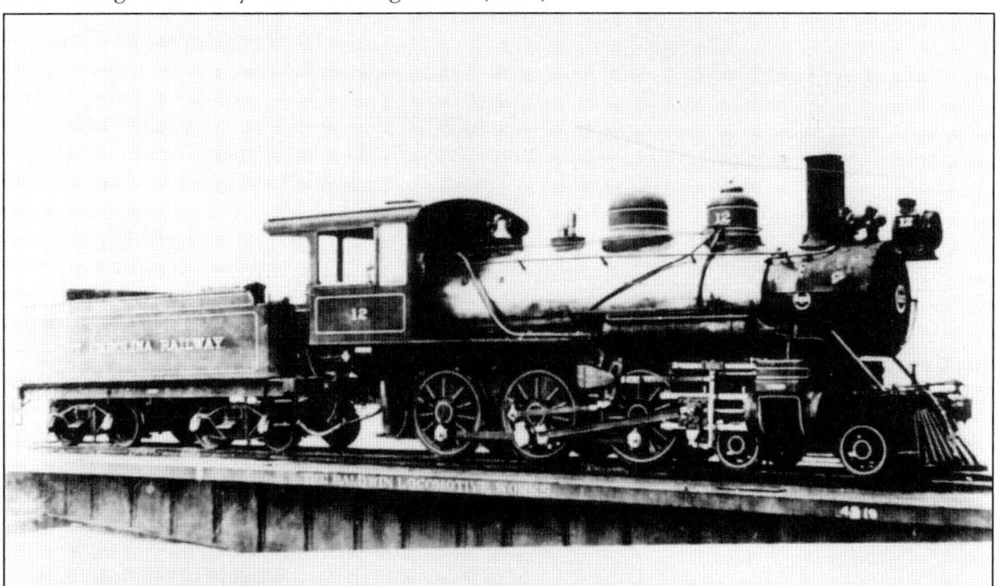

The East Carolina Railroad, founded by Henry Clark Bridgers, ran from Tarboro to Hookerton with stops in areas like Davistown, Pinetops, and Macclesfield. Trains first arrived in Edgecombe County in the 1840s and in Tarboro in 1860. (ECUSC Bridgers Collection)

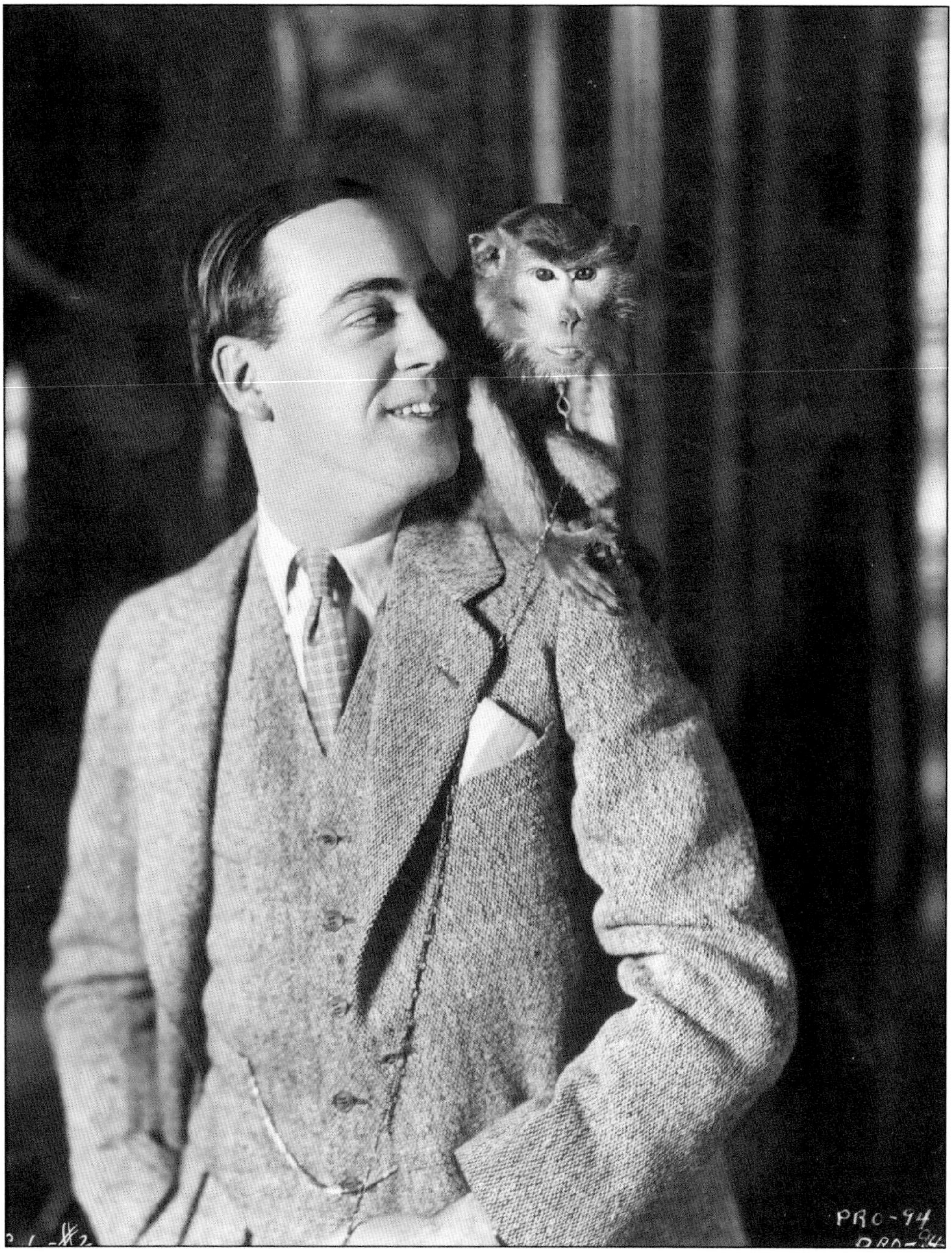

Silent film star Ben Finney poses with a pet monkey. Finney, the son of Tarboro native Elizabeth Bridgers, starred in dozens of films in the 1920s. His book *Feet First* describes the interesting life he spent with celebrities of the era such as Ernest Hemingway and F. Scott Fitzgerald. (PC Bridgers family)

Six

Citizens and Social Life

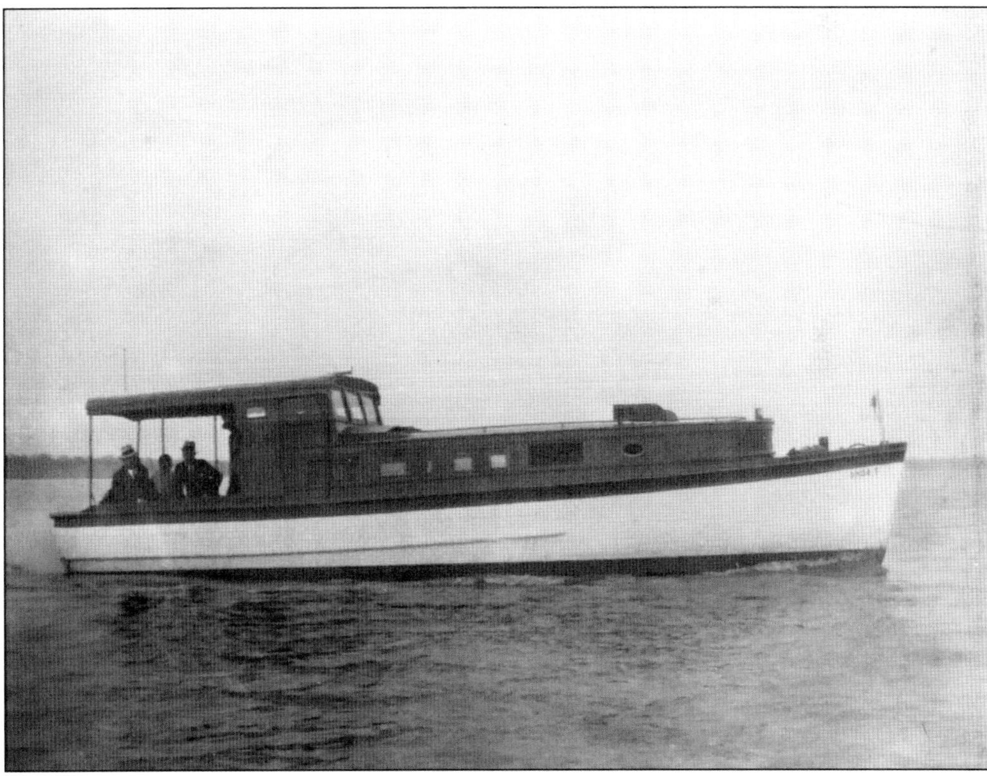

The Sea Horse, owned by Lyn Bond, took Edgecombe County citizens on excursions on the Pamlico Sound at the mouth of the Tar River. The craft was nicknamed the "Lost Boat" because the captain and his crew (usually Francis Jenkins, Pem Nash, and other adventurous gentlemen) had a habit of getting lost and having to be rescued by the Coast Guard. According to one story, Mr. Bond claimed that he was never lost; it was always the Coast Guard who couldn't seem to locate him! (PC Marrow)

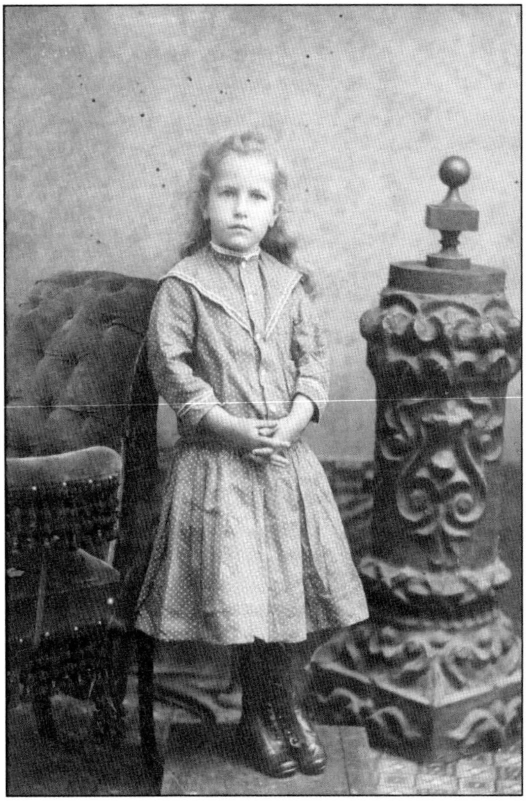

Mary Horne Bridgers, the daughter of John L. Bridgers, was born in 1882. She was a teacher in Tarboro for many years. Bridgers School is named after her and her sister Loulie. Mary died in 1964. S.R. Alley took this portrait around 1890. (PC Foster)

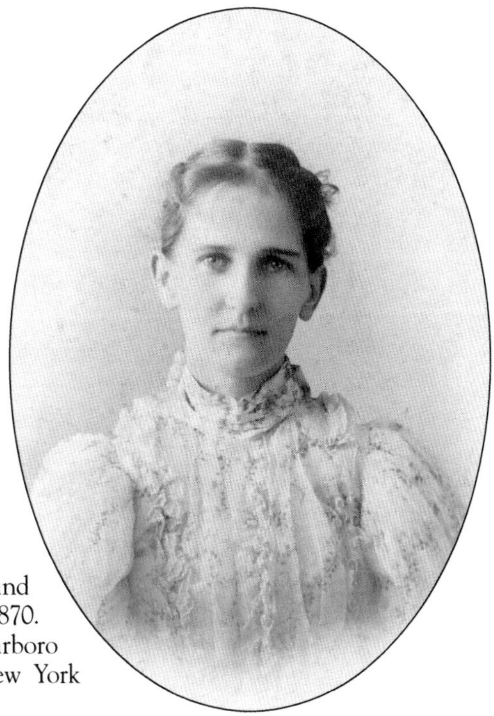

Loulie Bridgers, the oldest daughter of John L. and Mary Elizabeth Battle Bridgers, was born in 1870. She became a teacher and librarian for the Tarboro Public School. This portrait was made in New York around 1885. (PC Foster)

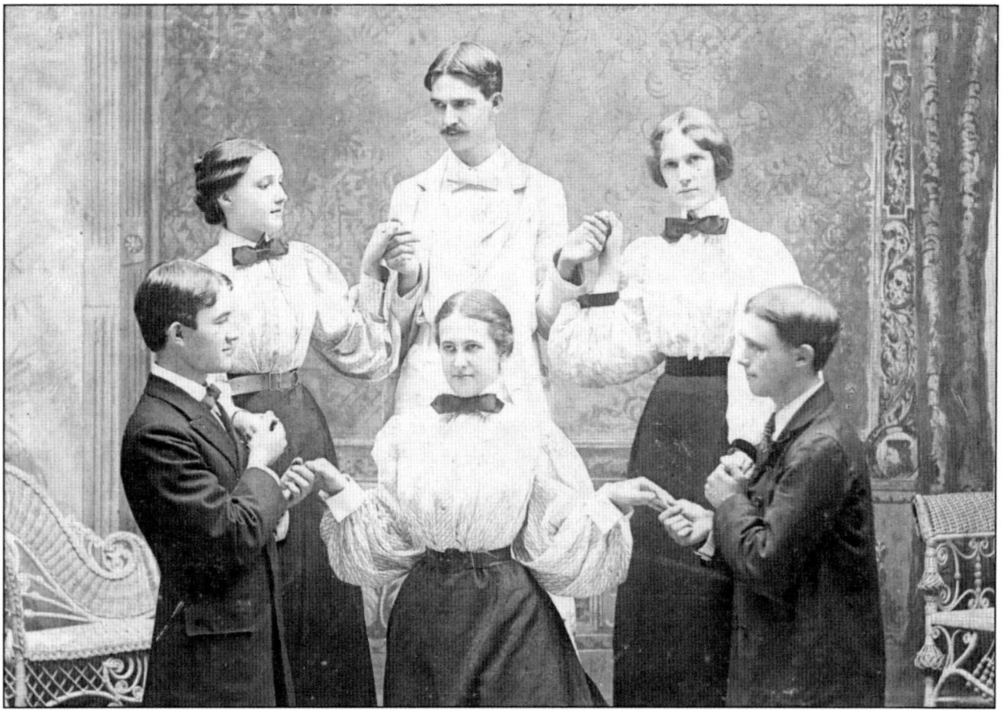

Stamps Howard, Mary Ferebee, Will Clark, Nan Clark, and Willie Howard pose for a photograph around 1894. (PC Howard)

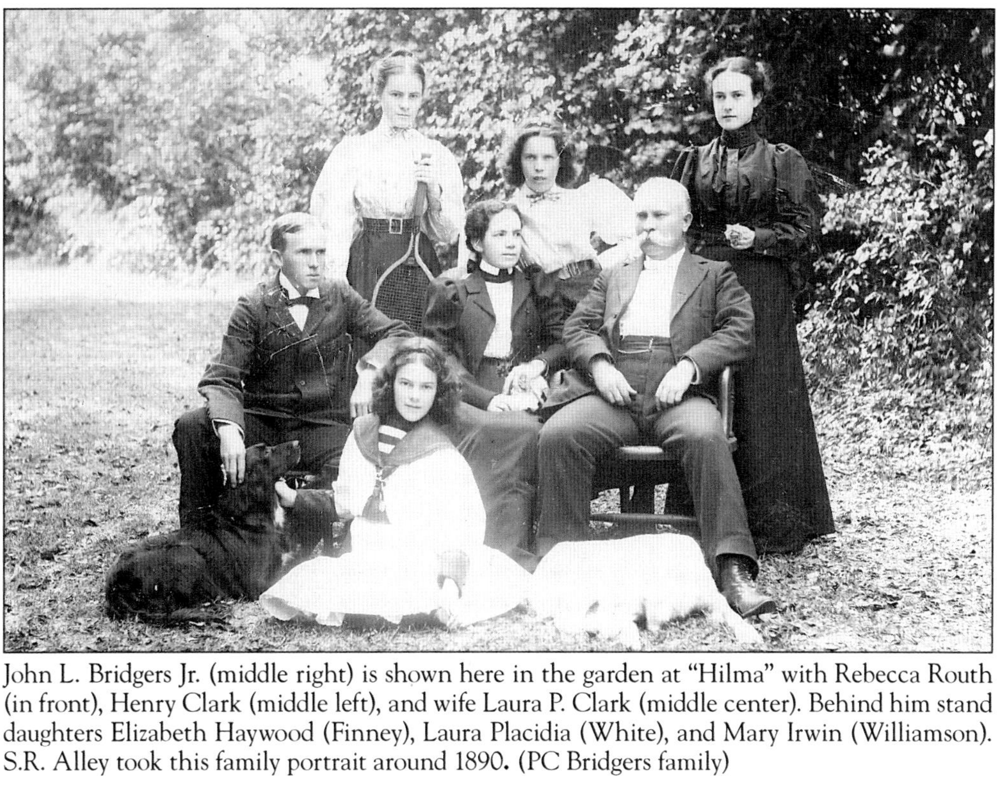

John L. Bridgers Jr. (middle right) is shown here in the garden at "Hilma" with Rebecca Routh (in front), Henry Clark (middle left), and wife Laura P. Clark (middle center). Behind him stand daughters Elizabeth Haywood (Finney), Laura Placidia (White), and Mary Irwin (Williamson). S.R. Alley took this family portrait around 1890. (PC Bridgers family)

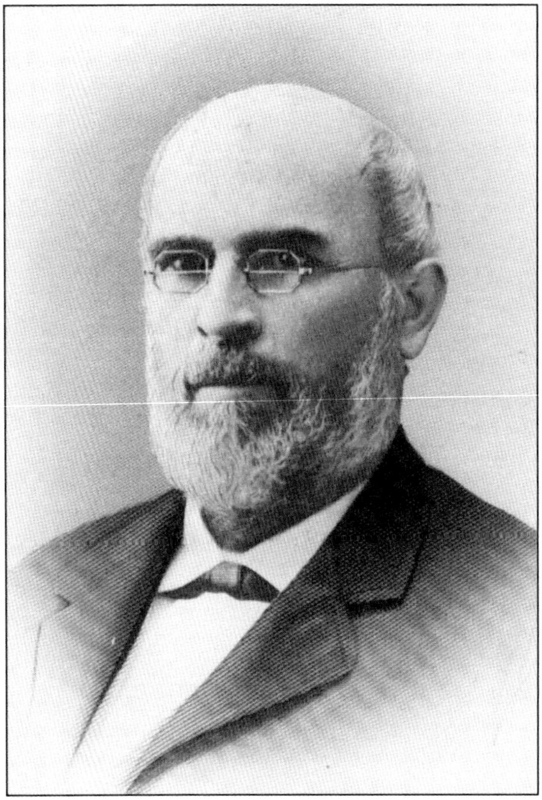

Robert Rufus Bridgers, the brother of John Luther Bridgers, was born in Edgecombe County in 1819. He graduated from the University of North Carolina in 1841 and practiced law in Tarboro. He was president of the Tarboro branch of the State Bank, and served several terms in the North Carolina General Assembly, as both leader of the house and as chairman of the judiciary committee. During the War, he served in the Confederate Congress. After the War, he was elected president of the Wilmington and Weldon Railroad and moved to Wilmington, where he died in 1888. (BBH)

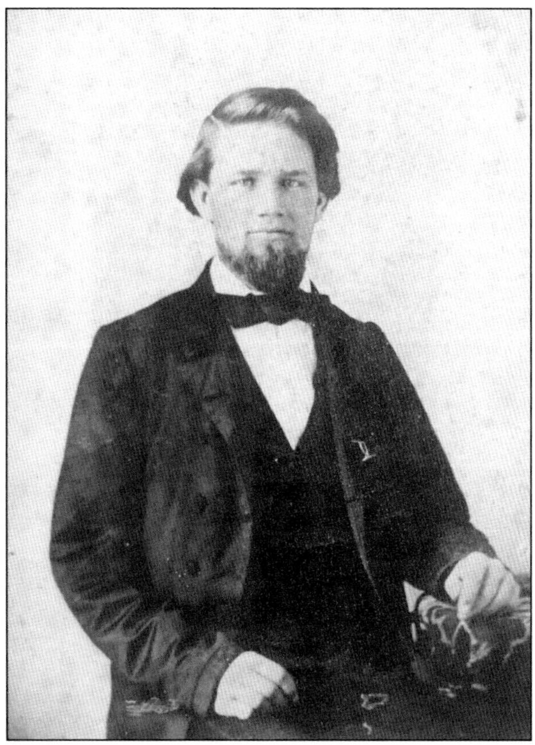

Born in 1840 to Baptist minister Milton Bourne, Henry Clay Bourne served in the CSA and was wounded at Shiloh. He came to Tarboro to recover and operated the Confederate Commissary on the railroad until the end of the War. After the War he married Florence Dickens. His second wife was Maria Toole Clark, the daughter of Governor Henry T. Clark. Bourne served the county as a magistrate, a justice of the peace, and a sheriff. (ECML)

Tarboro native John Spenser Bassett was the son of a building contractor who served in the Edgecombe Guards. Bassett attended Trinity College (later Duke) and graduated in 1888. He taught in Durham public schools, then became an English instructor at Trinity. He attended Johns Hopkins University and graduated in 1894 with a Ph.D. in history. Returning to Trinity, he taught for several years and published numerous articles on North Carolina and Southern history, including some of the first articles on African-American history and on the achievements of Booker T. Washington. His work drew the wrath of Raleigh editor Josephus Daniels, who demanded Bassett be fired. Bassett did go to Smith Collage, but eventually returned to Johns Hopkins. He founded the *South Atlantic Quarterly* and was secretary of the American Historical Association. He married Jessie Lewellyn of Durham. Bassett died in a car accident in Washington, D.C., in 1928. A historical marker on the corner of Wilson Street and Albemarle Avenue indicates his home site. (DUKE)

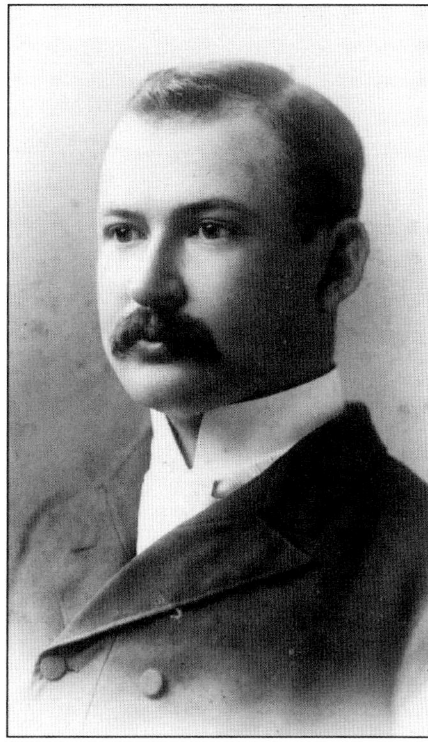

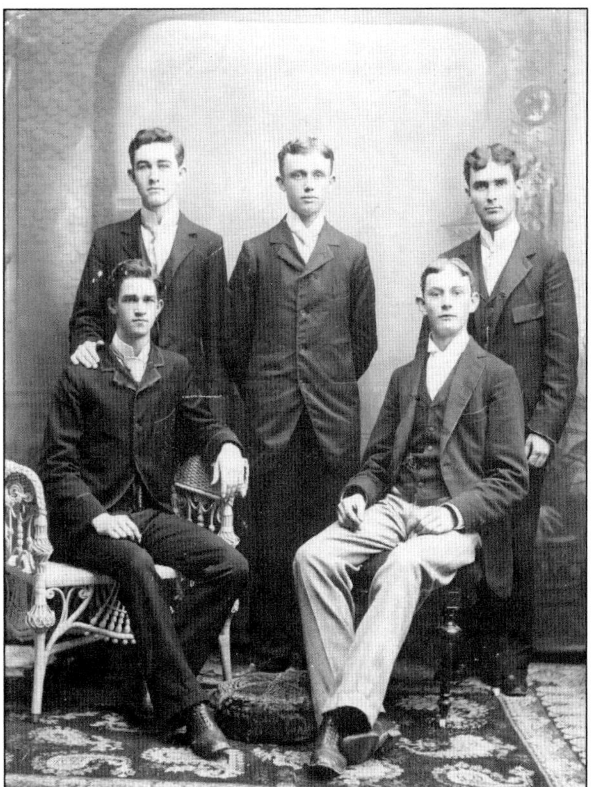

"The Bloody Five" in 1895 were Johnny Howard, Tom Gatlin, Stamps Howard, Bill Clark, and Lyman Cotten. (ECML)

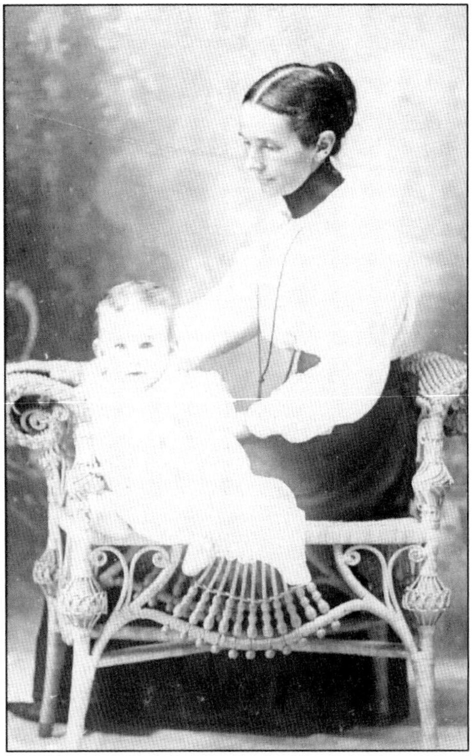

S.R. Alley took this photograph of a young Hobson Lafayette Pittman and his cousin, Alice Pittman, in 1900. Hobson Pittman was born in 1899 in Edgecombe County. As a youngster he moved to town and attended Tarboro schools under the guidance of the Bridgers sisters. Miss Mollie Rouse, his art teacher, recognized the artistic talent in Hobson and encouraged him to continue art training after high school. (BBH)

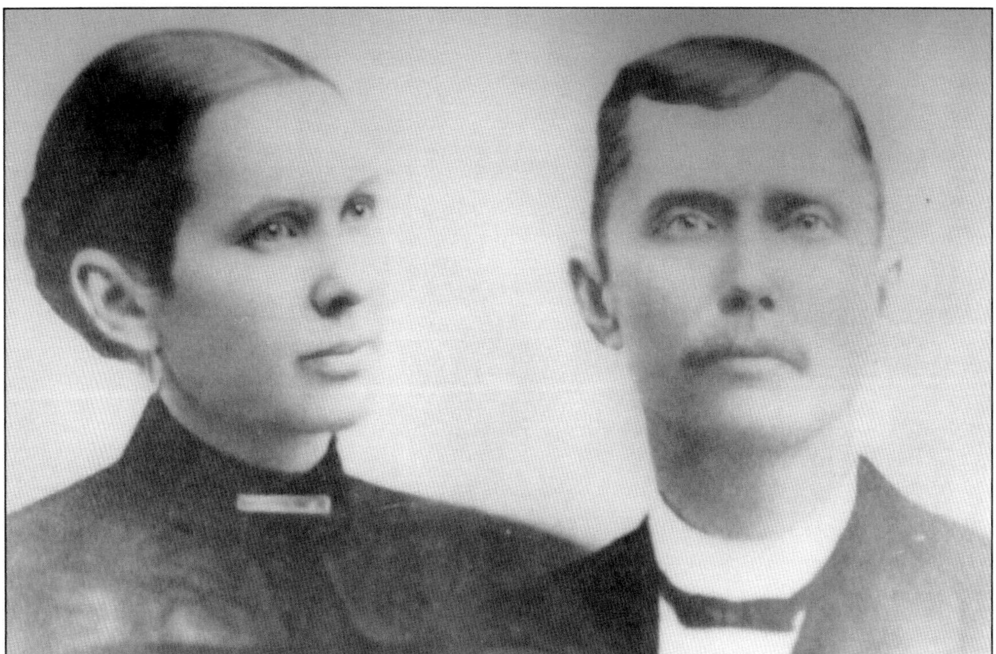

Alice Walston Pittman and Biscoe Pittman were the parents of Hobson Pittman, who grew up to become a noted artist. Hobson went on to study in Pennsylvania and eventually served on the faculty of the Pennsylvania Academy of Fine Arts. Mr. Biscoe Pittman operated a general store at Epworth, near Fishing Creek, where the family owned land. (BBH)

Hobson poses with his sister, Lena Pittman Weeks, a longtime stringer for the *News and Observer* and a dedicated missionary to local prisoners. By the early 1940s Pittman's work was being featured in popular magazines like *Life*, and he had become a recognized regional artist. (BBH)

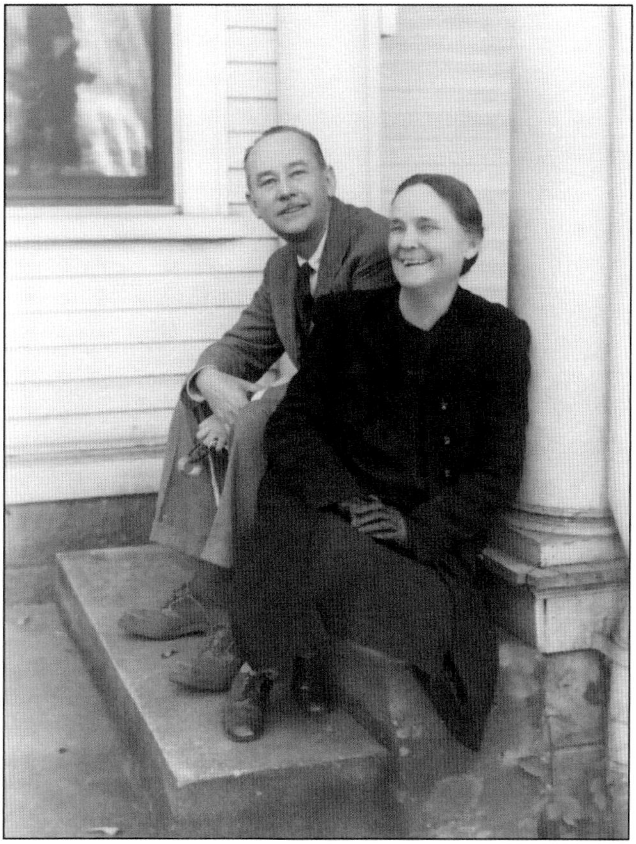

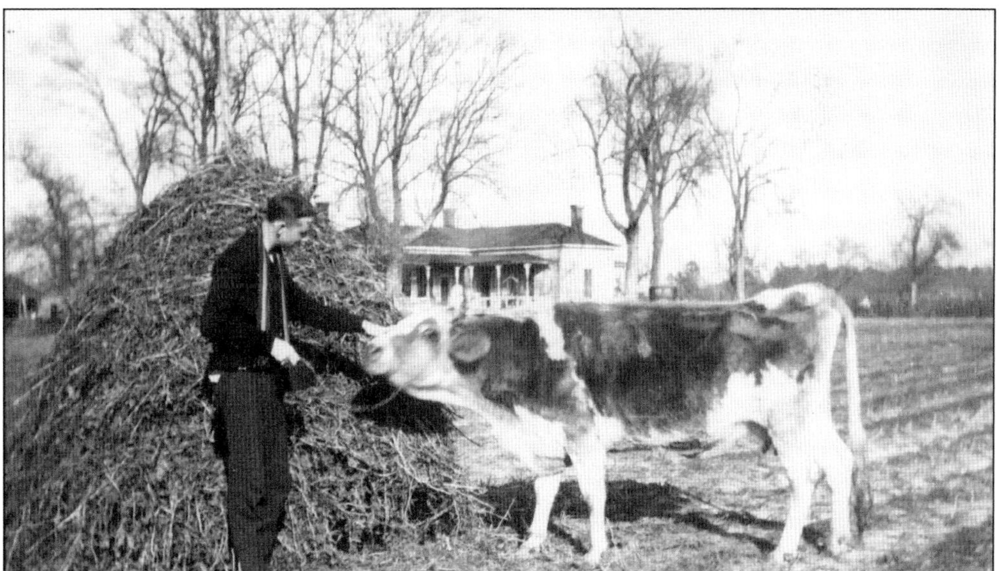

Hobson Pittman invites a cow to enjoy some peanut straw at his Epworth home. Straw stacks were important images in his early paintings. The Biscoe Pittman homeplace is in the background. (BBH)

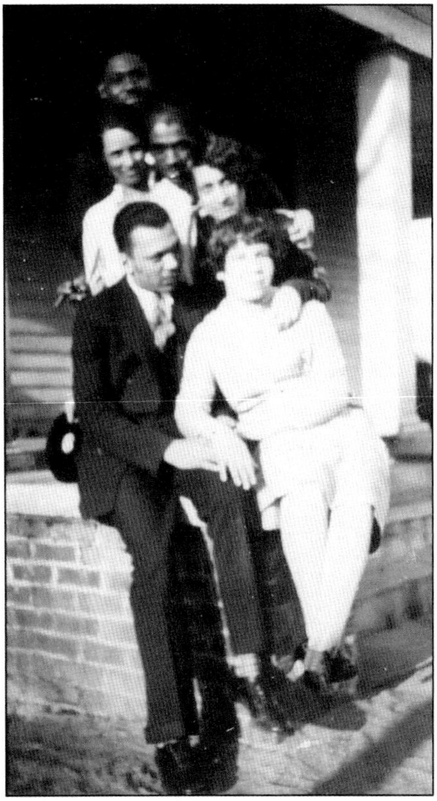

Mr. Richard H. Parker, Miss Helen L. Scales, and friends were photographed on the porch of 914 East St. John Street in the 1920s. (PC Parker)

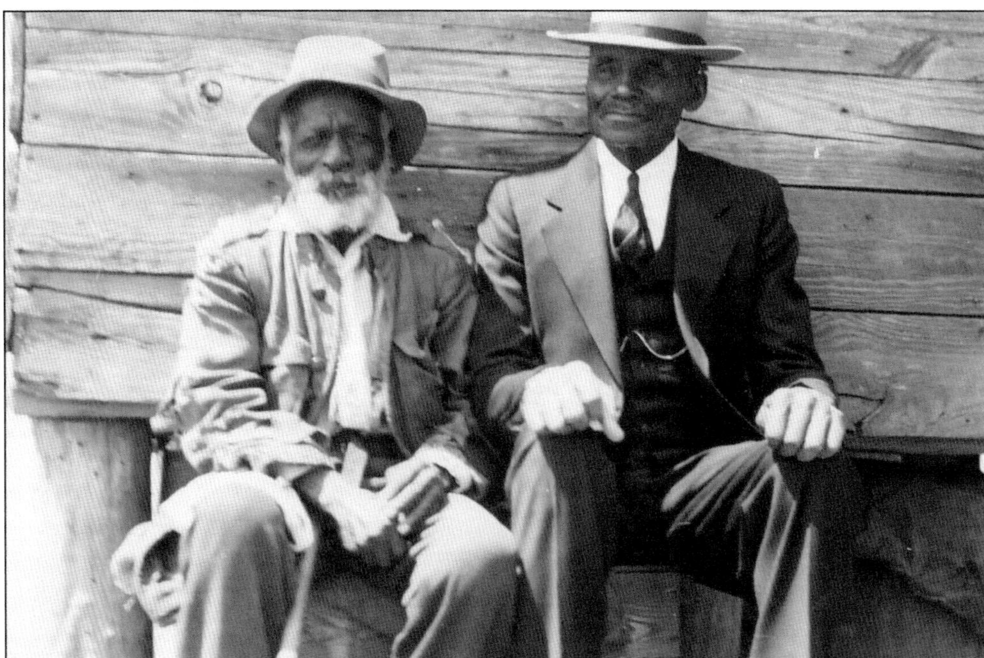

Primas Cherry (at the age of ninety-four) and his friend, Charles Key, sit outside the Winslow Livery stables around 1940. (PC Winslow)

Richard Parker, Hazel Scales, and friends pose in front of a 1928 Chevy belonging to Mr. Parker's father. (PC Parker)

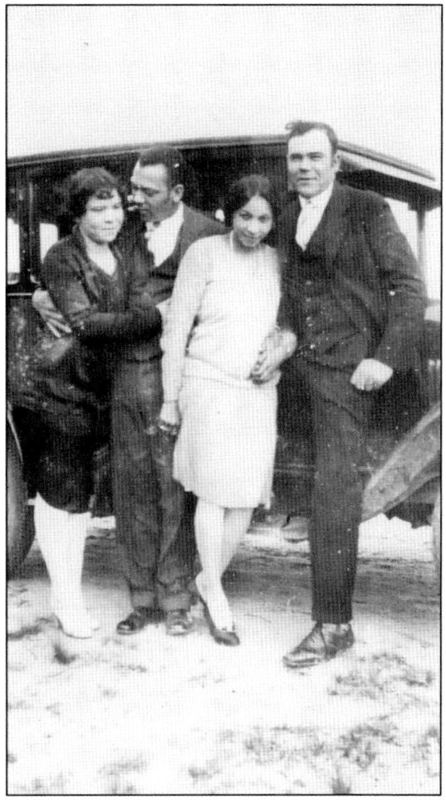

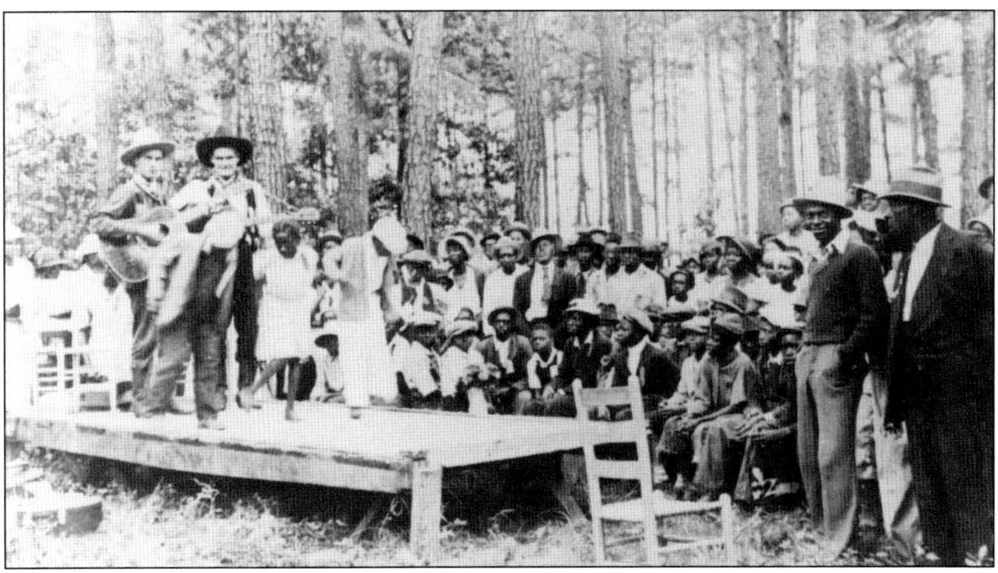

Live entertainment was not limited to the stage at The Opera House; traveling shows of all types made the circuit in the first quarter of this century. Here, three children dance on stage as a crowd enjoys the music of traveling singers. (ECML)

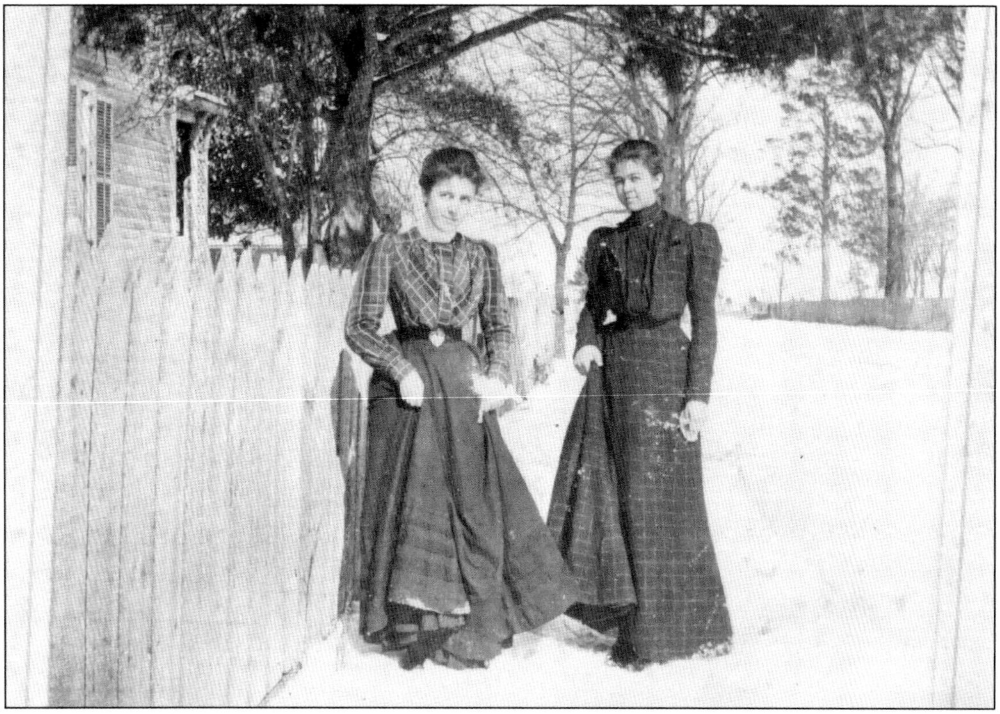

Two Tarboro ladies enjoy a stroll through the snow in 1899. This was one of many memorable snowstorms in the late 1890s. (BBH)

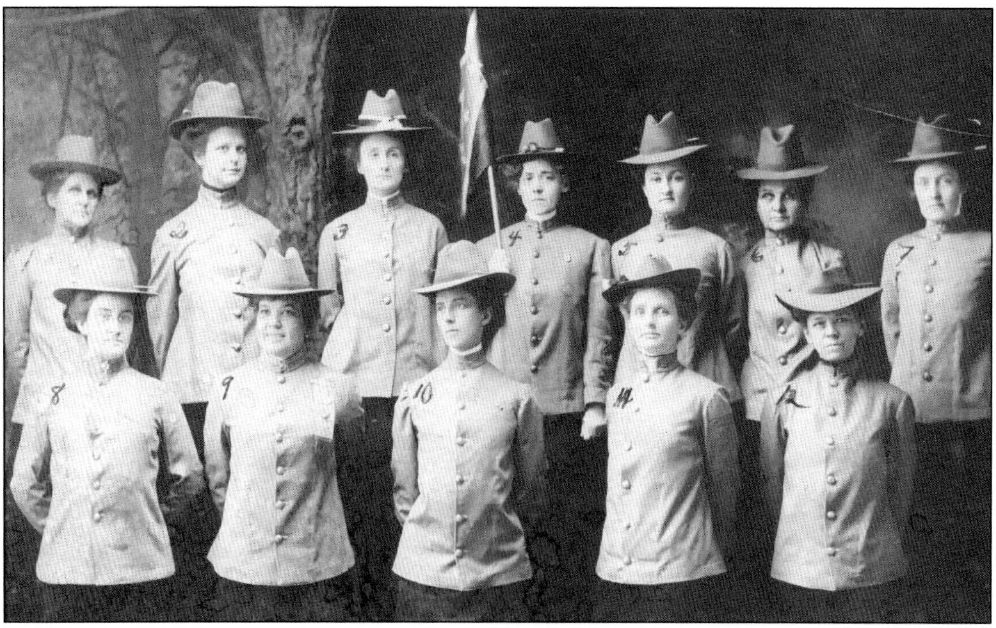

When this picture was taken, around 1900, the choir of the United Daughters of the Confederacy included, from left to right: (front row) Mrs. Jonie Dozier, Mrs Jacksie Daniel Thrash, Miss Mary Austin, Mrs. W.A. Hart, and Mrs. Ada Bass; (back row) Mrs. Seth Speight, Mrs. J.E. Morresette, Mrs. Minnie Williamson, an unnamed director, Mrs. McCraw, Miss Lucy Barlowe, and Mrs. Charlie Cobb. (ECML)

Miss Alice Braswell of Battleboro is shown here with a small girl, thought to be Elizabeth or Vivian Pearsall, who was visiting a neighbor. (PC Brown)

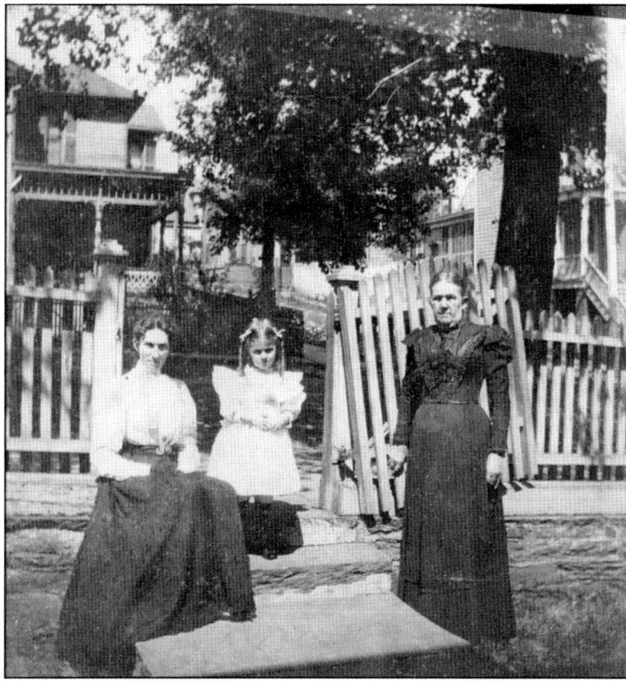

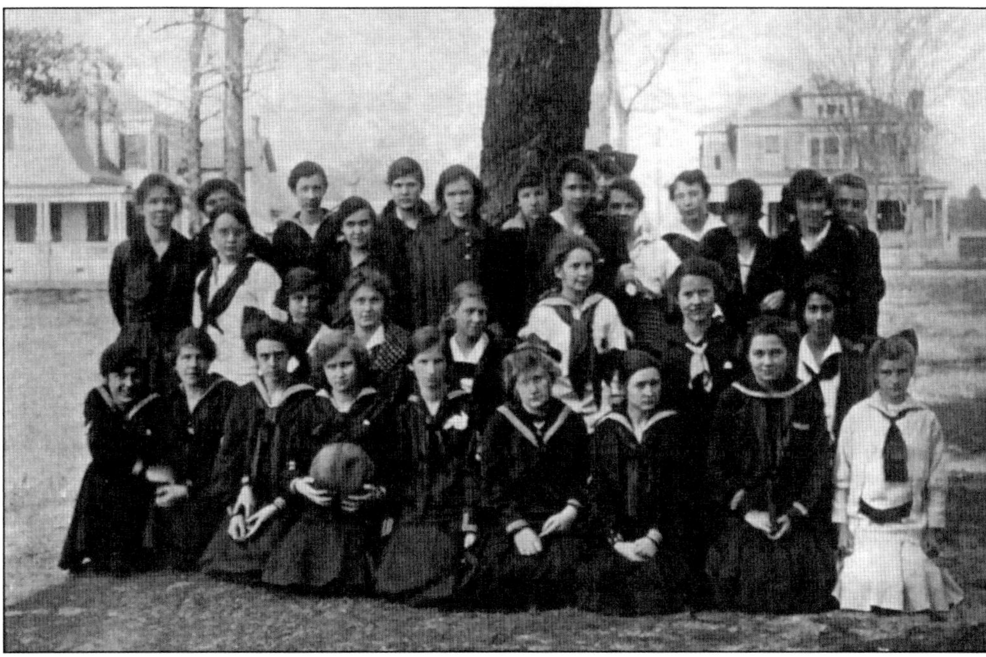

The Girls' Athletic Association appeared in the 1916 *Tarborah* yearbook. Members included Iva Andrews, Helen Battle, Katherine Batts, Elizabeth Bowden, Sarah F. Bryan, Annie E. Cobb, Catharine Cobb, Annie Fountain, Claribel Fountain, Fannie Gaskins, Nannie Hart, Reba Heilbroner, Frances Horne, Mary C. Howard, Annie E. Johnson, Vera Keech, Ellen Baker Leggett, Sophia Light, Lillian Liverman, Mabel Norfleet, Catherine Pender, Ella Pender, Sara H. Philips, Martha W. Powell, Lilla Rosenbaum, Beulah Strickland, Elise Taylor, Arlene Webb, Dorothy Williamson, Marion Wilson, and Elizabeth Worsley. (BBH)

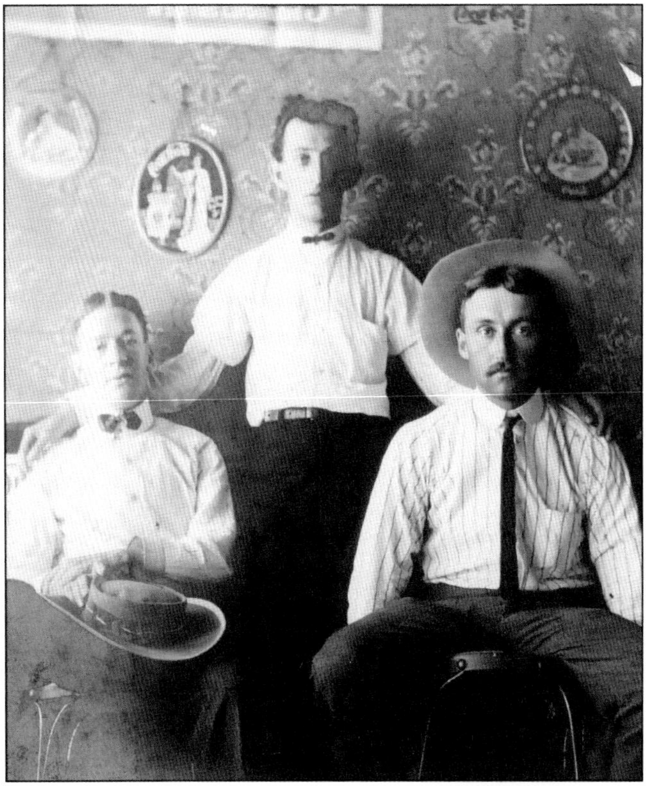

W.D. Bryan, E.C. March, and Charles Fountain Jr. posed in a barbershop around 1890. (PC Simmons)

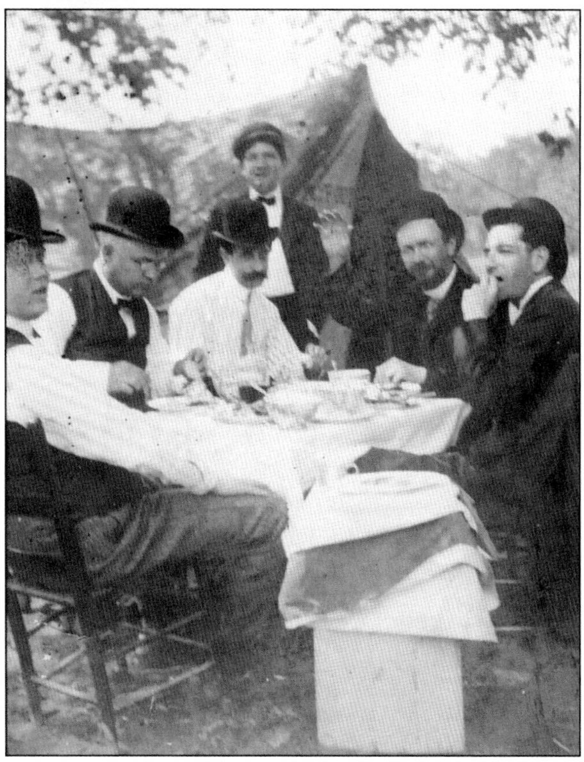

For entertainment, families often went down to the Tar River to camp out. Even though they were camping and had to improvise, they still managed to prepare full meals and serve them on china. (PC Simmons)

The meals were prepared over a camp stove. (PC Simmons)

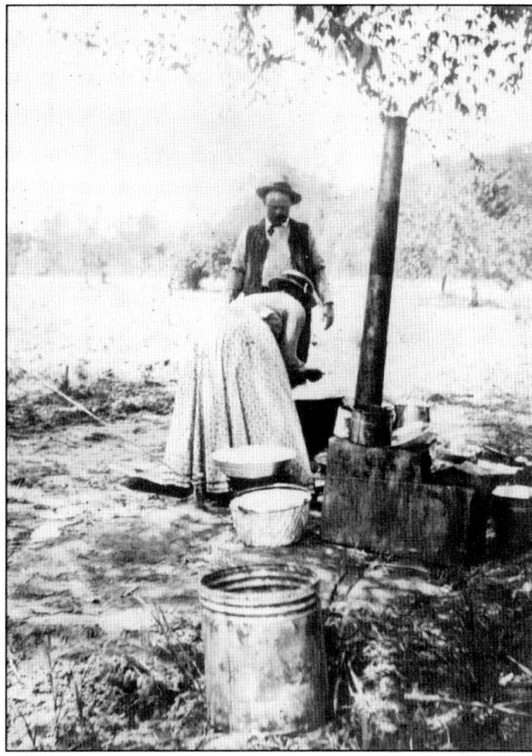

The camping group, including Willie Clark (lower right), enjoyed cards. (PC Simmons)

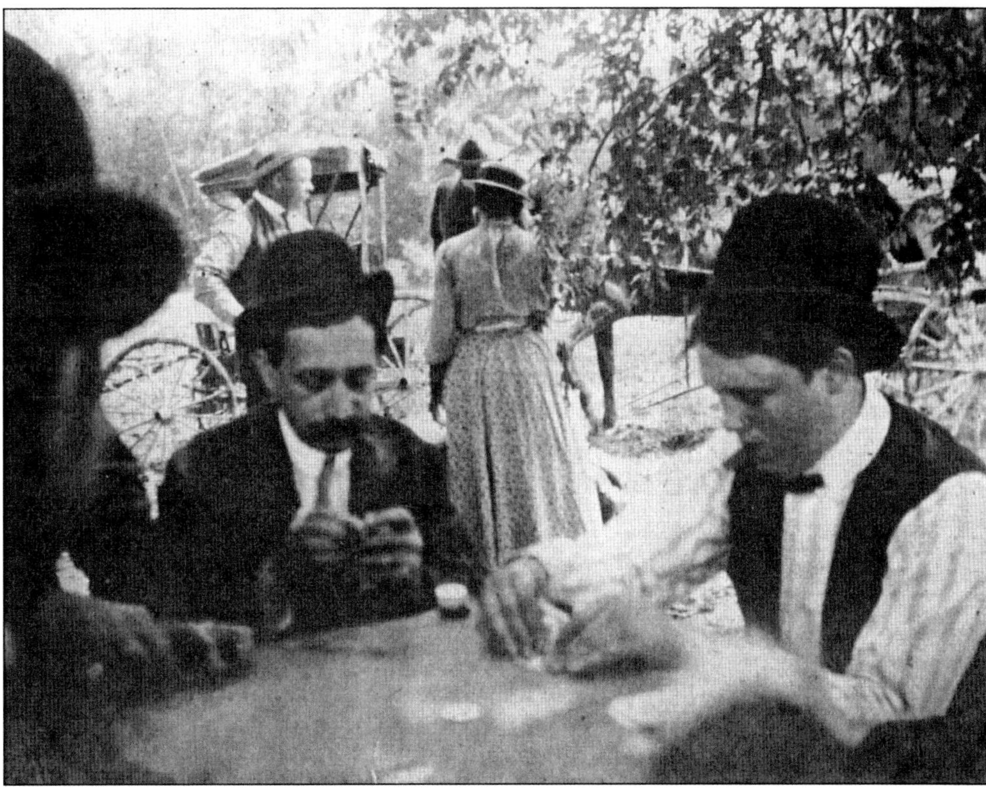

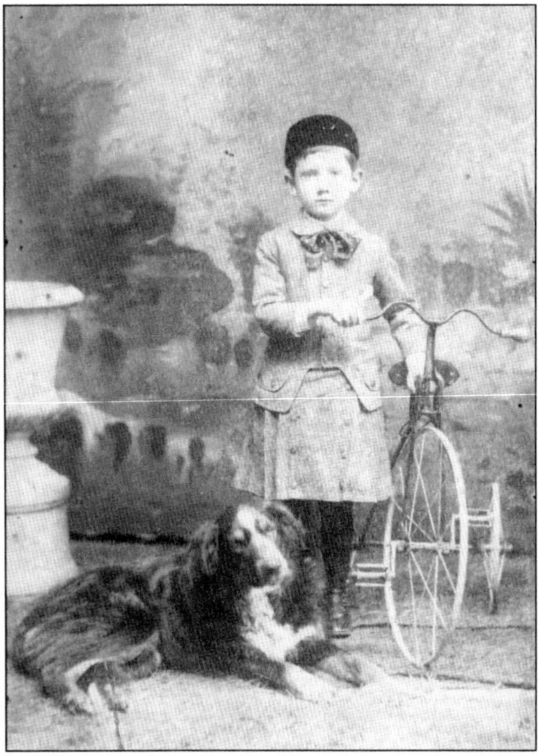

Marshall Staton visited S.R. Alley in his studio around 1900. The tricycle may have been a prop of Alley's, but the dog probably belongs to Marshall. (BBH)

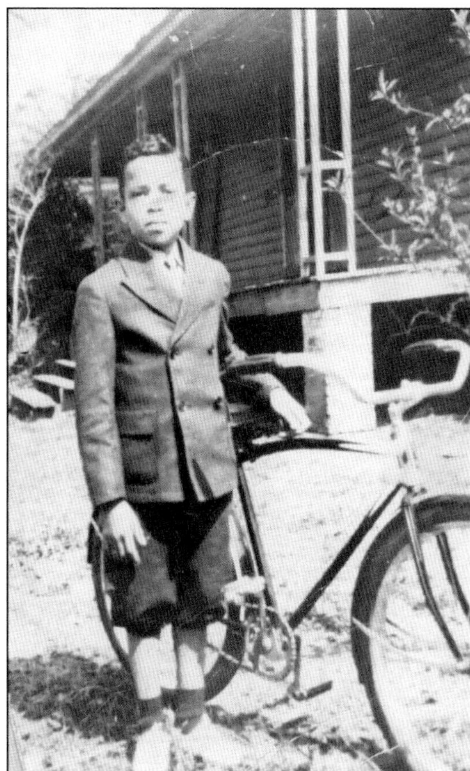

Richard Parker Jr. lived at 315 St. David Street in 1941. (PC Parker)

Wyngate Peters was another young man who visited S.R. Alley at the turn of the century. Peters was later killed in an automobile accident. (PC Brown)

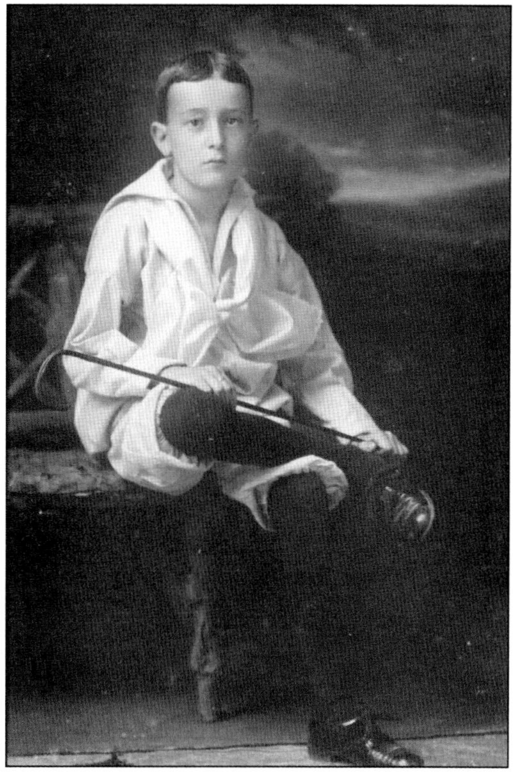

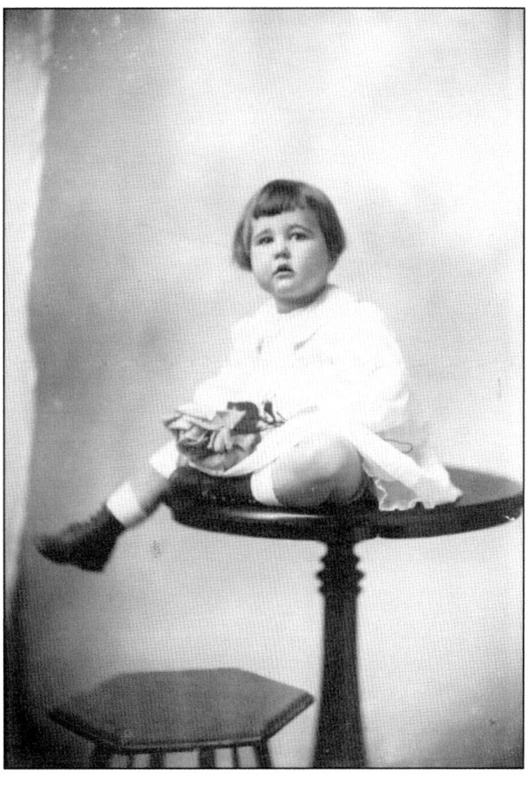

Mary Ferebee Howard was nineteen months old when she won the Better Baby Contest. She was rated 98 percent in health. Miss Howard grew up to work in the Red Cross in World War II, and eventually became a teacher in her hometown of Tarboro. (PC Howard)

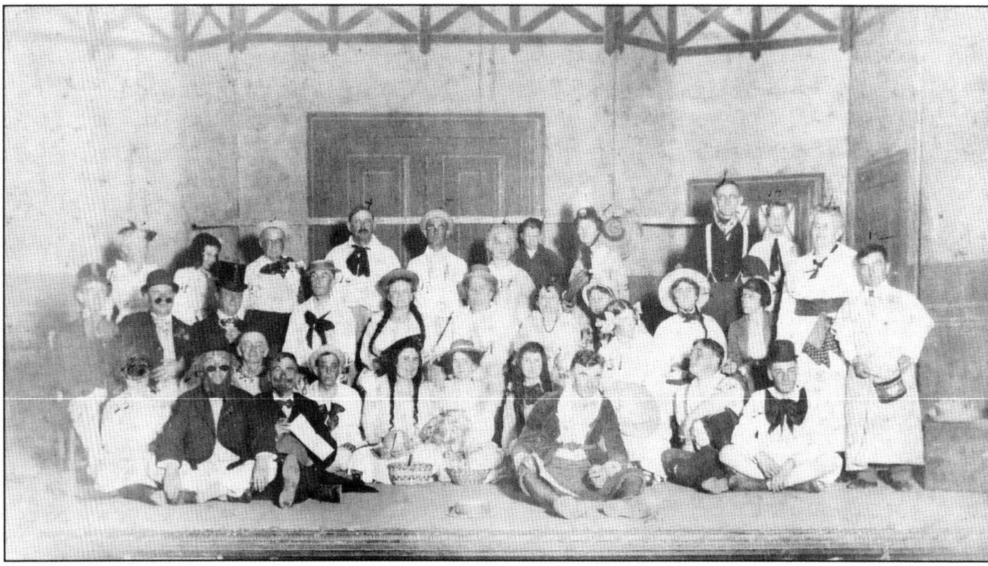

In 1912, the members of Calvary Church held a benefit to raise funds for the new fellowship hall. Some of the performers were, from left to right: (front row) Mrs. S.S. Nash, Mrs. W.S. Clark, George W. Rogers, Mike Edwards, Johnny Blow, Mrs. Frank Martin, Mrs. Harvey Lewis, A.D. Mizette, the Reverend Bertram Brown, Mrs. Farrar, and Mark Pitt; (middle row) Joe Pennington, Cliff Ruffin, W.G. Clark, Mr. Craw (a druggist), Mrs. C.M. Parks, Mrs. James Pender, Mrs. Frank Hart, Mrs. Mary Hester Howard, Mrs. Bertam Brown (with bows in her hair), Mrs. Minnie Williamson, and Mrs. Pearl Pennington; (back row) Mrs. Thigpen, Mary Matthews, Almon Hart, Chauncey Leggett, Irving Morris, Mrs. Frank Rives, Mamie Bryan, Evelyn Worsley, Haywood Foxhall, Sam Clark, and the Reverend S.W. Hale. (ECML)

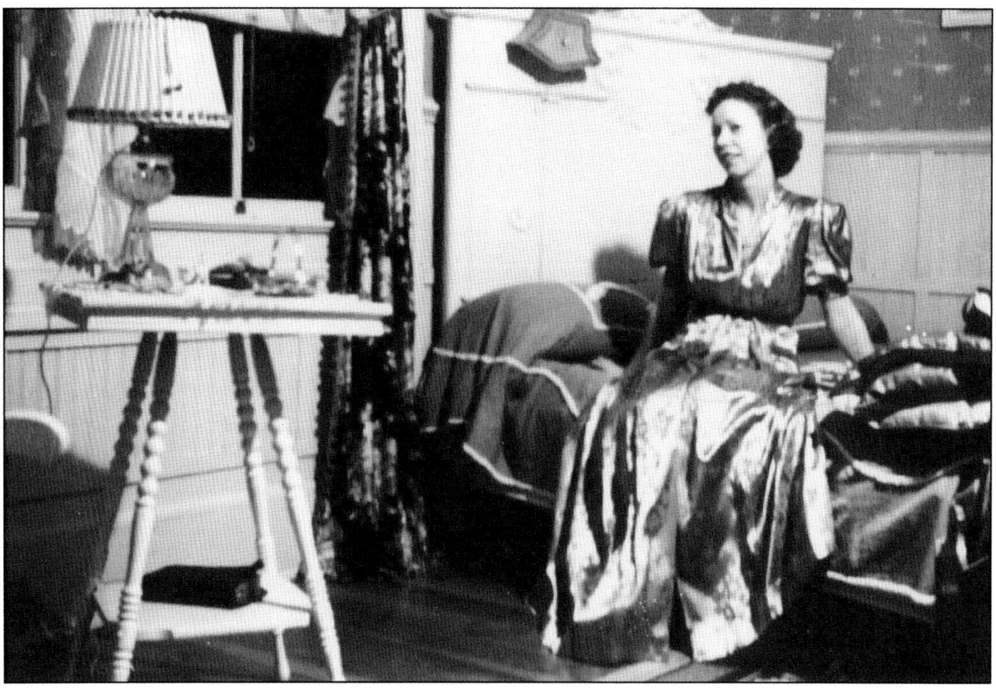

Jospehine Brown Nettles in "Adelphia" in the 1930s. (PC Brown)

Large or small, weddings always bring groups together for photographs. The wedding of Orren William's daughter in front of their Main Street home took place in 1892. (BBH)

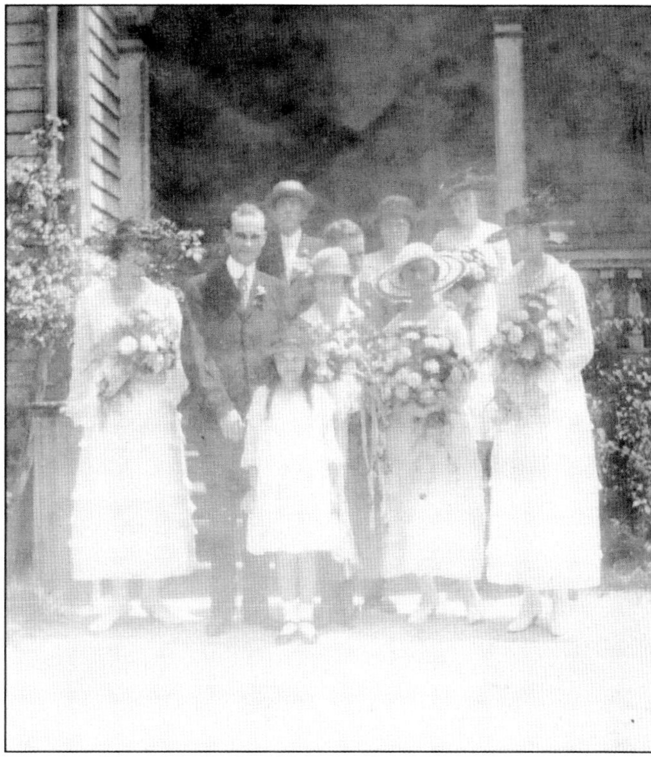

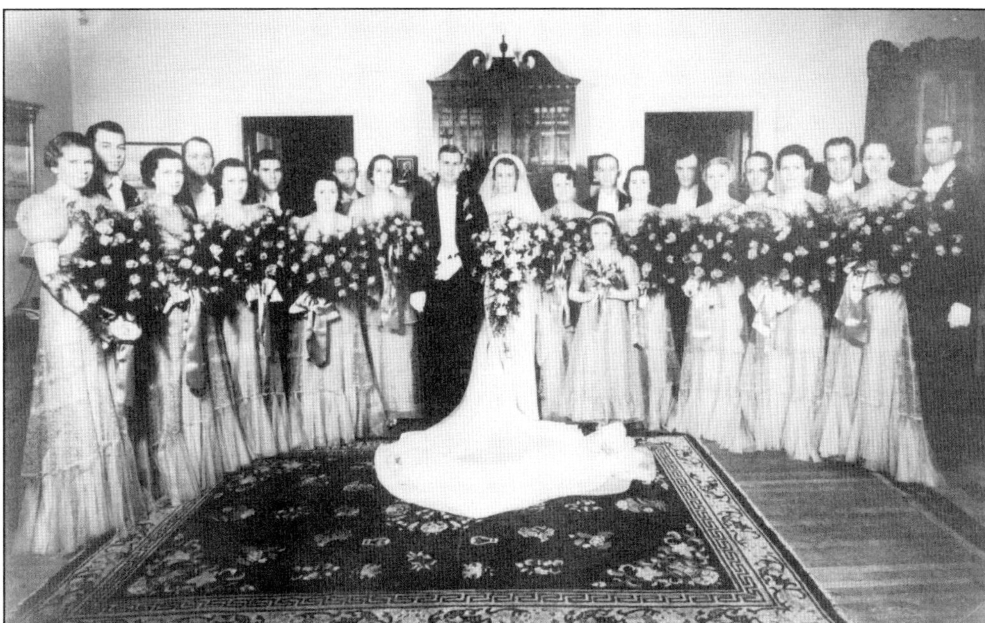

On January 30, 1937, Tarboro had one of the largest weddings of the decade when Virginia Clark married Francis P. Jenkins. The bridesmaids included Frankie Scholfield, Bella Johnston, Emily Ward, Isabel James, Jaquelin Nash, Mary Howard, Madeline Jenkins, Louise Green, and Ruth Clark. The groomsmen included Herb Taylor, Aubrey Parsley, Clark Bellamy, Bob Norfleet, Pem Nash, George Pennington, Dail Holderness, Perkins Morton, and Knox Porter. (PC Howard)

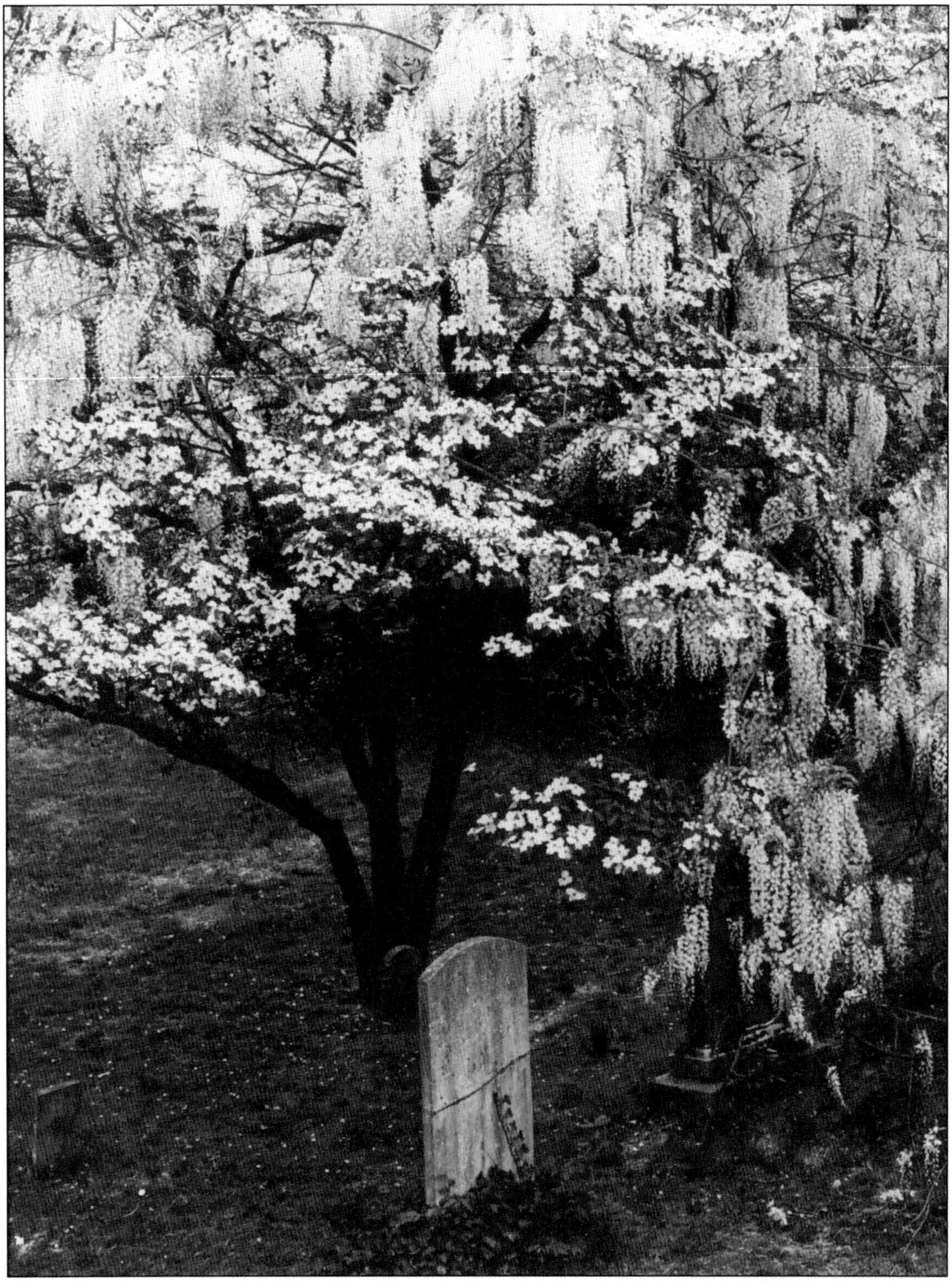

Draped with wisteria and framed by dogwood trees, the oldest graves in Tarboro are in the Old Town Cemetery located on the corner of St. James and St. David Streets, behind the Howard Memorial Presbyterian Church. Designated in the original town plan in 1760, the plot at one time covered the entire block. Many unmarked graves are the result of the wooden markers that were used in the late eighteenth century. Along with the Town Common, the Old Town Cemetery is the oldest surviving part of Tarboro and our final echo of Edgecombe County. (BBH)